CARROTS

CARROTS

True Confessions of a Hollywood Sex Addict

Dan Harary

BearManor Media
2022

CARROTS
True Confessions of a Hollywood Sex Addict

© 2022 *Dan Harary*

All rights reserved.

No portion of this publication may be reproduced, stored, and/or copied electronically (except for academic use as a source), nor transmitted in any form or by any means without the prior written permission of the publisher and/or author.

Published in the United States of America by:

BearManor Media

4700 Millenia Blvd.
Suite 175 PMB 90497
Orlando, FL 32839

bearmanormedia.com

Printed in the United States.

Typesetting and layout by BearManor Media

ISBN—978-1-62933-965-8

CARROTS

True Confessions of a Hollywood Sex Addict

Dan Harary

BearManor Media
2022

CARROTS
True Confessions of a Hollywood Sex Addict

© 2022 *Dan Harary*

All rights reserved.

No portion of this publication may be reproduced, stored, and/or copied electronically (except for academic use as a source), nor transmitted in any form or by any means without the prior written permission of the publisher and/or author.

Published in the United States of America by:

BearManor Media

4700 Millenia Blvd.
Suite 175 PMB 90497
Orlando, FL 32839

bearmanormedia.com

Printed in the United States.

Typesetting and layout by BearManor Media

ISBN—978-1-62933-965-8

For every guy who never got "The Girl"…
And for those who did…and wish they hadn't.

THE AUTHOR'S FAVORITE QUOTES

"I found that just surviving was a noble fight."
Billy Joel

"In the end, we're all alone, and no one's coming to save you."
Jim Caviezel, *Person of Interest*/CBS TV Show

"My ship isn't coming, and I just can't pretend."
Rush

"It's tragedy, with no one to love you. You're going nowhere."
The Bee-Gees

"When you're alone, you ain't nothing but alone."
Bruce Springsteen

"We have to find the LIGHT somewhere in our garbage, that's where it's hiding. When we can start identifying the garbage in our lives, it will eventually lead us to our divine purpose."
Kabbalah

WHAT SEVERAL TOP U.S. SEX THERAPISTS SAY ABOUT *CARROTS:*

"Imagine tossing Howard Stern's book *Private Parts* into a blender along with Woody Allen's script for *Play It Again, Sam* and Philip Roth's book *Portnoy's Complaint*. The result might be my friend Dan Harary's book *Carrots. Carrots* chronicles Dan's simple but lifelong challenge: how to navigate his desire and pursuit of alluring women while attempting to overcome crippling shyness and overwhelming self-doubt. Weave into that mix: a series of childhood traumas that affected Dan's earliest perception of females; his 25-year-long battle with (untreated) clinical depression; an 11-year-long marriage fraught with troubles; his wacky theory that he was cursed in a past life; a powerful sex addiction; and an endless series of 'really bad date' stories that quite often defy logic – or even belief. As a Clinical Sexologist and someone who's known him since 1984, I can attest that Dan's brutal honesty will leave the reader pondering: 'How on Earth was he able to accomplish so much?" – *Dr. Ava Cadell, Certified Love Coach, Clinical Sexologist, AASECT Certified Sex Counselor, and Founder of www.LoveUniv.com – Malibu, CA*

"I can honestly say I've never read anything like *Carrots* before. Dan Harary's book chronicles a lifetime of troubled relationships with women, some good, some bad, many ugly, but all told from a painfully frank point-of-view. Dan places the reader front and center as he describes in vivid detail the trials and tribulations of his odd history with the opposite sex. A gifted narrator, Dan is often witty and self-deprecating, but more often bares his feelings of longing, unfulfilled desire and heart-breaking disappointment like someone whose body has been cut open head to toe for major abdominal surgery. While he's not often the 'hero' in many of his stories, you have to give him credit for being brave enough to share six-decades worth of hugely personal and intimate encounters with his readers." – Dr. Nancy Sutton Pierce, Holistic Clinical Sexologist, Northern California

"In this absorbing read, Dan Harary candidly delineates his decades-long effort to find happiness and self-worth through sexual conquests. Ultimately, he finds meaning and himself through unexpected avenues, and realizes that his sexual preoccupation had led him astray for years. *Carrots* is a fun and quick read!" – *Dr. Maggie Carroll Vaughan, Psychotherapist, Founder & Executive Director at Happy Apple/NYC, NY*

"Dan Harary's book *Carrots* strikes a rare balance of being hilariously entertaining while simultaneously sad and painful. It is full of engaging tales of his ill-fated attempts to connect with women. You'll find yourself laughing out loud while shaking your head in disbelief at the equally humorous and tragic situations in which Dan finds himself! And you'll wonder, how can one man have so much bad luck?! It's enough to make you consider the possibility of a past life curse! *Carrots* is a brilliantly written look into the life of a man struggling with lifelong depression, sex addiction, extreme shyness and self-doubt, as well as several childhood traumas that shaped his perception of the opposite sex, the connection with whom seems to constantly elude him. Despite all this, Dan has still managed to have great professional success. And he tells his very candid and colorful true stories with a spirit of humor and perseverance that seems to transcend all that he has been through!" – *Dr. Kathryn Uzunov, Los Angeles, CA*

ACKNOWLEDGMENTS

The tales included in *Carrots* are 93% true, and accurate to the best of my rapidly fading recollection. I have changed the chronological order of some of the stories presented here for thematic reasons and have slightly embellished others for either dramatic effect or comic relief. While a few of these events might be hard to believe, each and every one is reality based.

I have also changed the first names of many of the women recounted here and blurred their faces in photos for the following reasons: I can no longer track them down; we no longer speak; they hate my guts and want me to die in a fire; or I'd prefer they not sue me.

To my mother, my ex-wife, Kim, former girlfriends, and any of the other women I've interacted with in the past 66 years who might read this book (and whose experiences in life have intersected with mine – for however long or short a period of time), I apologize to you here—in advance—for any embarrassment I may cause you. That was not my intention. My goal was simply to recount stories that often defy logic or belief. So, please brace yourselves.

Thanks to my publisher Ben Ohmart from Bear Manor Media for his bravery in publishing this book. And a special thanks to the countless therapists with whom I've shared most of these tales of woe since 1992; most notably Dr. Ava Cadell, Dr. Nancy Sutton Pierce, Dr. Maggie Carroll Vaughan and Dr. Kathryn Uzunov. Thanks for listening!

The roller coaster of my love life has been an extraordinarily bumpy ride, and I'm so very grateful for the steady support of my beautiful daughter, Anjuli. She will forever remain the only woman in the history of my life who could never possibly become a "Carrot!"

DJH
Beverly Hills, CA
Summer 2022

CONTENTS

PROLOGUE
My Mommy, the Carrot 1

CHAPTER ONE
The Rock, the Bush, the Sign, the Fence and
the Square Dance Lesson 5

CHAPTER TWO
First Girlfriend, First Kiss and Discovering
Playboy Magazines 10

CHAPTER THREE
The Call of the Wild, the Obscene Phone Call and
"20 Seconds in Heaven" 15

CHAPTER FOUR
Rock & Roll, A Guy Named Bruce and the Purple Bikini 22

CHAPTER FIVE
"Long Red" 29

CHAPTER SIX
The Unraveled Condom 35

CHAPTER SEVEN
The "Carrots" of Boston 40

CHAPTER EIGHT
"You Light Up My Life:" Snowy Adventures with Kim 47

CHAPTER NINE
The Belmar House, Jailbait Candy and
the Quick Fall of "Quick" 60

CHAPTER TEN
Boatshow Babes, the Furniture Store and
Heather/Larry at The Globe 65

CHAPTER ELEVEN
Sex In the City, Abe's "Ass Shorts" and
Babysitting Brooke Shields 78

CHAPTER TWELVE
Hello N.J., My Old Friend 84

CHAPTER THIRTEEN
"Jersey to Jacuzzi:" The First "Carrots" of Los Angeles 88

CHAPTER FOURTEEN
Eleven Years 103

CHAPTER FIFTEEN
Really Bad Dates 128

CHAPTER SIXTEEN
So, This is Sex?!?!? 137

CHAPTER SEVENTEEN
"Whack Shacks," Massage Parlors, Strippers and
Las Vegas Call Girls 154

CHAPTER EIGHTEEN
The Miracle of Prozac 167

CHAPTER NINETEEN
Ellen & Sharon 174

PHOTOS
Photos: 1956–2022 185

CHAPTER TWENTY
Attack of the Nymphos 215

CHAPTER TWENTY-ONE	
The Very Close Call	231
CHAPTER TWENTY-TWO	
Serial Dater	237
CHAPTER TWENTY-THREE	
Everybody Wants to "F" My Personal Trainer	248
CHAPTER TWENTY-FOUR	
The Comatose Three-Way and the Spanish Orgasm	254
CHAPTER TWENTY-FIVE	
Shiksa Blondes and the Missing "Zap"	262
CHAPTER TWENTY-SIX	
Bella and Lilly	273
CHAPTER TWENTY-SEVEN	
Marti and Tales of Auschwitz	283
CHAPTER TWENTY EIGHT	
Hollywood Hotties	290
CHAPTER TWENTY-NINE	
UFOs, Bethany and the Field of Orbs	298
CHAPTER THIRTY	
"These Are a Few of My Favorite Whores"	307
CHAPTER THIRTY-ONE	
Help! I'm in Love with A Supermodel!	320
CHAPTER THIRTY-TWO	
Meet My Dominatrix	336
CHAPTER THIRTY-THREE	
Sex Addiction Therapy and SAA	343

CHAPTER THIRTY-FOUR
Psychic Readings, Past Life Regression and
My Two Shamans   350

CHAPTER THIRTY-FIVE
Ten Years After: 2012–2022   358

CHAPTER THIRTY-SIX
The "Energizer Donkey" Retires   367

AFTERWORD
371

PHOTO CREDITS
373

PROLOGUE

My Mommy, the Carrot

When I was 23, I lived in Long Branch, New Jersey, a few blocks from the Atlantic Ocean. At that time, there was a terrific boardwalk nearby with rides, restaurants and novelty stores. One summer day, I noticed a shop with a sign that read "Spiritual Advisor." Having never encountered such a place before, and on a whim, I entered. A heavy-set, middle-aged woman said she'd tell me my fortune for $20. Although that was a chunk of change, I paid her. We sat, and I stuck out my hand. She stared at it for an uncomfortably long minute or so.

Slowly, she looked up, stared into my eyes, and spoke firmly: *"Many women are attracted to you. But something GOES WRONG with EACH ONE you meet,"* she declared. Then leaning closer into me, she added, *"The women you desire somehow elude you—they remain just beyond your reach."*

Her words were so completely accurate, I almost fell off my chair. How could this total stranger know my entire life story? I'd just walked into her shop at random. For all these many years since, I've been kicking myself in the ass—I never asked her "WHY?" Why did the women I desired most always seem to elude me? Why did things always "go wrong" for me with the opposite sex?

My first therapist suggested this phenomenon was tied to my earliest days with my mother. When I was three weeks old, my mother – who'd been sexually assaulted as a teen by her father in Brooklyn – experienced what she now calls "a break with reality." My birth had caused her (at age 21) to begin flashing back to forgotten months of her childhood spent in various orphanages and foster homes, while her mother was in and out of the mental hospital, and her father, a sociopath, was in and out of jail for raping various neighborhood women.

Post-partum depression triggered my mother's nervous breakdown. After she'd summoned the FBI to our house (telling the disbelieving agents who'd arrived there I'd been targeted as the intended victim of a "baby-kidnapping scheme,") my father had her committed to a mental hospital for a few weeks.

During her time away, my mother received electro-shock therapy treatments.

When she returned home, she was unable to breast feed me, and had developed an intense personality disorder. Now a classic narcissist, she began to find fault with everything and everyone, everywhere, at all times. (This condition continued until late 2020, when one of her doctors prescribed a "happy pill" to her. It worked and she became a much calmer person.)

As an adult, I came to realize that I'd never properly bonded with the first major female in my life. Without question, I understand that this early childhood situation has played a significant role in my pursuit of "Carrots" – desirable women who've crossed my path yet who remain just out of reach. Sociologists have long known that it's critically important for human babies, as well as numerous animals, including ducks, to either quickly bond ("imprint") with their mothers, or die.

Apparently, my imprinting was skewed (and screwed) right off the bat.

Although I did manage to get married and have relationships with a slew of subsequent girlfriends and lovers, every one of those interactions seemed organically pre-destined to fail. Between the ages of 36 to 56, my endless quest to find true love morphed, instead, into an overwhelming sex addiction. When I realized my little "hobby" had cost me well over a few hundred thousand dollars, I sought specialized therapy, and joined Sex Addicts Anonymous. I attended meetings, on and off, for several years.

While trying to piece together the puzzle that would explain my handicapped relationships with EVERY SINGLE WOMAN IN MY LIFE (except my daughter,) I realized that, as far back as early childhood, I occasionally felt an "otherworldly" influence within my midst – one which I believe has played a role in my peculiar phenomenon. I have pursued paranormal measures in hopes of explaining my odyssey with the opposite sex, having met with a number of renowned psychics, aura healers, and even two shamans. I've also experienced regressive hypnosis in this pursuit.

My conclusion? I know it sounds wacky, and I can't imagine there is any way to ever prove this conclusively, but I am 100% CONVINCED that some kind of "Curse" from a past life has followed me into this one!!

I truly believe this to be the case. Read on. And let me know if you agree?

CHAPTER ONE

The Rock, the Bush, the Sign, the Fence and the Square Dance Lesson

My very first memory – I'm three, living with my parents in a small house in Neptune, New Jersey, one town west of fabled Asbury Park. We were the only Jews on that block, and I was one of just three boys there. Most of the families in that neighborhood were Catholic or Protestant, and many had cute, little, Shiksa daughters running around.

My best friend and next door neighbor, adorable, blonde Donna, and I were on the lawn in front of my house kicking a ball. Without warning, Donna decided to stop playing. In a sudden burst of rage, I picked up a rock and hurled it, striking her in the forehead. It caused quite a gash. She put her hand to the wound, felt the blood, and stared at me for a second in silence, before letting out a scream that I can still hear today, 60-plus years later.

Donna's mother flew through her kitchen door, racing to her daughter's aid. She saw the blood and the rock, then shot me a terrifying glare. "Look what you did!" she screamed. "What's wrong with you? Such a bad little boy!"

The woman grabbed my arm and shouted through the screen to my mother. "Joan, Joan, come quick," she cried. "Look what your son did to my daughter!" My mother's face conveyed it all– despair and disappointment. "I'll talk to him," she said. As we heard, "I don't want him playing with my Donna again" through the screen door, my mother told me it was never OK to hurt a girl.

Having been banned from Donna, I next turned my attention to Mary-Barbara (MB), a larger than life, chubby brunette. When I was four and she was about six, MB said, "Let's take off our clothes." I had no idea why anyone would want to do that. Standing behind the large bushes in the front yard of her house, MB removed her shirt and pulled down her skirt, until she stood in just panties and shoes. My heart pounding, I was frozen, awaiting her further instructions.

Suddenly from nowhere, MB's mother (a short, Italian powerhouse with glasses,) appeared, parted the bushes like Moses at the Red Sea, and shrieked, "What on Earth are you doing to my daughter? You little pervert!" My shame, fear, and confusion were overwhelming.

Pulling me by the ear, the woman rushed me down the street to my house. Once again: "Joan, Joan come quick! We have a problem!" My poor mother answered the door and learned the news. "Stay away from the little girls, Danny. They are not your friends," she admonished. I was so utterly embarrassed. What had I done wrong? MB was the criminal here, not me! Yet, because I was the boy caught with a nearly naked girl, I was the evil one. The sicko. Clearly, the savage neighborhood rapist.

After this one-two punch, I decided my mother was right—neighborhood girls were trouble. I started palling around with two boys who had train sets, rang doorbells then ran away, and insulted ancient Mrs. Goodwin, whenever she pushed her walker past us on the sidewalk.

At five, I met a new neighbor – a young boy playing in his front yard. He invited me inside to see his Etch-a-Sketch. We played with several of his wonderful toys, and his mother brought in milk and cookies. I was in heaven. This was a wonderland. While we played, my pal's baby sister walked into his room, clad only in a diaper. Drinking from a bottle, she was probably about two.

Flashing back to the incident with MB in the bushes, I realized I needed resolution: "What on Earth do girls have 'down there'?" Deciding this baby wouldn't pose much of a challenge, I pulled down her diaper, and took a good long look. "Interesting," I thought. "I wonder what that thing is?"

My luck with mothers-of-friends having not changed even for this briefest instant, my buddy's mom walked in, saw what I'd done, and became hysterical. She swooped up the little girl, shouting, "You little bastard! Get out of my house!" I quickly made my escape, but remember thinking, quite clearly, that at least I saw a naked girl that time.

Two, cute, older Italian girls who lived directly across the street taught me how to climb fences and trees. One day, the three of us were climbing up inside the cross-beamed wooden structure of a large billboard sign promoting the drugstore around the corner. When we were rather high up, one of the sisters shouted, "Hey Danny, look at me!" and blew me a kiss. Startled, I FELL OFF THE SIGN, flew through the air, landed on my back and blacked out.

I awoke hours later, on a couch inside a stranger's house, many blocks away. I was never told how I got there. When I came to, no one was home. I distinctly recall thinking I'd died, and that my body had somehow been brought back to life, possibly by an Angel.

Third Grade. Two situations that have haunted me for decades:

During recess, a buddy and I wanted to "catch the girls" – a running game. A pair of identical twins, Wendy and Robyn, were willing to play, so I selected Wendy and began my chase. I was an extremely fast runner as a child, so I zoomed after her, sure I could tag her quickly. Wendy managed to stay ahead of me the entire time—I was never able to touch her. After a few minutes, Wendy sprinted away, turned her head over her left shoulder, and mocked, "You'll never get me, Danny," not noticing the fencepost railing dead ahead.

Wendy slammed her mouth, hard, into the railing, and came to a screeching halt. I stopped running when I heard that awful sound. Clearly in a daze, Wendy spat blood into her hand, then slowly lifted her face toward mine. Holding half of an adult front tooth in her open palm, her expression read, "Look what YOU did to me!"

As she ran off to the school nurse, crying, I stood alone in stunned silence. Once again, for whatever inexplicable reason, I'd "hurt" a little girl—this time, one I never even touched. And once again, I experienced the same terrible feelings of guilt I'd become accustomed to from my earliest days of childhood.

Another third-grade trauma involved square dancing, of all things. In gym class, we had an unprecedented, "boy/girl" session taught by our male coach, a real hard-ass, former Marine, and our lovely young teacher, who paired the boys off with the girls. My partner was a blonde cutie.

The coach had a record player at the front of the gym, and as the singer sang, "Swing your partners, Docie Doh, round and round and round you go," I did exactly as instructed, exuberantly swinging my gal pal. I distinctly recall her laughing – I'd never been happier in my life. Suddenly, the coach stopped the record player, blew his whistle, grabbed me by the shirt collar, and screamed: "What do you think you're doing?"

"Do you know what we do to boys who are too rough with little girls?" he admonished, inches from my face. "We take them to the woodshed and BEAT THE CRAP out of them!" His rage was overwhelming. His face, bright red, had steam shooting out from the ears. I glanced to my teacher for help, but she simply turned away. Stunned and speechless, I worked up the courage to look at little blondie, but she'd begun to cry. The coach had me sit on the floor in front of the class. "Stay there, you little ass. Do not move."

I recall telling my mother about this event that same afternoon. I was particularly upset by two things: First, I had no idea what I'd done wrong – and still don't, to this day. Second, I was startled to hear the words "crap" and "ass" – the first "dirty words" I'd ever heard in my life. Unfortunately, my mother didn't believe my story, and I was forced, once again, to subjugate my abject humiliation.

For the rest of my childhood, I did my best to steer clear of girls. As my father began to make more money working as an electronics engineer for Uncle Sam in the '60s ("I helped the United States win the Cold War," he'd later say,) we moved to a much larger house in West Deal, N.J., and my two younger brothers, Bobby and Michael, joined the fold. During this period, JFK had been shot, The Beatles played *The Ed Sullivan Show*, my father taught me how to mow the lawn, and my new (predominately Jewish and Italian) neighborhood provided me with a bunch of young boys to play with.

When I was eight, I became best friends with a "pre-maturely mature" kid I'll call Dustin, who lived a bit down the street. He and I would become in-separable for the next six years. Dustin and I built go-carts from scratch, rode bikes to watch Little League games, became obsessed with tropical fish tanks, snuck into "mature" movies, and, together, discovered the music of The Beatles and The Lovin' Spoonful, and the comedy LPs of Bill Cosby and Alan Sherman.

When Dustin and I were 10 – and *The Monkees* TV show premiered on NBC – we became obsessed with rock and roll. We'd ride our bikes to the local music store, and stare into the window, imagining the day he'd have his own bass guitar, and I'd have a drum set like my hero, Micky Dolenz. After two years of begging and pleading, our parents gave in, and bought us our requested instruments. Along with a friend from Hebrew school, Doug, who'd just gotten a Telecaster guitar, we formed our first rock band, "The Living Dead," rehearsing in my garage.

As unaccomplished as we were musically, playing drums in this band provided me with one of the happiest experiences of my youth. Of course, this brief era occurred just a hair before puberty kicked in and ruined my life forever.

CHAPTER TWO

First Girlfriend, First Kiss and Discovering Playboy Magazines

At 12, I was quite popular in school. During these "glory days," I was elected president of my 6th grade class, even though our teacher was a major bitch on wheels. She once asked me to deliver a report about Nasa's Gemini Space program in front of the class, criticizing me the entire time, and causing me to develop a fear of public speaking that would last for decades.

One night I got a phone call:

Me: "Yes?"
Caller: "Do you know who this is?"
Me: "No…"
Caller: "Stephanie" (a fellow sixth grader)
Me: "Why are you calling?"
Steph: "Who do you like?"
Me: "What?"
Steph: "Who do you like from school?"
Me: "What are you talking about?"
Steph: "What girl do you like?"
Me: "Girl? I don't like any girl…"
Steph: "You must like one girl in our class…Who is it?"
Me: "Nobody."
Steph: "We know you like somebody. What's her name?"
Me: Not wanting to sound like a total loser…. "Joanne, I guess."
Steph: (Giggling voices in the background) "Joanne, I knew it…OK, bye."

Like a deer in the headlights, I had no idea what had just happened. I shrugged off the call, then went to watch Tiny Tim sing "Tiptoe Through the Tulips" on NBC's *Laugh-In*. The next day, a gaggle of girls from my class cornered me on the playground during recess. They included Stephanie, and Joanne, a cute, round-faced blonde I'd only even noticed for the first time a few days earlier. Clearly the ringleader, Stephanie confronted me: "When are you going to ask Joanne to go steady?"

Poor Joanne was now the deer in the headlights. "What does that even mean?" I asked. Stephanie explained: "You get an ID bracelet with your name on it and give it to Joanne. Then she's your girlfriend. It's easy." As the geese gaggle fluttered away, Joanne looked over her shoulder, shooting me a seductive, parting glance. I instantly felt an electric twitch – I'd like to say it came from my heart, but, to be honest, I believe it came from my pre-pubescent testes.

I asked my father for some cash, something I dreaded, due to his lifelong insecurities about money. (My dad and his family once lived for a week on a sidewalk in Brooklyn during the Great Depression, when his parents couldn't pay their rent or utility bills.) I told him there was a girl involved, and he reluctantly handed me five bucks. Dustin and I rode our bikes to a stationery store that always smelled like pencil erasers, and I bought an ID bracelet engraved with my first name. It was much too big for my wrist, and during the ride home, fell off me several times.

End of school the next day: Before we could be dismissed by her majesty, our teacher, we had to stand in two lines – one for boys, one for girls – and wait for the bell to ring. All eyes were now laser-honed onto my face. Stephanie whispered: "Do it, Danny, come on!" My heart racing, I removed the bracelet, turned to Joanne, and, in my best Don Juan impression, said, "Here, you want this stupid thing?" Tossing it, Joanne caught the bracelet, put it on, and gave me an enormous smile. The other kids were psyched. I was a pioneer—not just the 6th grade class president and the leader of my peers, but also the first kid in our class to be going steady. The bell rang, we all dispersed, and I realized I wasn't in Kansas anymore.

A few days later, our shithead teacher called on Joanne to answer a very hard question. Joanne choked and had no response. The woman, devoid of one ounce of humanity, kept hounding her: "Why don't you know this material, Joanne? What's wrong with you? Didn't you study? Why are you in my class?" Joanne turned beet red and started to cry. Teacher: "Are you a cry baby now?" The eyes of every single student then shot over to ME, as if to say, "Your girlfriend is embarrassing YOU! What are YOU going to do about this?"

A very pretty brunette who sat just in front of me (and with whom I credit my first sexual fantasy based on a person I knew in real life,) turned and said, "Some girlfriend you picked! Good luck with HER!" For whatever reason, I didn't call Joanne that night, simply because I'm an inconsiderate putz.

That weekend, Stephanie threw a boy/girl party. I arrived with Dustin and was instantly confronted by several guys from class. "Danny, Joanne really embarrassed you the other day. She can't be your girlfriend anymore, she's a cry baby. You need a different girlfriend. She's a loser." I was besieged by these brilliant words of wisdom. Feeling cocky, and egged on by Dustin, I thought, "They're right. I don't want a cry baby for a girlfriend. She really DID embarrass me." Marching up to a smiling Joanne, I demanded my bracelet back.

Stunned, heartbroken, and crying once more, Joanne reluctantly handed the silver jangler back to me. My friends started laughing. My first relationship, which had lasted maybe two weeks, was now over. I walked away thinking, "Why on Earth did I just do that? I really liked this girl."

Half-way through seventh grade, my parents drove my brothers and I to Washington, D.C., for a family vacation. My mother turned around: "Which little girls do you want to invite to your Bar Mitzvah, Danny?" Girls? The thought of GIRLS suddenly scared me to death. I didn't know why, but at twelve and a half, the thought of "girls" terrified me. In the backseat of the car, I literally began shaking…my entire body trembled. Instinctively, I knew something was wrong, but I couldn't name it, nor describe it to my parents.

"Girls are stupid," I replied, masking my terror. "I don't want any stupid girls at my Bar Mitzvah." "Your other friends will probably have little girls at their parties," my dad chimed in. "Nah," I said, "I don't like girls…who needs 'em?" My parents laughed, and I realized I'd entered a new era with them.

My Bar Mitzvah was fairly uneventful. A trained monkey, I recited my Hebrew in a trance, having studied the same prayers four days a week for a million years in advance. I could have sung them blindfolded, in an upside-down chair, while being chain whipped. Looking out over the crowd in temple that morning, I recognized only a few of the 100 people assembled. Dustin, was there, of course, trying to make me laugh. I was too terrified to do so.

After the ceremony, my parents and I stood in a reception line, greeting a bunch of alter-cocker Jewish relatives from Brooklyn, most of whom I'd never heard of. Toward the end of the line, Jamie, a classmate from Hebrew school, came up and said, "I am so proud of you!" She quickly pecked me on the lips and smiled into my eyes. A girl kissed me! My very first kiss. A highly memorable experience – by far the day's highlight. (We've remained friends to this day!)

Shortly after our Bar Mitzvahs, Dustin and I hit puberty—hard, which coincided with our discovery of his father's *Playboy Magazine* collection. Since the only naked girl I'd ever seen in my life up to that poin had been wearing a diaper, the fact that I was now exposed to voluptuous women showing me their humungous boobs, shapely asses, long legs, and mysterious "down there" stuff, was more than just a little overwhelming. I was mesmerized. Dustin would grab a few of his dad's mags, and, together, we would sneak off into my attic. Meticulously studying each page, we wondered what those weird looking "vaginas" were all about.

One afternoon following a particularly inspiring *Playboy* review session, life threw me a curve ball. Dustin and I stood in my driveway, where my mother's car was parked and unlocked. "I want to try something," he said. "You be the 'girl' and I'll be the 'boy.'" I had no idea what he was talking about. "Lay down on the back seat," he ordered. Curious and naïve, I did as I was told. (We were both fully dressed.) He then positioned himself on top of me, held me in his arms, and started sucking my shirt, pretending I had "tits."

Dustin then began grinding his crotch against mine, and humped me, thrusting his hips up and down. Although I was frozen, I concurrently got my very first hard on. After a few minutes, he and I both climaxed in our pants at about the same time. He got off me, and we exited the car.

"Thanks for the sex, see ya later," he said, nonchalantly walking back home. I stood speechless in the driveway, watching him leave.

My first boner. My first orgasm. My first sexual experience. What was this sticky stuff in my underwear? And this big stain on the front of my jeans? "Thanks for the sex," Dustin had said to me. "What is "sex?" What the fuck???

It took me well over 30 years to remember that this event had ever happened.

CHAPTER THREE

The Call of the Wild, the Obscene Phone Call and "20 Seconds in Heaven"

After Dustin deflowered me in the backseat of my mother's car, I invented masturbation.

I had absolutely no idea what this private paradise was all about, what it was called, nor why I wanted to do it so often. I just knew that at some point during the night, I was going to wake up with a hard weenie, take off my pajamas, and slowly and methodically pull on myself. I imagined the body on the pretty brunette from sixth grade and would experience an all-embracing comfort that was indescribably wonderful and completely overwhelming.

I honestly thought I'd discovered something no one else on Earth even knew existed! Clearly, I was a genius!

I also became a thief. Once a month, I'd ride my bike to the local drugstore after school, steal the new issue of *Playboy,* and frantically ride away, shaking and sweating. After several years, I built up quite a collection, which I carefully hid in the crawlspace, underneath my bedroom closet. Several times a week, in the middle of the night, I'd take out my "girlfriends," and methodically lay their photos on my floor in collage-like fashion. I would then walk over them, naked, studying every inch of their bodies, and in the process, make sweet passionate love to my left hand in their honor.

One night while sound asleep during this era, I heard a noise that would have startled Boris Karloff. A deep, loud, mournful, "Call of the Wild" seemed to be emanating from outside the house. I lay in bed frozen, convinced that a wild animal had become injured, and was now trapped on our front lawn.

Sitting up, I placed my ear against my bedroom wall, and came to realize that this painful sound was not coming from outside, but rather from <u>inside</u> the house—from my parents' bedroom! Could it be that the sound of a bull moose bleeding to death was actually erupting from my FATHER??

"What on Earth could they possibly be doing in there?" I wondered. "Is my mother killing him?" I fully expected that, in the morning, I'd find my father's corpse, and a blood-stained butcher's knife on my mother's dresser.

After hearing "The Call" on many nights during the ensuing months, I realized that my parents must be doing "sex stuff" with each other. I still had no idea about intercourse, or about sex acts of any kind—no one ever bothered to teach me. I only knew that sticky white stuff comes out of a penis when you play with it for a few minutes. My parents must be doing something "penis-related," I presumed, but was too horrified to ask them.

When I was 13, and home alone one day with my brother Bobby (9,) we decided to explore our parents' bedroom, a no man's land throughout most of our childhoods. I found a shoebox at the top of my father's closet, hidden by a towel. I took down the box, Bobby and I sat on the carpet, and together we inspected our contraband treasure.

My father's porn stash contained perhaps the most confusing imagery I've ever seen, to this day. Inside were French nudist colony magazines, and a deck of black and white playing cards of naked people doing things to each other that defy description. These photographs were so grainy and disgusting, it was remarkable that anyone in their right mind would actually have paid money for them.

As Bobby said, "What are those people doing?" I realized that I'd gotten a boner. "Hey, wanna see something?" I pulled down my pants, spread out my father's playing cards, got onto my knees, and jerked off in a matter of seconds. My brother: "Wow! That was really cool. Do that again!" I told him it was a "secret magic trick," and I could only do it once. Without another word, we repackaged the porn stash back to its original state and replaced the forbidden shoebox to its proper place atop my dad's closet. (The incident was never again discussed.)

My mother (now an over-achiever) had become a noted teacher, actress, singer, musician, and playwright in the community. Hormones flying, I began to notice that she also had some very physically attractive girlfriends. My parents entertained in our house quite often, throwing cocktail parties for other married couples on a regular basis. Bobby and I loved these parties, because our father let us be the bartenders, and taught us how to mix whiskey sours, martinis, and Tom Collins cocktails. The couples would dance to "Cha-Cha" and Chubby Checker "Twist" records, while my brother and I would sneak sips of J&B Scotch (or "Jewish Booze," as one of the adults called it.)

Several of my mother's girlfriends were voluptuous blondes, with long hair, blue eyes, and rather large breasts. (Legend has it that, during more than one of these parties, my mother caught my dad, drunk, making out with some of these women, under the trees on our front yard.) I would surreptitiously "drink in" –visually – the bodies of my mother's friends during these shindigs. I'd then sneak off to the bathroom, fantasizing that these women were unsnapping their bras and watching, as I showed them the "secret magic trick" I could do with my penis.

For my 14th birthday, my parents gave me the greatest gift any budding, young masturbator could ever have asked for in the early '70s—a TV set in my bedroom! As ever male baby boomer well knows, a plethora of "babes-to-beat-off-to" starred on the tube then: Barbara Eden from *I Dream of Jeannie*, Tina Louise from *Gilligan's Island*, Goldie Hawn in her bikini on *Laugh In*, and the "Gold Diggers" who would shake their white-leather, mini-skirted asses right into the camera lens on *The Dean Martin Show*. I honed an ability to "time" my orgasms to the sexiest moments of any TV show – I instinctively knew when "Jeannie" would be leaning forward so I could best see her cleavage, or when "Ginger" would be wearing a coconut bikini. But my career best "cum timing" was always in conjunction with the Raquel Welch movie *Fathom*, in which that timeless sex symbol would strut her stuff in a lime green bikini.

I "had" all of those TV goddesses, many, many times.

"Look what I've got," said my friend Barry, who came flying into my house one day, waving a scrap of paper through the air. "What's that?" I inquired. "Janet's phone number." Through some miracle, he'd gotten the number of one of the hottest girls in 8th grade. "What do we do now?" I asked. "We call her, you big pussy." I led my buddy into my parents' bedroom, where he secretly dialed. I picked up the extension phone in the kitchen, so I could voyeur-istically listen in.

"Hello?" Janet answered. In a "disguised" voice, Barry said: "What color are your cunt hairs?" I was stunned. What did he just say? What are "cunt hairs?" Janet: "Who is this?" Barry: "Listen up, bitch, you heard me…what color are your cunt hairs?" At least he was consistent.

Janet: "I know who this is…and you're an asshole." She hung up. My pal raced into the kitchen, and fell to the floor, laughing hysterically. Repulsed, I felt like I'd just been physically violated.

The next day at school, Janet approached ME, gently gliding a piece of paper onto my desk. "You should read this," she said in disgust. It was a page from a police handbook, describing the criminal offense of making obscene phone calls. How did she know I was involved? I didn't call Janet! There was no "Caller ID" back then! I never asked her, nor was I able to face her again for a very long time. Through my association with an imbecile, I'd betrayed a beautiful girl. And now, once more, I was the one feeling guilty.

Shortly after the Dustin backseat incident (which I locked inside a "mental strongbox" for decades,) I met a short kid named Steve, who had a cherry red Fender guitar and was an accomplished musician. Before we knew it, Dustin and I joined with Steve and another friend, Sammy, to form "Radiation," a pop/rock band. Our repertoire consisted of an array of then current hits by the biggest bands.

Quite often while rehearsing in my attic, Radiation would attract a number of local girls from my neighborhood. They included: an adorable Jewish girl with very large breasts who lived down my block; two of the hottest blonde cheerleaders from school; and my backyard neighbor, who, for years, had tried in vain to rile my interest by wearing extra short cut-offs. Unfortunately, neither I nor any of my band mates ever had the balls to chat up these girls, much less the courage to ask one of them out for a date.

Allan from Hebrew school approached me one day: "Hey Danny, wanna have a boy/girl party at your house?" The idea stopped me in my tracks. I didn't have that kind of courage. The basement in his house had flooded, and he needed a new venue for his 14th birthday party. "Mom, Dad, can I have a boy/girl party here Saturday night?" My parents were excited. "We've been waiting for you to show some interest in little girls." The party was a go.

(Side Note: My request also triggered an unexpected parental response. A few days before this party, my father decided to have "The Talk" with me. The ONLY portion of this conversation I remember was: "Don't let anyone ever tell you that when a woman orgasms, nothing squirts out. That's simply not true."

Huh? What the fuck was he talking about? When I was in my 30s, I asked my mother: "Why didn't you or dad ever have the sex talk with me?" Her answer, "Your father told me *he did*." I then asked my father the same question. "I *did* have the talk with you," he recalled. "You turned bright red and ran out of the house." That was some talk, Dad. Really cleared everything up. Very meticulous. Great job, thanks.)

Allan and I produced a joint venture at my house, comprised of six boys and six girls, among them a sultry little beauty named Bonnie, who I'd never seen before. Allan taught us how to play spin the bottle, and as we sat in a circle, I noticed Bonnie smiling at me. After a series of other party games, Allan told us about "Seven Minutes in Heaven." He'd pair each boy with a girl, and, together, each couple would then enter my garage for seven minutes of bliss. Allan designated me the time-keeper, as I was the only kid there with a watch.

Allan and a pixie little blonde went first, and then one couple, after the next, after the next, each had a full, solid, seven minutes of making out behind my garage door. Since I was clocking these sessions, I'd inadvertently become the last boy to participate. Finally, Allan took Bonnie's hand, placed it in mine, and said, "OK, Romeo, have fun out there."

My heart pounding out of my chest, I was about to experience my "coming of age" – the moment when I would forever leave behind my childhood, and become "a man." (Just as Bonnie and I were walking toward the garage door, I glanced at the mirror in our den. My VERY FIRST ZIT, right in the middle of my forehead, had magically appeared from nowhere.)

Bonnie stood before me at the foot of our attic stairs in the garage, trembling slightly. I stroked her hair and hugged her tight. Here was a real live girl, in my arms—a first. I slowly and deliberately closed my eyes, and gently placed my lips against hers. She smelled like fresh linen. We kissed. Her lips were nice and moist. I "saw stars" from behind my closed eyes. I could swear that I also heard music playing. The kiss was heaven... It was bliss...

And it only lasted about 20 seconds.

Bonnie's father had arrived, far too early – and completely unexpectedly – to pick her up. Allan raced into the garage, panicked, and grabbed my arm. "Danny! Bonnie's father's here!" I thought he was playing a particularly cruel joke. Why was my new best friend busting my chops? Then, through the open garage door, we saw a man in an overcoat. Bonnie: "Oh my God, my Dad! I am so sorry, Danny." Bonnie fled, hooked up with her father, and split the scene moments later.

After the party guests left, my parents entered the room. "So, did you meet any nice little girls?" my mother asked. How was I supposed to answer that question? I'd just experienced the most magical moment of my life. And then, in a flash, it was gone. In the blink of an eye. Just like that.

A few weeks later, Bonnie's father was transferred to another city, and her family moved away. I never saw or heard from her again.

CHAPTER FOUR

Rock & Roll, A Guy Named Bruce and the Purple Bikini

For close to two years, Radiation had a solid run as one of the most popular grade-school rock bands in our community. We played at countless school dances and private parties. Steve and I became inseparable friends along the way, later splitting Radiation off into a new group, "Grain," by dropping Dustin and Sammy, and adding a brilliant bassist/singer named Scott.

One night after a Grain rehearsal in Steve's basement, and after Scott had gone home, we were walking his dog. Two attractive young girls appeared across the street. "Hey, you're Steve, the guy with the band, right?" asked the taller one. "I'm Andrea. This is my friend, Ginger." Steve turned to me and whispered, "Let's get these chicks back to my house."

This was really a bold move for either of us sixteen-year-old kids, but especially for Steve, who was remarkably shy, except when he was onstage. Steve (to the girls): "Hey, my parents are gone, and I've got some liquor…why don't you come over?" Andrea conferred briefly with her friend. "Yeah, sure, OK." They crossed the street, and we entered Steve's place.

I was a nervous wreck. Steve and I were alone with two girls—an unheard of situation. With a sentence that came from nowhere, I said, "I need to get drunk." My pal pointed out a brand new bottle of Manischewitz grape wine in his fridge. "Drink that," he advised. I downed about a third of the bottle rather quickly, and, for the first time in my life, got bombed. Steve's father had a cool little bar in their den, and Steve played bartender to these girls, mixing them each a drink. He, himself, hated liquor and drank nothing.

Clearly, Steve had his eye on Andrea, the far better built of the two. Making his move early, he put his arm around her, and said, "Let me show you my room." Cute, in a "foreign" sort of way, Ginger, now alone with me, was perhaps Middle Eastern, and much more exotic looking than anyone else I'd ever previously known.

"What do you want to do?" she asked. Me: "Urgh, ahhh, we could watch some TV?" Steve's den was one of my favorite places on Earth, because his family actually had color TV. (My family had only B&W television my entire childhood.) Sitting side by side on the couch, Ginger asked, "So, what's your story?" The wine was hitting me hard, and I became uncharacteristically cocky. "I'm the drummer in Grain, the best band around. Maybe if you're nice to me, I'll invite you to watch us play next weekend at a dance." "How can I be nice to you?" Ginger giggled. I glanced at her blouse, saw two buttons open, and noticed that her red bra was partially exposed.

"Well, I'd like to see more of those!" I said, disbelieving my own courage. "You like my girls? Yeah, most guys do." Ginger removed her top and unhooked her bra. "Is this better?" Her breasts, although small, were now fully exposed. They were quite beautiful – the first breasts I'd ever seen in real life.

"Those are amazing! I wonder what they feel like?" Ginger: "You've never had a girlfriend, have you?" "Uhm, no," I admitted. "Well, why don't you touch them, and tell me what you think." An invitation to handle some real breasts…I must be dreaming. I gently, but firmly, squeezed one, then the other. Ginger: "Not so hard, easy. Be nice." Doing as I was told, I continued feeling Ginger up. It was great—a true highlight of my teenage life.

Suddenly imitating a drunken sailor, I began to scream at the top of my lungs: "Hey, Steve! I got tit! I got tit!" Like the village idiot, I was roaring my conquest to my buddy, half-a-house away at the time. Ginger didn't take too kindly to my boasting. She quickly stood, re-dressed, and said, "Well, you're a real Creep-O, aren't you?"

Ginger decided to leave, and called for Andrea, who came down from Steve's room, zipping up her pants. Ginger: "Let's go. He's drunk and obnoxious." Andrea: "Yeah, OK. Bye guys." She winked at Steve, and the girls split. Steve was grinning. "I touched her bush," he proudly announced.

Bush? Really? I was so proud of myself for simply touching a girl's tits, and here was Steve, miles ahead of me, establishing his sexual prowess.

My burgeoning sexuality smacked me hard after the night I felt up Ginger. In my horny little imagination, the girls and women in high school began to appear like pages of *Playboy* come to life. Suddenly, I could spot – from miles away – every girl wearing a mini-skirt, hot pants, or a low-cut top. Our English teacher, who instructed us while sitting atop her desk, notably never wore panties – I'd crane my neck for the best angle. And the most beautiful blonde in school once mocked me, after I'd accidentally walked face first into her breasts in the stairwell. "Enjoying the view?" she asked in disgust, before fleeing.

Eventually, Grain attracted three cute brunette groupies—Laura, Cheryl, and Lisa. I got my driver's license before my friends and would borrow my parents' cars. I played chauffer to Steve and these girls, driving them to parties, midnight showings of Marx Brothers movies, and rock shows at the concert hall where he and I worked after school.

For over two years, Steve and I were the stage managers of a local concert hall in Asbury Park called "The Sunshine Inn." We worked stage crew and theatrical lighting for dozens of concerts, featuring a number of rock bands that were already quite famous at the time:

Mott the Hoople, Edgar Winter, Procol Harum, and Deep Purple, as well as others that would become VERY famous just a few years later: Fleetwood Mac, KISS, and a local guitarist named "Bruce."

Steve and I saw Bruce Springsteen perform—solo and with different bands—in various clubs and bars for <u>years</u> before he became a legend. At one of his shows (Feb. 1973) we ran his lights and set up his equipment—at the end of that performance, he looked at us and growled, "Hey, you cats were incredible!"

In early '73, Bruce's sax player, Clarence Clemons, asked Steve and I if we'd like to join their road crew. "Gee, Clarence, we don't even drive yet," Steve said, to which I added, "And I'm pretty sure our fathers want us to go to college." (Was this the "big break" in my life that got away? Was I meant to schlep amplifiers for Bruce Springsteen and the E Street Band for decades, becoming a deaf hunchback with enormous biceps along the way? I suppose the world of rock and roll will simply never know.)

Up until now, Steve and I were never alone with just one of our groupie girl-friends. There was no hooking up—or pairing off—yet, just hanging out sessions "en mass." But all that changed after a remarkable event in the school cafeteria. Laura and I were sitting together one day having lunch. "Can I talk to you?" Looking at her face, I saw the word "STEVE" prominently displayed on her forehead. It appeared to me like a neon sign for about five seconds. "If I wanted someone to ask me for a date, should I tell him?" Me: "You mean Steve, right?" Laura: "How did you know that?" Me: "I just read your mind."

I relayed the message to my best friend, who was pretty taken aback. "Really? Laura wants to date me?" Up until that point, Steve and I lived for just one thing, Rock and Roll. Our bands, instruments, LP collections, long hair, light shows, and stage crew work at The Sunshine Inn had consumed our every waking moment for the past five years. Now, suddenly, the dynamics between us were about to change forever.

Steve and Laura fell in love in about ten minutes. I helped him buy condoms at the local drug store, so that the lovers could quickly lose their virginities to each other. Lucky me, I was often asked to drive them to clandestine locations for their lovemaking sessions. Boy, did that suck! I'd be sitting in my father's car, waiting for hours listening to the radio, while the two of them were going at it at a party or on the beach. I recall looking up at the moon, more than once, and asking God, "Why am I SO alone right now? Why Steve, and not me?" The psychic pain was overwhelming. Suddenly, I was the "third wheel" to my best friend. It was a role I simply dreaded being forced to play.

One night after a particularly strong band performance at our high school talent show, groupie Cheryl drove me home. Parked in front of my house, she said, "You are so talented and smart and funny. I really like you." Not remotely realizing that Cheryl was making a <u>move</u> for me, I replied, "Thanks…I like you too. You're cool." We sat in the front seat of her car for at least an hour. Cheryl: "I love your long hair." Me: "Yeah, it's almost as long as yours, huh?" Not getting the hint. Simply NOT making the connection. This girl was MINE for the taking, and I was completely stuck in "friend" mode. Friend, Friend, Friend. A friend would never want to kiss me. A friend would never want to be my girlfriend. Sex is only for girls who pose naked in *Playboy Magazines*.

After an interminably long time, Cheryl said, "Well, I'm kinda tired. I guess I should go." Me: "Sure, thanks for the ride. I'll see you later." I got out of the car and watched her make a slow u-turn before me. She rolled down the window, stared longingly into my eyes, and said, in a very sexy voice, "Goodnight Danny." The SECOND she drove away, I had an epiphany. Did Cheryl "Like me, like me?" Was she coming on to me? No way, I thought. No girl with boobs that big could possibly want to be with <u>me</u>!!

The next day, I had lunch once again with Laura. "Poor you," she said. "Cheryl got back together with her ex-boyfriend, Tom, last night. She told me she was so horny for you she couldn't stand it, but you didn't make a move...so she got back with him. She really likes you, you know, but she needs sex. I guess you're too late now." Laura walked away; I sat there stunned. I'd "lost" the one girl on the planet who actually desired me sexually.

A complete and total putz, I've never forgiven myself for this fiasco...nor will I ever be able to do so. If and when Aliens come to Earth to reveal themselves to mankind, and offer us a Time Machine, this is the first moment from my life that I'd truly like to "do-over."

At that point, Cheryl left the gang, and just as thoughts of Lisa, our last little groupie, were about to enter my head, one of Steve's buddies made his move, and beat me to the punch. He and Lisa hooked up in a flash. Now I was driving Steve & Laura AND Bob & Lisa around town. The couples referred to me as "Dan, Dan, the Taxi Man." Ever the chauffer, I had to endure my buddies and their girlfriends getting lucky in the backseat of my father's car, as I sat alone upfront, suffering in silence.

After high school graduation, all of the guys who'd played in our various bands went their separate ways. I worked as a stock boy for a summer goods retail store, located in a distant beach town. The owner, a friend of my parents, was the only employer I could find who would hire a teenage boy with hair as long as mine (more than halfway down my back.)

While stocking store shelves with Coppertone sun lotion, inflatable rafts, and floppy hats, I wallowed in a level of misery and self-loathing unprecedented in my life. I was consumed with regret—the whole "Cheryl thing" was killing me. What had I done to piss God off so deeply?

On the last day I worked there, a very pretty girl in a purple bikini about my age came into the store. She bought a soda, took it up the counter where I stood, and shot me an amazing smile. "Wow, you're cute!" she said, "You live around here?" Overwhelmed by her beauty, and mired in my hellish sorrow, I simply said, "No. Fifty cents please." She paid, laughed, and left, as I watched her unbelievably perfect ass walk through the front door. My ancient boss, standing just behind me, sighed: "Ah, to be young again." Minutes later, he locked the place up, and drove me home.

The ride in his car was interminable. "Nervous about college?" he asked. I didn't reply. Trapped in a hell of my own making, I began having thoughts of suicide for the very first time. And while I never saw my little summer goddess again, thoughts of her "purple bikini'd ass" would continue to haunt me for some time to come.

CHAPTER FIVE

"Long Red"

After the end of a long, tortuous summer, my parents schlepped me an hour north to Rutgers University, in New Brunswick, N.J. Rutgers was the only college I applied to—or had ever even heard of—because, quite simply, my father went there. Now it was my turn to continue the family tradition.

I was 18 years old, with incredibly long hair, and a drummer without a band. I was still a virgin, while all my friends had been getting laid for most of the previous year. My acne was beyond belief—there were days when chunks of "salsa" seemed to be dripping from my face. To top things off, I'd become deeply, seriously depressed, while having no idea what depression was. (My mother neglected to tell me that clinical depression ran rampant throughout her side of the family for generations.)

My parents brought my suitcases up to my dorm room, hugged me goodbye, and split. I watched their car pull away, realizing I was now in an alien universe. In my entire life, I'd only ever slept away from home one night – at the age of 10, in the woods at summer camp—an experience that scared me to death. Suddenly, my parents, my brothers, my drums, Steve, The Sunshine Inn, my music buddies, and the only girls I'd ever spoken to, had all vanished. I was utterly alone.

An older student popped his head into my room.

"Hey man, I'm Carlos. Wanna get high?" – were the very first words I ever heard at college. "No thanks, man. I don't smoke pot." Carlos stared at me in disbelief. "Oh, you're into acid? Pills? Coke? Whatever you need, let me know, I can get if for you." Me: "Sorry, Carlos, no, I don't believe in drugs." Carlos: "With that hair, are you serious? We were taking bets out here you were a heroin addict." It took me a while to convince him. "OK, man, whatever," he said, retreating into his room at the end of the hall. Moments later, Jimi Hendrix blasted "Purple Haze" out from Carlos' room, as a massive cloud of marijuana smoke wafted through the cracks in his door.

That night, a "Welcome Freshmen" dance was held at the student union. Having been alone most of that day, I attended in hopes of making some new friends. A DJ played records, and a large crowd had assembled. A bunch of overweight girls were dancing with each other, while several guys, none with hair anywhere near the length of mine, were drinking beer. A few couples danced.

And then I saw HER on the dance floor. Alone. Swaying to the music. Her eyes closed. Her <u>incredibly long red hair</u> flowing over her shoulders and breasts, and nearly down to her ass. I gasped – electricity in my brain firing in all directions.

Instantly in love, I named this wonder girl "Long Red." Staring at her—from afar—for over two hours, I never once approached her, nor spoke to her. I watched as a number of guys did dance with her, though, each giving her one or two songs, and then politely moving on. I was frozen in place. Mesmerized. No beer, no alcohol, no drugs. While watching this wondrous creature sway before me, I became completely and utterly catatonic.

The dance ended, the crowd scattered, and Long Red began walking—alone—back to her dorm building. Like a mental patient, I trailed about 15 yards behind, stalking her, watching her hips sway and her hair flutter in the breeze. This woman was a vision to me, a goddess. I was certain "Long Red" was "The One."

Virtually every day for the next four months, I'd visually scan the gatherings at Rutgers, looking for my dream girl, and would see her quite often in the cafeteria. As I stood staring from a safe distance, food tray in hand, she and her girlfriends would be seated together, laughing. During one of these stalker sessions, Long Red looked up from across the room, and caught me staring. She shot me a quizzical smile, as if to say, "Who <u>are</u> you? Why don't you come over and talk to me?" Almost dropping my tray, I scurried off in another direction.

My roommate and most of the other guys on my dorm floor knew about my obsession. I'd get Long Red "sighting reports" – what she was wearing, who she was with, etc. A dorm friend, Keith (the first openly "gay guy" I ever met,) was eventually able to learn that her first name was Meryl.

A few months into my freshman year, my mother became concerned about my mental health. She'd call on the dorm's payphone and would hear me fighting back tears. I told her I was in love with a girl I couldn't even talk to, and was thinking, quite often, about suicide. Realizing I was having a mental breakdown, my mother made an appointment for me to see a shrink during the upcoming Thanksgiving break period.

Dr. L. asked me to draw a house, a family, and a tree. He also asked me to draw Long Red. I thought he was an imbecile. We only had two sessions together. Never explaining to me that I had clinical depression, a MEDICAL ILLNESS that ran in my family, he simply told me to take some of his pills. "You'll feel better."

"Drugs? I don't do drugs. Drugs are for losers," I snapped. Dr. L.: "These pills will elevate your mood. You don't need to feel sad all the time. You should try them." Me: "Yeah, sure whatever." My parents filled the prescription, and I went back to college, tossing the pills away.

"Fuck that bullshit," I thought. "I don't need any fucking drugs. Drugs are for losers. I'm no drug addict."

In the naivety of youth, I didn't understand the difference between drugs as medicine and drugs as recreational distractions. **Without question, this decision was to become the single biggest mistake I would ever make in my life.**

While most of the guys in my dorm were, like me, total losers with women, two were incredible exceptions. Not only were these guys both unbelievably good looking, but they played guitars together beautifully, and sang like angels. Billy and Ronny were our heroes—our Gods—while their girlfriends were among the prettiest women in all of Rutgers.

One evening while my roommate and I were studying in our room, Keith knocked on my door. "Long Red's upstairs at the coffee house. Billy and Ronny are playing. She's alone." I looked up, my heart racing. "Oh my God, is tonight the night you actually meet this mystery woman?" my roommate, Fred, scoffed. Keith: "Come on. You have to talk with her. Now!" My pals had to almost literally pry me out from my desk chair and lead me upstairs to our dorm's social gathering.

As the elevator doors opened, I saw candles everywhere, and heard Billy and Ronny performing. Keith had me sit with his friends, and subtly pointed out Long Red. She was sitting alone, next to a cement column a fair distance away, chewing gum, and swaying her head to the music. Once again, her eyes were closed. "This is your chance," my roommate encouraged. "She'll like you. Go for it." Keith: "We're right here for you. Nothing bad will happen. You need to do this. Tonight is your night."

A million thoughts raced through my mind: "What's my opening line? What on earth can I possibly say to the woman I've been obsessed with for the past six months?" I re-positioned myself on the floor about four feet from where she sat, pretending not to notice her. However, I could see from the corner of my eye that she was keeping tabs on me as well.

With each new song, I managed to forcefully glide my ass a bit closer to my dream girl. After perhaps six tunes, I was finally in a position just inches from her right shoulder. I was sweating – what should I say? "What's your name?" No, too stupid. "I'm Danny." Who cares? "Got another piece of gum?" Not bad…that one could work. "I love your hair." Too forward. "These guitar players live on my floor." So what? What the fuck? The lines were swirling like cotton candy, constricting any iteration of normal thought.

"Do it for God's sake!" Keith had insisted just a few moments earlier. "This is it. You will meet Long Red right now. You will talk to her. You will have a conversation. She smiled at you once, remember? You CAN do this. You will do this NOW." I turned to my left. Long Red turned to face me. Now scant millimeters apart, our eyes locked.

"Urghhhahhhuhmmmm." Nothing. No words. No semblance of anything resembling the English language. A low, guttural, laryngitis-type noise emanated from my constricted voicebox. (Medically, this condition is called Dysphonia.) Six months planning this moment, and the best I could do was make a virtually inaudible sound that I didn't even recognize. I'd never heard it before.

Long Red furrowed her brow, stared into my face, and tilted her head to one side like the RCA Victor dog. I stared helplessly into her eyes. Still nothing. No words or other sounds. I was a helpless fucking loser, madly in love with a goddess "Carrot."

Mercifully, Long Red stood after not too long, and walked away. My friends came up to me. "She's not your type anyway. I don't see what the big deal about her is," said Keith. "I couldn't do it. I just couldn't," I croaked.

My obsession with Long Red continued throughout the rest of my freshman year. I never once—ever—spoke to her. Keith took it upon himself to tell her I was in love with her but was just incredibly shy. "Yeah, I know," Long Red told him. "It's too bad, because I think he's cute, and I like his long hair. But I'm looking for a boyfriend with some balls. Apparently he doesn't fit that criteria."

Throughout the remainder of my freshman year of shit, I confided solely to my mother the details of my horrifically painful life. Realizing my sanity was at risk, she insisted that I transfer colleges the next year. "You should live near Steve. You need a friend who'll watch out for you," she said. "You should go where he is."

My father completely freaked out at the idea of my transferring colleges for two reasons: First, HE'D gone to Rutgers, so I was supposed to go there, too. And secondly, my new school was going to cost a fortune. He and my mother fought bitterly over this controversy for months. Fortunately, my mother won out.

Steve had spent his freshman year attending the Berklee College of Music in Massachusetts. My next stop that fall would be Boston University.

CHAPTER SIX

The Unraveled Condom

I cut off my long hair during my summer break between freshman and sophomore year. While I'd originally grown it extremely long to be a "rock and roll freak," I now felt simply like a "freak of nature." Back along the Jersey Shore, I worked as a busboy at a top steak restaurant, while Steve worked at his father's coat factory. On a night we weren't both working, Steve and I went to a nightclub in Asbury Park called "The Warehouse," with a simple goal in mind – to get me laid. I needed all the help I could get in that department. While I was clearly incapable of managing that feat on my own, Steve, in the interim year, had become "The Fonz," having developed the ability to score with almost any girl he desired, virtually at will.

After a few drinks, Steve and I noticed a not particularly "svelte" girl, with reddish-brown hair, drinking alone. Steve elbowed me: "Ask her to dance. She's alone." Me: "She's too heavy." Steve: "Are you kidding me? Who the fuck are you, Clark Gable? Ask her or I'll punch you." I approached this girl, we danced, we drank, we talked, and she gave me her digits. Steve: "You did it. You finally got a girl's phone number. Mazel Tov." "You think I should call her?" Steve: "She'll fuck your brains out, I can tell. She's horny. She'll be your first fuck."

A few days later, I had my legendary date with Claudia.

I drove about half an hour to pick her up, and we spent the afternoon at her friend's B-B-Q, drinking tons of beers. When dusk fell, she offered me a joint. (I had "caved" on my "Just say No to Drugs" crusade half-way through my freshman year. Since I was the only person in my entire dorm building who didn't smoke weed, I had completely alienated myself from my peers.

I told the guys on my floor that I would try it once, hate it, and never do it again. Much to my own surprise, I loved it immediately, and continued to smoke it for the next decade.)

Claudia and I returned to her house and went downstairs to her den. Her parents were awake, watching TV. The Dad: "So who's your new friend?" Claudia: "This is Danny." Me: "Hi, nice to meet you." Drunk, and stoned off my ass, I was amazed I was able to speak English. The four of us watched *Barney Miller,* her parents in matching Lazy-Boy recliners, Claudia and I on the couch. Holding hands, we tried hard not to burst out laughing.

The show ended. The Mom: "Goodnight, Danny, so nice to meet you." Me: "Yeah, thanks." The Dad: "What show do you kids wanna watch next?" Claudia: "Dad, don't you think it would be a good idea if you went upstairs with Mom now, too?" The man eyed me with "Dad Eyes," and said, "OK, I guess I can do that. Don't stay up too late. Goodnight Dan." The Dad shook my hand and left as well.

"God, I thought they'd never fucking leave!" Claudia said. With that, she removed her shirt and bra, and pulled me hard next to her. "Suck my big tits," she demanded. "I'm so fucking horny for you right now." "What?" I had NO idea what was happening. This was SO far out of my realm of reality. Enormous tits in my face? You have got to be kidding me.

We kissed briefly, but then she had me sucking and squeezing her titties, hard. She liked it—I was overwhelmed. "Take everything off, now! I want to suck cock." Me: "Huh?" Again, shock and amazement. Steve was right, though, I was going to be getting laid tonight; actually I was going to be getting laid right now. (He'd given me one of his condoms – my first.)

Claudia and I were both naked. She got on her knees and started sucking me. I looked at the top of her head—this was, without question, the most amazing scene ever, but I was so drunk and stoned, I couldn't get a full erection. She looked up. "What's the story? Aren't you attracted to me?" Me: "Of course…I never have this problem at home." Claudia: "OK, then, maybe just eat me out instead?"

Huh???

Claudia lay on the couch on her back, legs spread. "Can you get into it with your tongue?" Me: "Excuse me?" Claudia: "Can you get into my pussy with your tongue?" I had NO IDEA what this girl was talking about. None whatsoever. "What do you mean?" Claudia: "Put your tongue on my clit. Flick it back and forth as fast as you can. Suck it hard. Eat me out. Make me cum."

"Clit?" I was in Russia and didn't know the language. Claudia pushed my head into her crotch: "Lick me clean, Danny boy." I leaned over and forced my face into her vagina. For a second. The smell of "Fisherman's Wharf" was overwhelming. I saw black. I almost threw up.

"I don't think this is gonna work out for me," I meekly offered. Claudia: "What's wrong?" Me: "I just don't wanna do that right now, sorry." Claudia: "Well, are you gonna fuck me at least?" I looked down at my cock. He was nearly microscopic. I cursed him. "What is wrong with you?" I inner-voice screamed. "All the times I've played with you at home, and now a real girl is here, and you've stop working? Traitor! I'm never speaking to you again."

Claudia, a woman on a mission, was once more on her knees. "I've never had a guy not get hard for me." You've heard the expression, "That chick could suck chrome off a trailer-hitch?" I'm pretty sure Claudia inspired it. My reproductive system was so deep in her mouth, I prayed she wouldn't bite it off.

After about five minutes, my penis decided to respond. I got hard. Sort of. "You got a rubber?" Me: "Ahh, yeah, actually, I do." I got off the couch, picked up my jeans, and frantically searched the pockets for Steve's magical condom. Found it! I'm going to be getting LAID RIGHT NOW. Wow! Finally!

Sitting back on the couch, I next made one of the biggest mistakes in the history of my sex life. I ripped open the package, and unraveled the condom, all the way out, in mid-air. I'll say that again. I UNRAVELED the condom all the way out, IN MID-AIR, BEFORE I tried to force it onto my flaccid penis. Guys, try doing that some time.

Claudia: "What's wrong?" Me: "I'm trying to put this stupid thing on." Claudia: "You don't unroll it <u>first</u>…you unravel it, very slowly, right directly onto your hard dick." Me: "Really?" Claudia (disgusted): "You're a virgin aren't you?" Me: "Ah, yeah, I guess so." Claudia: "Shit. Just my luck."

I was so desperate not to completely fuck this opportunity up, I somehow managed—through sheer will power—to get firm enough to secure about one third of the condom onto myself. "Fuck me, Danny, now, hard and deep! Make me scream!" With a partially protected noodle doing his impression of a question mark, my penis was now as close as he'd ever been to the promised land.

With my Johnson mere inches from Claudia's snatch, we heard the loud noises – a door slamming upstairs, followed by footsteps stomping down the nearby staircase. Slowly, deliberately, one stomp at a time. "Oh, my God, my father! He'll kill us both!" Like "The Flash" comic book character, a terrified Claudia flew off the couch, gathered our clothes, pulled me by the arm and raced us into her adjacent bedroom. She locked the door and began hyperventilating.

"You have GOT to leave here, right now! If my father sees us naked, he'll kill you! He'll throw me out of the house!" Claudia's face was contorted—she was scared to death. Our eyes darted about the room. Claudia opened the window and tossed out my clothes and shoes. I tried to kiss her goodbye, but she was too busy shoving me through as well. Naked, I got re-dressed in the bushes in seconds, ran my ass across the street, bolted into my car, and drove away, shaking.

While I'm not 100% sure, I do believe I saw Claudia's father moments later, glaring at me through the open portal.

A week later, I called Claudia to arrange another date. "No thanks, Danny, I don't think so. It's just not gonna work out between us," she said, hanging up abruptly. Sadly, I was never given a second chance at "thrill fucking" Claudia in her father's den.

CHAPTER SEVEN

The "Carrots" of Boston

Relocating my life to Boston was quite a feat. The summer prior to living in my new city involved my parents fighting—bitterly—about the costs involved in my transferring to Boston University. Unfortunately, these fights would lay the foundation for their impending divorce.

My father moved me into a B.U. dorm room, where we met my new roommate. Brad became a real ally to me. A guitarist, we talked about rock music, girls, and goals in life. He'd had a few girlfriends before college, was shocked to learn that I hadn't, and was even more surprised to hear that I was still a virgin. "I just haven't found the right girl yet." Brad: "You're at B.U. now. There are a million girls here. If you can't get laid at B.U., you simply can't get laid. Period."

During that first week at B.U., Steve and I attended a dance where we met two freshman girls: Wendy and Gail. Steve instantly put his arm around Wendy, the brunette, and far cuter of the two, and walked off with her, while I was left standing with Gail, who had very short blonde hair, a somewhat mannish face, and a rather husky build.

The four of us spent some time together drinking beers, then Steve and I got their phone numbers. Walking back to my dorm, Steve said, "I'm gonna take Wendy out for dinner this week and fuck her." "I believe you," I replied, "But what do you think about that Gail chick?" Steve: "I think she's a dyke."

I knew nothing whatsoever about homosexuality – had never even heard of it. Steve, once again, was light years ahead of me in all areas of sexuality, and explained that some guys suck cock and some girls have sex with other girls. "How do they do that without a dick?" I innocently asked. "They eat pussy," Steve explained—info I certainly could have used the previous summer with Claudia.

True to his word, Steve had a date with Wendy a few nights later, and they had sex. During her sleepover, he had a dream in which Wendy said, "Gail and I have lesbian tendencies." Steve called me the next morning to share the news. "Terrific," I said. Steve: "You should still ask her out, maybe my dream was wrong." I arranged what I assumed was a date with Gail, and she met me at the student union. After a few drinks, I talked her into coming back to my room.

I locked the door, sat next to her on my bed, and, while shaking almost violently, put my arm around her. Gail: "What are you doing?" Me: "Trying to kiss you?" Gail: "Are you serious? I don't fuck dudes. I'm gay." I retracted my arm. "Steve dreamed that - about you and Wendy." Gail: "Yeah, Wendy told me she screwed Steve - that's cool. She goes both ways. I only like pussy." Me: "Then why did you come up to my room?" Gail: "Ever hear of just making friends? Not everything's about sex, ya know."

My very first girl in Boston = Brand New Carrot # 1.

Brad and I would often eat together in the dorm cafeteria, and during the early weeks of school he pointed out a very cute girl with light brown hair, alabaster skin, and bedroom brown/green eyes. One morning, Brad forced me to sit next to her, and I did.

Her name was Morgan.

A communications major from Maryland, Morgan was a bit reserved, had a low, husky voice and a naturally sexy aura. I was completely smitten, and determined NOT to let Morgan become another Long Red. I was going to date her, make her fall in love with me and parade her as my girlfriend for the next three years of college.

Morgan and I often bumped into each other walking down Commonwealth Avenue, to or from classes. Several times, she'd come to my room fairly late at night, to get my help with her homework. As was my way, I became obsessed with her, and after a few weeks, the "incident" took place.

A huge party was to be held off campus. Brad and I got an invite, and he suggested I bring Morgan as my date. "You think she'd go with me?" Brad: "Of course. She digs you. Just find some balls." I took the elevator to Morgan's floor in our building and walked the long hallway to her room. I lifted my hand to knock on her door. I was going to make my move on Morgan – I was going to ask her out to an amazing party. She was absolutely going to say yes.

Then it happened.

With my hand up in a knuckle-clenched fist three inches from her door, about to knock, I stopped – completely and totally frozen. I could not take that simple next step. My innate negativity and intense shyness engulfed me: "What if Morgan says no? What if she rejects me, right here, in the hallway, right to my face?" There was no way on Earth I could have handled that. So I stood there. Alone. Four minutes. Five. Nothing. "Do it, or don't do it. But you can't just stand here." Another minute, maybe two more. "Loser. Fuck you. Go back down and tell Brad what a loser you are."

"What the fuck? I've never seen anyone with less courage than you," Brad scolded. "I know. I just couldn't do it," I confessed. Cut to: The party. Brad and I were having a great time – the drinks were bountiful, lots of free food, and the music wasn't too loud. Then Morgan walked in, with an incredibly handsome guy on her arm.

Brad: "Oh God, no." I wasn't looking into a mirror, but I'm sure all the color flushed right out of me. I felt sick. How could Morgan do this to me? Didn't she know I was the guy meant to be with her? She and "Mr. Perfect" walked right past me, without a glance. Either she didn't see me (quite possibly,) or didn't want to flaunt this guy to my face. I was unable to speak. Brad found some empty, glass beer bottles, grabbed my arm, and said, "Follow me outside. Now."

We left the party and walked into an alley behind the building. I was almost catatonic. Brad: "Here, take this, and throw it as hard as you can." He handed me a bottle. I stared at it, and then at the flawless brick wall. Enraged, I threw the bottle as hard as I could. The "smash" was amazing. The glass shards flying everywhere symbolized my anger, shame, and embarrassment. After throwing two more bottles, Brad and I looked at each other and burst out laughing. We walked together back to the dorm, our friendship forever cemented in broken glass, brick and stone.

I was taking a history class – a slightly hefty Jewish girl sat next to me. One day, I was doodling in my notebook, drawing zombie-like faces of men with horrific arrows and spears through their heads, blood dripping from their wounds, and "Harry Potter" like Z scars all over their bodies. These poor zombie men were having a terribly bad time.

This girl saw my doodles, glanced up, and said, "Wow… you must be <u>so</u> sexually frustrated." Here was a normal girl, blatantly coming on to me, and I was too stupid to take a hint. We became friends, occasionally taking walks together, and I knew she clearly had a crush on me. When she'd take my hand, I'd cringe – chills ran up my spine. I just wasn't attracted to her—she simply "wasn't" Morgan.

Brad and I inherited his older brother's apartment across the street, and we continued another year as roommates. I began classes at B.U.'s School of Public Communications. There were some sexy girls at that school, but perhaps none hotter than Marla. After a journalism class, I walked outside the communications building to a sunny Boston afternoon. Marla, wearing tan velvet short shorts and a low-cut top, stood in front, eating an ice cream cone. She was gently licking, and some of the vanilla cream began dripping. She was the most beautiful girl I'd ever seen in Boston.

Too stunned by her beauty to talk, I quickly walked past her, shocked when she said "hi," and stopped in my tracks. Then—together —we watched as a blob of ice cream gently dripped down from the cone and directly into her cleavage. She scooped up the drippings with her fingers, sucked them like she was giving a sensual blowjob and winked at me. "I know, I know – fucking hot, right?" she laughed, then slowly scurried away. I made a mental "videotape" of the scene for future masturbatory purposes.

Brad met an attractive, curly-haired blonde, Carol, in one of his classes, and told me she was looking to meet "a nice Jewish guy." He took it upon himself to fix me up. I took Carol for dinner, and we wound up back in her dorm room. "My roommate's gone for a while, but why don't you lock the door, just in case," she said. I did as instructed and Van Morrison's classic "Moondance" LP was placed on the stereo. We then sat together, side by side, on her bed, talking. And then we listened. And listened. And listened. And listened.

Side one of that fucking "Moondance" LP played over and over again, in its entirety, at least four times. I sat there, completely paralyzed. Carol was staring at me, waiting for me to make a move. I couldn't. Again, fearing possible rejection, I was a roboton, flashing back to those fleeting seconds of panic when I sat beside Long Red, or tried to knock on Morgan's bedroom door. Half my brain: "Go for it, she's waiting for you! How could she NOT want to kiss you?"

Other half of brain: "She's too good looking for you. Who do you think you are?

She's not going to kiss you back. If you put your arm around her, she'll laugh in your face, push you away, scream rape, or tell you she's gay."

Carol didn't make a move on me either, unfortunately, which would have ended this incredibly awkward stalemate. When "Moondance" was about to play for a fifth go-round, she stood. "You should probably go now, I guess." What a relief. I could end this torment. I walked to her door, and then, with a sentence that defies belief, even to me, even to this day, I actually said, "Well, can I get a good night kiss, at least?" "I can <u>not</u> believe you just said that!" Carol exploded, abruptly slamming the door in my face.

I relayed tales of the evening to Brad. "Oh brother, what is wrong with you? She was a sure thing! Oy vey." He and I sat there, incredulous. Carol never gave me a shot at a second date, and, to this day, whenever "Moondance" plays on the radio, I have to switch stations immediately.

That summer ('77,) I worked back in New Jersey at a radio assembly factory. It was also during this time frame, the infamous "Summer of Sam" (the David Berkowitz killings in New York,) that I met Steve's cousin, Randi. At 17, Randi worked as a hair model for a local beauty salon. She had gorgeous red curly hair, a beautiful face, and quite a little figure. We met one night at a party and were smitten with each other, instantly.

Randi became my first girlfriend. Sort of.

Other than fleeting seconds kissing Bonnie or Claudia, Randi was the first girl I ever made out with that elicited real passion. We had a few long sessions in my bedroom. One night, I put Bread's "Greatest Hits" LP, featuring the song "I Wanna Make It With You," onto my turntable.

Randi and I were lying side by side on my bed, kissing intensely. We were both completely clothed. I started rubbing her "area," thinking I was stimulating her. "You're rubbing my pubic bone," she alerted. "Why?" Me: "Oh, er, uhm, I heard that chicks like that." Randi: "No, you're supposed to rub me here." Moving my hand a bit down lower, Randi showed me how to rub just above her special spot. She began to moan.

I maneuvered Randi so that she was now under me, and I got on top. We were dry humping, and as the "Make It With You" song was ending, we climaxed together. Unfortunately, my little brother, Michael, walked into my room just at that moment – horrified at the scene, he fled.

During the next weeks, we repeated our "clothes-on" lovemaking maybe a couple of times. About our second month together, I realized I was falling in love with Randi. So one night, I said those magical words every woman longs to hear: "Ahh, Randi, do you think we could have sex sometime soon?" She replied firmly, "Well, you know we're both going to different colleges in September. I'm not sure we should be moving in that direction. Let me think about it."

The next time I saw her, Randi handed me a greeting card. Inside, she'd handwritten the lyrics to a Bob Dylan song: "It Ain't Me, Babe, No, No, No, It Ain't Me, Babe. It Ain't Me You're Looking For, Babe." She looked into my eyes. "I decided that I'm not ready to have sex with you. I'm only 17. You've already been 'around the block' with other girls. But I'm still a virgin, and I want to wait a while longer. Sorry."

Randi had no clue that I, too, was still a virgin at that point—I was too embarrassed to admit it.

We stopped dating. I went back to Boston for my senior year, and Randi went off to her freshman year at Rutgers. A short time later, I heard through Steve that she'd lost her virginity during her first few weeks away.

As Don Adams used to say on the old *Get Smart* TV show: "Missed it by that much!"

CHAPTER EIGHT

"You Light Up My Life:" Snowy Adventures with Kim

During my last year at college, Brad chose to study abroad in Israel. Before he split, though, he hooked me up with his buddy, Michael, who would take his place in our apartment, becoming my new (unanticipated) roommate. On our first day together, Michael waltzed his girlfriend, Pam, into the place. He'd neglected to tell me about her in advance but did share that she'd be staying over with him "quite often," and that they'd be sleeping on the sofa (pullout) bed in the living room.

That first night, I relived my parents' "Call of the Wild." Michael and Pam should have been porn stars, because their fuck sessions were mind-boggling. At 2 AM, on a nightly basis, I'd hear: "Oh Michael, oh my God, Michael!! Fuck me, baby, fuck my pussy! Harder, Michael, harder, fuck me deep and hard!! Shove your big hard cock deep inside me, baby! Fuck me, Michael, oh my God, Michael! Make me cum baby, make me cum. Michael, I'm gonna cum, oh Michael, here I cum! Oh my God! Arrarghhhgghhhhhh-hhhhh!"

God forbid, if I had to pee in the middle of the night, I'd have to quietly unlock my bedroom door, and silently tiptoe to the bathroom down the hall. I'd become a prisoner in my own apartment. The two of them were clearly sexual acrobats who apparently loved torturing me.

Months later, I got my revenge.

Just before Christmas break, I lined up an internship, working in the newsroom of WNAC-TV, Boston's local ABC affiliate. I needed an internship to graduate, and this one was a cherry. I was going to work for the producers of the 11PM evening news, by re-writing wire copy, and operating the teleprompter, from which the news anchorman would read, live, on-air.

But first, I was back in New Jersey for the holidays. Steve and I spent most of our nights at our favorite place on earth—a nightclub called "The Royal Manor." The hottest chicks on the planet danced there, the drinks were incredibly strong, and the band, "Holme," was our own Beatles. The place simply worked – "Disneyland for Young Adults." Steve had scored with girls there a number of times, and even I managed to briefly kiss a few on the dance floor occasionally. (Invariably, though, one of us, Steve or I, would usually end up getting too drunk, and puking his guts out in the bushes at the front entrance.)

The highlight of our Royal Manor era took place that New Year's Eve, 1978. I was the designated driver that night. I arrived at Steve's house, and his younger brother, Dean, greeted me. "We've got a problem." Steve was sick. He had a 102-degree fever and had just thrown up. His Mom: "Steve's not going anywhere tonight, boys. He needs to stay home." His Dad: "I don't want Stevie out tonight. He stays in bed." Steve was hyper animated and pissed. "No way! It's New Year's Eve! I'm not staying home! I'll stay in bed tomorrow. I'm going to the Manor with Danny." Resigned to his decision, Steve's mother said, "Please Danny, be sure Steven doesn't die tonight."

Steve, Dean, and I zoomed off to the Manor, and once inside, downed our first round of Long Island iced teas. The women at the club that night were super hot, with skintight pants, low cut tops, and open toed heels, even though it was like 29 degrees outside.

Steve, coughing his ass off, was determined that nothing was gonna slow him down, here in our magical escape from reality.

The place was fucking packed solid. It was hard to move after about 10 o'clock, which was kinda fun, because it meant grinding bodies up against every girl that passed by. Steve, Dean, and I were all getting some terrific looks from the girls we were squished up against, and one French kissed Steve outright, probably dying of pneumonia the next day. The band was playing songs we all loved – the greatest hits from The Beatles, The Beach Boys, Boz Scaggs, The Stones, and Van Morrison (yes, even including the dreaded "Moondance.")

Around 11:30 PM, the three of us were dancing with an assortment of girls in every direction. Balloons and confetti were omnipresent—people blew noisemakers wildly. From the corner of my eye, I saw Steve chatting up a girl with long, perfectly straight, white-blonde hair. He approached me: "There's a cute girl over there – her name is Kim. You should talk to her." Steve started coughing again and walked off toward the bathroom. The girl he'd mentioned stood in the middle of the dance floor alone, sipping a cocktail. Completely out of character, I walked up: "Hey Kim, I'm Danny. Wanna dance?" Almost in slow motion, Kim looked up from her drink and stared into my eyes. "How'd you know my name?" "Tonight's magic," I said, "Just go with it." So we danced.

Midnight: The lead singer from Holme announced the countdown: "Ten, Nine, Eight, Seven…" Kim and I were making out like bandits. If we'd squeezed each other any tighter, I would have been standing behind her. Kim's tongue was so far into my mouth, I almost choked. Her hands all over my ass, she was grinding herself against me.

"Six, Five, Four, Three…" I led Kim to the back part of the dance floor and pressed her up against a wall. The chemistry we had was undeniable and overwhelming. I felt like I'd found my life partner – my missing link. "Two, One, Happy New Year!" Holme played "A

Hard Day's Night," and the place erupted. A few girls threw bras into the air. Dean was at the opposite end of the dance floor kissing his partner. I motioned to him, "Where's Steve?" Dean indicated he was in the bathroom, heaving his guts out.

"Listen, my best friend is really sick. Can you stay here for a minute?" Kim: "Of course. I'm not going anywhere. I won't leave you, Danny." Her smile was electric—really phenomenal. Dean and I retrieved poor Steve, who'd been sitting next to a toilet on the men's room floor. "You better not fucking die tonight, buddy, I promised your mother." Dean and I each grabbed one of Steve's arms and lifted him. Approaching Kim, I said, "I have to get my pal home. Give me your phone number. I want to see you tomorrow." Jotting on a napkin with lipstick, she stuffed it into my pocket. Kim: "Tomorrow. I can't wait. Feel better Steve."

Steve was incoherent. Miraculously, Dean and I managed to get him back home, before any permanent brain damage from his fever – or alcohol poisoning – had set in. I arrived at my mother's place about two in the morning. (My father, who'd been having an illicit affair with my mom's best friend, had moved out of our family house a few months earlier.) Completely wired, a million thoughts swirled around my noggin. And then I remembered – I had to fly back to Boston on January 2, so I could start my internship at the TV station on the third. Fuck! I'd just met this sexy blonde girl who wasn't repulsed by my presence, and I only had another 24 hours to see her again!

January 1, 1978, saw an incredible blizzard hit New Jersey – I didn't care. Fuck snow. There was no way on Planet Earth I wasn't going to see Kim that day. No way. I called her, got her address, and told her I'd see her "soon."

After somehow convincing my mother that I was capable of driving her car through supernaturally tall snowbanks, I shot out the door, and my little adventure began. I would have had a solid hour of driving in normal weather, but with this bullshit snowstorm, who even knew? The trip was hell. The snow and ice were so compacted, I didn't "drive" that night, I "slid" my mother's car across the Garden State Parkway and the New Jersey Turnpike. It took me two and a half hours to get to Kim's house, with virtually no other car in sight.

I finally arrived, parked, and trudged through a snowdrift to reach Kim's house. The moon was full, the air was incredibly cold, and the street was silent. Christmas tree lights shone through the windows of pretty much every house on her block. She greeted me at the door, wearing a fluffy white sweater and jeans. Her long blonde hair was a sight to behold. "I didn't think you'd make it!" Me: "No big deal." Kim: "Come on in, I want you to meet my folks."

Kim led me inside. In the kitchen, her father, cigarette dangling from his lips, was frying an enormous mound of bacon in a skillet. It occurred to me that he looked EXACTLY like Lee Harvey Oswald. He shook my hand and seemed nice enough. I then met Kim's mother and brothers, all of whom were watching TV.

Kim decided we should take a walk, so we could be alone. Her Mom: "Are you two seriously going outside? You'll freeze to death." Kim: "I want to show Danny the stables. We'll be right back." The night air hit us hard, and our smoky breaths were everywhere. I held Kim's mitten-clad hand, and together we walked the crunchy street. The moonlight was intensely bright, and the icy road beneath our feet twinkled from the reflection of multi-colored Christmas lights. We didn't talk. I heard music—I LITERALLY heard the song "There's A Kind of Hush" by Herman's Hermits, playing in the sky above:

"There's a Kind of Hush, all over the world, tonight.

All over the world, you can hear the sound, of lovers in love." (I swear this is true.)

Kim led me to the next block, where we entered stables, pet some horses, and sat on bales of hay. We were shivering…violently. I leaned in, we kissed. The looks in our eyes were magnetic—hypnotic. We were mesmerized by just the sight of each other. Shaking from the intense cold, but mesmerized.

"Kim, I can't wait to make love to you. I can't take it. I want to be alone with you so badly," I somehow managed to say. Kim: "I know. I want you too. But we can't. Not here, not now. It's too cold. And my father will be looking for me if we don't get back soon. Sorry." Me: "I can't believe I met you – this amazing girl – and I have to go back to Boston tomorrow." I explained my internship situation to her – silence followed. Kim: "That's not fair. I don't want to be here without you."

During those fleeting moments, I also learned that Kim, who had just turned 20, was a junior nurse in a local area hospital.

We sat on the hay bales for maybe 15 minutes, tops. Our kissing was deeply passionate, but our noses were getting frostbite. We stood, and slowly walked back to her house in silence.

I took Kim to her front door and kissed her goodnight. Her younger brothers were watching through the window, laughing. "When can I see you again?" Me: "I'll be back at my mother's place for spring break. I promise, we'll be together in April." Kim: "I can't wait to make love to you either." She winked. One last kiss for Dannyboy, and back into mommy's car I went, no longer aware of the shivering. The feelings I had at that moment were the most powerful I'd ever felt in my life. Kim waved goodbye, blew me a kiss, and shut her door. I skidded off, "slip sliding" away, honestly not knowing if I'd ever see my little blonde girl friend again. I'd been at her place for less than an hour. It took me another almost three to get back home, lost in conflict, emotion, and a blasting defogger the entire way.

I began my internship at the Boston TV station on January 3rd, as scheduled. Other than working there on weeknights, I was completely alone – it was still Christmas break, and everyone else at B.U., including my porn star roommates, were away. When I got home each night after midnight, I'd lay in bed like a lox, wide awake, hour after hour.

After a sleepless week, my phone rang at 3 AM one night. Kim: "Danny, I haven't slept in days. I can't take it. I need to see you." Me: "I can't sleep either. I can't stop thinking about you." Kim had saved enough money (she was working at a local, NJ, hospital) to fly up to Boston. I was ecstatic. I'd been completely alone and now a GIRL was flying to see ME?? Unheard of.

That Friday afternoon, after buying some condoms for the first time in my life, I took a subway to Boston Airport, arriving hours early. I waited until Kim's flight landed, and when she walked through the gate, I saw she was carrying daisies. I stood still, in awe of her. She practically leapt into my arms and kissed me. "These are for you," she said.

Kim accompanied me to my internship that night, and moments after the newscast ended, we took a taxi (a rare luxury) back to my apartment. The minute we got inside, clothes flew off in every direction. We jumped into my bed, where we would remain for the next 12 hours, straight.

That day was highly memorable to me for three reasons:

Hubert Humphrey had just died.
I'd finally lost my virginity.
It was a Friday, the 13th.

Kim and I made a "whole lotta love" that day. We had sex nine times, to be exact! The next morning, Kim said, "My God! I never knew sex like that was even possible!" Me (the Pro): "I know, right?" All weekend, we trudged through the snowbanks of Boston, ate at some great restaurants, had lots of drinks, and enjoyed massive amounts of sex. The longer we were together, the less we talked. Our communication was instinctive—words were not important. She stayed until that Tuesday morning, when I took her back to Logan Airport.

As we waited for her plane to board, I said, "Kim, I have something to tell you, you might not believe. I was a virgin until you got here." Her face said it all. "Are you kidding me? I had no idea. Wow! For a virgin, you sure knew what you were doing!" Me: "Well, I've had a tremendous amount of practice – with myself." She kissed me forever. "I'll come see you again soon, OK? I promise." Me: "Bye, kiddo. You're the greatest."

I watched her board. Outside the airport, I waited until her plane took off and hurtled deep into the sky. My lover was on that plane, I thought. The one woman on the planet who really, truly, cares about me is on that plane, and now she's gone. On the subway ride home, I cried.

Kim and I spoke by phone every night from that point on. Soon thereafter, college was back in session, and students, including my porn star roommates, were back in town. I was attending my communications classes full time and working five nights a week at the TV station. Exhausted, and lonely for my wonder girl, I once again had to endure Mike and Pam's audible gymnastics. But this time, I was less affected by them. I, too, now had a sex partner of my own.

Two weeks later, Kim had saved up for a second trip to Boston. Again, I met her at the airport and brought her to my place. Mike and Pam were shocked. I hadn't let them in on my little "secret," and when I told them Kim would be staying with us for several days, they were none too thrilled.

On those nights when Kim and I were having sex, I urged her to scream as loud as she could. I told her about the way my fuck-head roommates had been torturing me for months, and how I longed to get back at them. Kim and I were as obnoxious as could be, screaming and moaning, panting and groaning. One night, we heard the door slam in the dead of night—we'd driven Mike and Pam out of the apartment.

Score!

During that second weekend with Kim, I took her to the top of the Prudential Building (Boston's tallest structure,) to a romantic nightclub called the "Top of the Hub." Kim and I found an intimate place to sit and ordered white Russians. A small jazz trio was playing in the corner of the club. Kim: "Aren't you going to ask me to dance?" Holding her in my arms, I slow danced for the very first time. The band played soft, smooth music. We were, by far, the youngest couple there. Then, the trio began to play an instrumental version of "You Light Up My Life," a huge hit song at the time.

Kim and I were slow dancing. The song was romantic. She kissed me. The moonlight was shining through the over-sized windows. Candles lit the inside of the club. The drinks were hitting me, hard. Everything was coming together. I became overwhelmed with emotion. This was, without question, the most joyous, romantic and miraculous moment of my life.

"Kim. I love you."

She looked into my eyes. "Really? Wow…I love you too, Danny boy."

I began to cry. Sob, actually. I began to sob, uncontrollably. "I have to sit down." Kim walked me over to our seats. "Here, you need this?" she asked, handing me a few cocktail napkins. I was a mess. I didn't know feelings like this were possible. She gently laughed. "Looks like I fell in love with a big ole girl, huh?" she mocked, as I wiped away tears. "I think it's sweet. I think you're sweet," she added.

That night, we made the best love, ever.

I told Steve and Brad that I was "officially in love." They howled with laughter. Steve: "Love? You're just in lust!" Brad: "You finally got laid—that doesn't mean you're in love. You're confusing sex with love." Me: "Bullshit, you guys. This is the real thing. I'm in love with Kim, she's in love with me. You're both just jealous." More laughter.

In early February, Kim flew to see me a third time. Another weekend of sightseeing, walking through snowdrifts, and eating at restaurants I couldn't afford. Mike and Pam had decided to "boycott" us this go round and were spending their nights at Pam's dorm room. (Up until then, I didn't even know Pam HAD a dorm room.)

Kim and I became more experimental with our lovemaking during that third weekend together. Kim had already been with a few guys previously, and was willing to impart some of that know-how to yours truly. Kim became my sex-ed teacher – my own personal porn star.

On the last night Kim stayed over during this trip, I had an idea. "Let's screw on Mike and Pam's bed!" Kim was all for it. "Yeah, let's drip all over their sheets, those selfish, fuck-heads." I put on my favorite LP at that time, Dan Fogelberg's "Souvenirs," lit some candles, and pulled out the mattress from Mike and Pam's sofa bed. Kim and I got under the sheets and had sex for many hours, enjoying every conceivable act (except anal, which I didn't know existed.) We were sweating and cumming, dripping and spinning, twirling and screaming. This was sex for the ages. Sex from the Gods. This was the sex I'd been in desperate need of since I first discovered my penis in 1969.

Early the next morning, Mike and Pam entered the apartment, and caught Kim and I sleeping in THEIR BED. The look on their faces was priceless. "Oh, hey guys," I said, nonchalantly, "Back so early?" Wordlessly, they split, in complete and utter disgust.

Later, I brought Kim back to the airport. We said our passionate goodbyes, professing eternal love for each other. This time we both cried when she had to board. This was a wonderfully magical time for us. She blew me another kiss goodbye, and then, once again, Kim was gone.

I came back to the apartment, took the used "cum sheets" off Mike and Pam's bed, tossed them into the laundry hamper, and replaced them with fresh sheets from the linen closet. I ran some errands, then went off to work my internship.

Returning home that night, I saw Mike and Pam lying in their sofa bed, reading. I also noticed that they'd put the used "Dan and Kim sheets" BACK ONTO THE BED, thinking that I hadn't switched them with clean ones! They were mistakenly laying in our sex juice. I loved the situation with all my heart!

"Oh, ah, hey guys," I said, trying not to laugh, "You know, those were the sheets Kim and I used last night, right? I had clean ones on there already." Again, the looks on their faces, especially Pam's, were absolutely fucking priceless.

Score!

Kim and I continued our nightly phone calls for a few days after her third visit. And then, suddenly, nothing. Must be my imagination, I thought. But after four consecutive nights of "no Kim," I phoned her. The conversation went something like this:

Me: "Hey Kim, how are you?"
Kim: "Danny...I was just thinking of you..."
Me: "You OK? You stopped calling."
Kim: "Yeah, uhm, I have to be honest with you about something. Totally and completely honest."
Me: "Of course...what did you do, rob a bank?"
Kim: Silence
Me: "Kim?"

Kim: "Having sex with you these past few weeks has made me so incredibly horny, I've been going out of my mind. I never knew sex could be so intense and addicting. Not having you around whenever I need it is killing me…"

Me: (Not getting her point) "Yeah?"

Kim: "Well, I need sex, Danny, I need it badly. You've really spoiled me. So a few nights ago, I went to the Royal Manor, and I met a guy – Billy. You'd like him."

Me: "Huh?"

Kim: "Yeah, so, I have to be honest with you. Billy took me to his place and we fucked for a few hours. He made me cum a bunch of times. But you have to know this, Danny, I want you to know this…"

Me: "Huh?"

Kim: "Every time he made me cum, I was thinking about YOU!"

I felt sick to my stomach. Kim was fucking ANOTHER guy? She was so horny for ME that she was fucking ANOTHER GUY? What the fuck was THAT about? I didn't understand. I couldn't comprehend this betrayal. How could she possibly do this to me? I told her I loved her. She was the first girl I ever said "I love you" to. And now she's fucking BILLY?

Kim: "Danny, are you OK? Please, please understand. It's just so hard for me to be away from you. I want to see you again in a few weeks. But, in between, I need to fuck Billy, too. Please tell me that's OK? I love you, Danny."

I felt like someone just told me my family had been killed in a car crash. The room was spinning – my stomach churning. I'd been stabbed in the back by my lover, the only woman in the universe I ever truly loved.

Me: "Uhhh, Kim, I can't deal with this right now. Sorry, I have to go." I hung up.

Although I was emotionally shattered, I surprised myself by never shedding a single tear for the end of this romance. I was deeply shocked and hurt by Kim's betrayal. But instead of crying, I internalized the pain and became a techno-drone, locking the hurt deep inside my mental strongbox, and tossing away the key. I felt completely removed from reality.

Much, much later, it occurred to me that during those magical weekends in Boston, I'd simply fallen in love with the idea of love itself. The blonde girl I knew as Kim was merely a transitory figure, one whose significance in the history of my life wouldn't be revealed to me until EXACTLY four years later!

CHAPTER NINE

The Belmar House, Jailbait Candy and The Quick Fall of "Quick"

My college graduation was fairly dramatic. Since my parents had divorced just a few months previous, the wound in my mother was still fresh. She wanted NOTHING to do with "that fuck, your father," so I had to plan separate post graduation celebration dinners for my family. It sucked. I was graduating from Boston University's renowned School of Public Communications. (While I was there, future radio shock jock Howard Stern attended as well, two years ahead of me. However, I was too lazy to wake up early to listen to his now legendary morning radio broadcast. I'd meet him ten years later, in Hollywood.)

Now both college grads, Steve and I left Boston, and moved back in with our parents along the Jersey Shore. While sitting together on the beach one day, he had a big idea: "Let's rent a house, start up a new band, and rock this town!" He convinced me that after four years of having our lives on hold for college, we should regroup, form a kick-ass, brand new rock band, and play all of the local clubs. "We can be the new 'Holme,'" Steve declared. "We'll have fun, make money, and pick up tons of chicks."

Steve and I found a wonderful old house in Belmar, a block from the beach, and near the soon-to-become infamous "E" Street, of Bruce Springsteen fame. Our fathers signed our lease for us, as we had no income of any kind. We set up my drums, Steve's amps, and our PA system in the living room of "the Belmar House," and shortly thereafter added a keyboard player ("Steve 2,") and a singer to our ensemble. We rehearsed nightly.

After one such rehearsal, "My Two Steves" and I took a walk on the Belmar boardwalk. It must have been about 10 PM. They were engrossed in talk about chord changes and repertoire, and about where this little powerhouse band could go. However, I was in a chronic "daze." With a college degree now in hand and the realization that I was qualified to do absolutely nothing, my clinical depression had returned, big time. On top of that, my parents were constantly hocking me to "go out there and get a good job." I felt like a lost sheep, alone in the deep, dark woods.

A teenage girl with a large dog on a leash walked toward us. She smiled. Steve: "Hey cutie, where you going?" "Just walking Chester," she replied. Steve 2: "You live around here?"

"Yeah, next block over." Steve: "You want to walk with us a while?" Girl: "Sure." My best friend, Arthur Fonzarelli, was at it again.

I walked behind the four of them (counting Chester), lost in my own depressive thoughts. Then, the girl turned, stopped, and waited for me to catch up. "You're sad, huh?" she said. "I'm Candy." Candy, Chester and I then began walking together, making small talk, while the two Steves reengaged in band chatter, and continued walking in front of us.

When it got too cold, we headed back to the house. We all assumed Candy and Chester would split. The Steves: "So long Candy. See ya." Me: "Wanna come in?" Candy smiled. "Sure. Can you help me tie up Chester, first?" The Steves were amazed – Candy had a thing for ME!

I found some clothesline, and Candy and I secured Chester to our backyard fence post. We went inside, and sat together on the living room couch, as the Steves continued music talk. They were pretending to pay no attention to Candy at this point. I held her hand. Steve 2: "Hey Candy, how old are you, kid?" "Sixteen," she replied. Steve: "Jailbait, huh!" The Steves laughed. Me (to Candy): "Wanna see my room?" "Yes!" She stood and led me by the hand up the stairs. The Steves watched the unfolding scene in horror. "Jailbait!" Steve 2 shouted up at me with sincere concern: "Careful bro!"

Candy and I entered my room. She kicked off her shoes and lay down on my bed. "Kiss me," she said, and I did. She was adorable. "I'm a virgin," Candy confessed. "But I don't wanna be. Can you teach me about sex?" I was deeply flattered by her request. Miraculously, I had a few condoms in my nightstand drawer (left over from my Kim days.) I slowly removed her clothes. Rock hard, I took a condom and gently (and correctly) installed it. Candy spread her legs. "Like this?" she asked. "No, let me show you." I positioned her with my hands into a better pose, and then, very slowly, entered her. She winced a bit. "You OK? You want me to stop?" I asked. "No! I want you inside of me," came her childlike reply. I maneuvered myself inside and started to pump away.

It was great. Really fucking terrific. Her body was tight, and she smelled like soap. As I was thrusting, a tear gently rolled down her cheek. I came. "Thank you," she said. "That was better than I thought it would be."

We talked for an hour or so, until I got hard again. "Fuck me, Danny." Another go-round, better this time. More powerful. More animal. I came again.

More talking. Chester began to howl outside. "Do you have to go?" I asked. "No way," she said, "I'm not leaving you. Can I spend the night here?" "Of course," I told her. "That would be great." Third go round, doggie-style. Fabulous. We fell asleep. The next morning, we awoke to the sounds of Chester, wailing away. "Shit," Candy said, "My parents will probably kill me."

Just then, it hit me. "Parents?" I'd fucked a "jailbait" minor three times, and she'd slept over in my bed. Her family lived around the corner. If she told her father, I'd be a dead man. "Uh, you don't have to tell your folks about me, do you?" I pleaded. "I don't think they need to know, right?" Candy: "Don't worry, I'll tell them I spent the night at my friend's place. They won't care. They're probably too drunk to notice I wasn't home last night, anyways." I walked Candy downstairs, past the Steves, who were in the kitchen drinking coffee. No words from them were spoken. We untied Chester, she kissed me goodbye, then vanished.

Candy was never discussed further. She didn't leave her number, and I never saw her again. Candy seemed to have been a personal apparition just for me – God had thrown me a "Here, maybe this will help cheer you up 'Carrot.'" The second girl I ever had sex with, Candy remains perhaps the most tender, and mysterious, lover I've ever encountered.

After a few months rehearsing in anonymity, our band, now called "Quick," managed to get a gig at a popular bar. Virtually every human being Steve and I knew in New Jersey planned to attend our debut. However, just two days before our coming out show, our singer, who was truly gifted, quit the band, deciding to embrace his homosexuality by moving into Manhattan to live with his new boyfriend. We had to substitute him at the last possible minute with an opera singer who knew nothing about rock 'n roll.

Quick sucked out loud. Beyond horrible. Words alone could not possibly express the level of suckage here. (Steve tape-recorded the show. To this day, we've never once had the courage to listen to it, more than 40 years later.)

After our second set, the owner of the club approached Steve 2 off to the side of the stage. After a secret talk, S2 returned and whispered, "We've been fired, guys. We need to split after the third set. Plus, we're not getting paid." Crushed, we bravely trudged our way through our final set. Stevie Wonder's "Golden Lady" was a wonder—of strangeness, "Two Tickets to Paradise" rivaled a Pavarotti tune, and the ominous "Moondance" could have won an award at a comedy show. At the end of our performance, I announced, "OK, folks, that's it for Quick tonight. We need to leave now. Thank you all for coming."

Having stoically endured our "performance," our guests were stunned. Steve and I had obviously blown our triumphant return to the Jersey Shore. Sympathetic pity read on the faces of our parents (including my dad and his new girlfriend,) ex-girlfriends, high school buddies, cousins, and closest pals. We packed our gear, and drove back to the Belmar house, in silence.

"Clearly," I thought to myself, "I'm never gonna make a living as a rock star." The next morning, I told the Steves I was quitting the band.

It was time for me to get a "real job."

CHAPTER TEN

Boatshow Babes, the Furniture Store and Heather/Larry at The Globe

Once I'd officially resigned as a musician, my parents gave me some advice: "Get a job doing what you studied in college." The problem was that I had no marketable skills of any kind. The only thing I truly "studied" in college was how to jack-off quickly, and without getting caught.

One day, Paul (Steve's cousin) came to visit the Belmar house. Paul was hilarious—a truly unique, comedic character – a crude blend of Jerry Lewis, Larry David, and Howard Stern. "Larger than life," people from far and wide would drop by Paul's house at all hours of the day and night to sit at his feet and listen to him pontificate about everything under the sun. But Paul's gossip was mostly centered around "who's fucking who." He LOVED any talk about sex.

Bonding instantly, Paul hired me to become the art director with a monthly boating magazine for which he sold advertising space. The pay was $140 a week, a remarkable pittance, but, to me at that time, a small fortune. My new boss, a much older man also named Danny, happened to have a severe case of Tourettes Syndrome.

During the year and a half I worked at the "Boater," Paul and I became more than best friends – we became inseparable. We confided EVERYTHING to each other, no subject was taboo. Sex, jerking off, girlfriends loved and lost, everything was discussed and analyzed. In retrospect, I'd have to say that Paul was my first real therapist.

"I love sex," Paul said to me. "If I looked like you, I'd be getting laid left and right." Paul thought I resembled a movie star. (This actually was the best "looks" era of my life. My acne had subsided, and having worked out with weights for years previous, my body was in great shape.

Girls kept telling me I had "bedroom eyes." Paul: "You can never ever tell anyone this, but when I'm out of town, I cheat on Carol. I've fucked women all along the East Coast."

I was shocked. "You cheat on your wife? The nicest woman on the planet? How can you possibly do that to her?" I'd never met a "cheater" before. Paul explained, "She's the best wife anyone could ever want, but she doesn't turn me on. I need adventure, excitement. I must have fresh pussy. I simply can't live without it."

In addition to my job as the Boater's art director, I was also required to attend various Boat Show Conventions. These were well-attended promotional events during which new subscribers were gleaned, existing advertisers were ass-kissed, potential advertisers were wooed, and new ideas for editorial stories were uncovered. However, Paul had a different agenda: "Boatshow babes are the sexiest broads you'll ever see."

Our first promotional boatshow was in New York City. Paul and I drove up together, meeting the rest of our team at the Javitz Convention Center. "Go find me some new advertisers," Tourettes Danny would call out to us, in between fits of violently loud, horrific, and vulgar "Fuck! Fuck! Prick! Prick!" outbursts.

Over the course of the next three days, Paul became my "older brother," someone determined to lead me to the next level of my burgeoning sexual development. Together, he and I visited every display booth at the boat show. Paul flirted shamelessly with every woman in sight – young, old, black, white, fat, thin, disgusting or goddess. To him, it didn't really matter. "A hole is a hole, don't ever forget that," this equal opportunity wife-cheater instructed.

Since I was younger than Paul, and much better looking, the models manning the booths at the show were flirting back with me. I'd entered a new world. Girls were giving me their phone numbers, posing for pictures with me, and kissing me in front of Paul. I could tell he was proud (he knew what a total loser I really was,) but at the same time, also a bit jealous. He yelled at me once: "You're good looking and you don't even know it! You waste so much time worry-ing if a girl is gonna reject you. Grow up. You should be fucking every woman in here. If I looked like you, I'd be. But, lucky me, I get to look like Arnold Stang."

On our last night in NYC, Paul, and Lloyd, the editor of the Boater (and Tourettes Danny's son) took me out to dinner, where we all got drunk. "I can't go back to Jersey without getting you some 'action,'" Paul glared at me. Lloyd chuckled. A wisp of a man with big, thick glasses, nerdy Lloyd could have been the founder of the "Geek Squad." Paul never mocked Lloyd, simply because he was too easy a target, most probably a virgin, and, more importantly, his boss's son. "After dinner, we're gonna walk Seventh Avenue, so I can get you laid."

The three of us walked the streets of Manhattan in the freezing cold—this was January. Bundled head to toe, our breaths clearly visible in smoke, we were shivering. Blocks later, we saw a rather attractive redhead, 40-ish, bundled in a coat, standing under an enormous sign of a neon Earth. We were at the foot of the Globe Hotel, in God-only-knows-where, New York City. Paul went right up to her: "Hey, I'm Paul. These are my little brothers, Danny and Lloyd. Danny needs some action. How much?" The woman scanned me up and down. "He's kinda cute," she said, "I'll take care of him. It'll be $100." Paul opened his wallet and paid Heather the dough. I was astonished. A hundred dollars? That was a HUGE amount of money to me. Almost a week's salary. "Paul, you don't have to do this…that's way too much!" Paul wouldn't hear of it. "Someday, you'll thank for me tonight," he winked. Lloyd stood in silence, mortified.

Heather took my hand and led me up the rickety, narrow staircase of the Globe Hotel. We approached a tiny little window of the office – an elderly man sat behind it. Heather: "Give us half an hour Max," she said to the ancient guy, who presented me with a sign-in sheet. Panicked, I invented an alter-ego, singing my name "Dana West." "Twenty bucks, kid," Max said. I looked at Heather. "Pay the man." I had maybe $40 in my wallet, MAYBE. I gave Max a precious $20 bill. Heather again took my hand and led me down the most disgusting hallway I'd ever seen in my life. We entered a shitty little room. Heather removed her enormous fake fur coat, but kept on a thick, red sweater, and a scarf. Clearly a babe in her younger days, Heather's body was still killer, but now, she kinda looked like a haggard Ann-Margret.

"Your buddy Paul tells me you need to be taken care of. So how do you judge that?" Me: "Huh?" Heather: "How do you rate being 'taken care' of?" I had NO IDEA what this woman was talking about. I shrugged. "Well, just take off your clothes and let's see what happens." Here I was, the biggest loser on the planet, shivering in a room about 50 degrees. I was naked but for black socks, with a tiny, not-even-close-to-hard dick, while lying on a rat-infested bed, in a total shithole hotel, staring at a well-worn whore asking me questions I had no ability to answer.

Heather: "You like getting your dick sucked?" "Sure, I guess so." The look of pity in Heather's face said it all. Clearly, I was a pathetic little fish in a new pond, devoid of all clues.

Heather pulled a chair up next to the bed, leaned over, took Mr. Limp Cock into her hand, stuffed it in her mouth, and started sucking. I felt like I'd entered a Hoover vacuum cleaner. It was intense—I thought I was shedding skin. After no more than four minutes, probably less, I shot my load. I don't think I ever actually got HARD, but she did make me cum, for which I was extremely grateful. Heather stood, smiled, walked over to the rust filled sink (situated in the middle of the room,) spat, brushed her teeth, and said, "OK, lover, you can get dressed now. We're done." Re-dressed in a flash and shaking, I walked with her back down the hallway of hell. Downstairs, I re-joined my brethren, who'd been freezing their nuts off on the sidewalk in front of the Globe, awaiting my return.

Paul: "So, Heather, how'd my boy do up there?" A good sport, Heather replied, "A real pro—a champ. Turned me on like crazy." Heather brushed my cheek with her gloved hand. "Goodnight, champ," she said. As she walked away, she turned her face over her shoulder: "So long, boys, don't forget me."

Paul, Lloyd, and I walked back to our hotel, giggling like little kids. Paul: "I want to hear everything. Every single fucking detail, no matter how small." I said, "Let's go to the bar – I really need a drink. Then I'll tell you guys what happened." Lloyd, suddenly big man on campus, said, "You better. I want to hear just how pathetic that was." Like Lloyd had ever been blown in his life.

We sat at the hotel bar, shaking the shivers from our bodies. Paul got us drinks. Me: "OK, guys, before I say a word, you both have to SWEAR that you will never tell ANYONE?" Lloyd: "We swear, we swear…now tell us already." I then relayed, in graphic detail, exactly what had happened, from my encounter with Max, to the shitty hallway, from the disgusting, rat-infested bed and my black socks, to Heather spitting my love juice out into the rusty sink in the middle of the room. Not one gruesome detail was spared.

Paul: "Hold on, Romeo, there's one thing you haven't told us yet. What did Heather look like without her clothes?" "Yeah," Lloyd chimed in, "Did she have nice big boobs?" I was stunned when I realized, for the first time, that Heather had remained CLOTHED during our entire encounter. I had to reveal the truth. "She never took her clothes off, only her coat," I confessed. "I never saw anything more than her face and her hair."

Astonished, Paul and Lloyd looked at each other for about five seconds in absolute silence, and then burst out laughing. Or should I say howling. Unforgettable, hysterical, incredibly loud laughter.

Tears shot out of Paul's eyes horizontally. Lloyd almost fell off his bar stool and onto the floor. "You never saw her naked body?" Paul managed to squeal, "Are you fucking kidding me? I paid a whore a hundred bucks, and you never even saw tits or pussy or ass? I can't believe this!." More hysteria. Other patrons sitting at the bar joined in—Paul's laughter was highly contagious.

Lloyd: "For all we know 'Heather' could have been a transvestite!" Shrieked

Paul: "Yeah, she was PROBABLY a MAN named LARRY!" Paul and Lloyd fell to the ground, crying. They couldn't stop. Paul practically announced to the crowd: "YOU JUST GOT SUCKED OFF BY LARRY THE WHORE!" Mayhem ensued – even the bartender, who had no idea what we were talking about, had tears of laughter streaming down his cheeks. I got caught up in the lunacy as well. It was the hardest I'd laughed in many years.

Back in New Jersey, I called the girls from Manhattan who'd given me their phone numbers. However, the "Carrots Curse" started kicking back in. Each girl had one excuse or another (Tourettes Danny called them "Bubba-Meisers"—the Yiddish word for "fairy tales.")

They ranged from, "Oh, you live too far away," to "My grandmother's really sick," to "You're cute, and I wouldn't mind fucking you, but my boyfriend just moved back to town," etc.

A few weeks later, the Asbury Park boat show arrived. Paul and I attended the press conference, during which the new boat show queens would be revealed. During this event, an older blonde beauty, Joanne, and her petite, brunette friend Megan, approached Paul and I. Joanne was undressing me with her eyes: "Hello, handsome. Who are you?" We talked for a while, and she told me that she'd been a boat show queen years before, but still enjoyed attending the conventions. I got her number. Paul beamed onto Megan like a laser. "I'm Paulie, your new lover," he told her. She laughed. He grabbed her arm, and together they walked off, disappearing for half an hour.

On the drive home, Paul told me, "Megan blew me. She wants me to visit her this weekend. She's divorced." Me: "What about Carol?" "I'll tell her I'm working on something with YOU, so don't blow my cover, OK?" Paul explained. "We'll pretend to go out of town together. Then, you can wait for me in the car." Me: "Why would I do that?" Paul: "You want me to tell everyone we know about 'Larry'?" "Alright, deal, no problem," I meekly replied.

Later that week, we drove to Megan's place, about an hour away. When we arrived, Paul smoked a quick cigarette, and splashed some cologne on his acne-pitted face. (For all his incredible bravado, Paul was not remotely handsome.) "How do I look?" he asked, the one time I'd ever seen him vulnerable. "Like a guy who's about to cheat on his wife." "Good," he said. "Wait here." Paul entered Megan's house, while I remained in the car, listening to the radio and waiting.

After an hour, during which time I recalled my days in high school waiting for Steve to finish with Laura, I went to stretch my legs. The only place open on the street at that time was an enormous, discount furniture store. I walked in, and slowly reviewed the merchandise for quite some time. I was there so long, in fact, the owner brought me a cup of hot chocolate and a donut. "Take your time, son, no rush." For close to two hours, I pretended to shop for cheap, unfinished, pine wood furniture.

FINALLY, Paul met me back at the car. "My God," he was breathless. "That chick REALLY knows how to fuck! Best sex I've ever had in my life! That bitch is an animal in bed…probably because she has cancer and doesn't know how much longer she has to live."

Cancer? "Yeah," he continued. "Her body is covered with surgery scars everywhere. She's had like seven or eight operations to remove tumors. Her body's a mess…so I insisted the lights stay off. As long as I didn't have to look at her, the sex was perfect. Really fucking amazing."

After Paul's experience with Megan, I figured I had a pretty good shot with Joanne, her best friend. She picked me up one night for our date in her little, yellow, sports car convertible, her long blonde hair flying in the breeze. We ate, I paid. I then managed to lure her back to the Belmar house. We went upstairs to my room, and I walked her onto the second floor balcony. We kissed in the moonlight. It was hot. She was hot. She pressed against me. I got hard. The Steves downstairs were impressed with this chick. All systems go.

"Is THAT your CAR?" she shrieked. I had an old, total piece of shit, 1970 Ford LTD, with rust on the sides, parked just in front of the house. "Urgh, uhm, yeah, that's mine," I confessed. She looked at me sideways, incredulous. "THAT's your CAR? Are you serious?" Joanne was completely annoyed. "Wow…ah, well, I should probably head home now." I walked her downstairs, and she split, never to be heard from again.

"She judged YOU for your CAR?" Paul screamed at work the next day. "She can go fuck herself!!" And for the rest of the time I worked at the Boater, Paul, Lloyd and I referred to Joanne as "She Who Deserves No Name," and later, simply, as "No Name," for short.

Another boat show beauty Paul and I met then was Ramona, a professional model who, today, I'd compare to Jenny McCarthy. One day Ramona asked if I'd like to take her roommate, Jane, out for a date. "She's very cute," she said. "You'll like her." "Beautiful as you?" I asked. "Honey, no one's as beautiful as me," she joked. "But trust me, I'm sure you'll like her." Ramona handed me Jane's number, and the date was set.

I took Jane to a romantic restaurant in Asbury Park, overlooking the lake. We had a terrific time. She was a tall, thin, blonde, and very attractive. After dinner, she asked, "You are gonna take me back to your place, right?" I led Jane upstairs to my room at the Belmar house. Once again, the Steves were impressed. She took off her shoes, hopped onto my bed, and asked, "You got any disco records?" The Steves and I abhorred disco, but I managed to find a Donna Summers record, and put it on the stereo.

Jane and I made out for a short while. It was fun – really great. Then, I began unzipping her tight jeans. "No, no, don't, please don't!" Jane implored. I was stumped. A few minutes later, I tried again. "Please, please stop, please don't," she begged. I was baffled. Her body was telling me "Yes, yes, yes," while her words were clearly not in sync. I tried to unbutton her shirt. "Stop, I need you to stop, please don't," she insisted. I sat up in the bed. "Janey, don't you want to make love with me?" I asked. "Huh?" Jane was dumbfounded. Silently, she got off the bed, put her shoes on, and said, "Please take me home now."

Days later, Ramona led me aside. "Just because a girl tells you 'no, no, don't, don't,' it doesn't mean you stop trying to screw her! It's just a game we play. Janey totally wanted to have sex with you, and you blew it, Charlie! She couldn't believe you stopped trying. And then you said something about 'making love?' Who talks like that?" Ramona walked away in a huff. "Thanks?" I called out meekly.

The summer was approaching, and Steve and I had to bail out of the Belmar house, as our lease was set to expire. I rented a new apartment in Long Branch, N.J., near a fun area called "West End." (Before his fame, Bruce Springsteen hung out there, usually alone. In the early '70s, I'd see him sitting on the beach, staring into space, probably writing "Jungleland" in his head.)

I was now living much closer to work, but still had zero "mojo" going on with the ladies. One evening after the Boater, and especially horny, I went to a 7-11 to buy a new *Playboy* (at least I wasn't stealing them anymore.) I tossed the mag on the counter. A very cute girl in her 20s working the register saw my purchase, looked directly into my face, and asked with concern, "Wouldn't the 'real thing' just feel a whole lot better?" I stared back in dismay. Too naïve to pick up on the hint, I was far too depressed even to simply respond.

Dear God, once again, I'd give my kingdom for a time machine.

One summer day on the beach, I bumped into Lori, a girl I knew from high school and Rutgers. We spent hours talking and reminisced about our past. We hadn't seen each other in five years. Lori looked incredibly attractive. She'd lost weight, had a terrific tan, and had grown into a very sexy figure. Surprisingly, Lori had become a major babe.

We went directly from the beach to a restaurant for dinner. There, we devised a plan: We'd jointly produce a mini high school reunion that next weekend in my apartment. Between us, we were still in touch with dozens of high school colleagues. We agreed to split the costs of food and liquor, and Lori offered to cook her "famous quiches" in my kitchen.

Days later, as we were setting up for the party, I asked, "Lori, did you happen to go to our senior prom?" "No," she replied, "Did you?" Me: "No, I didn't." I hesitated, then added. "The reason I didn't go, was because I was too shy to ask out the girl I SHOULD HAVE ASKED." Lori: "Someone I know?" I pointed at her. "Yeah…YOU."

Supernatural magnetism. We flew into each others arms, and began rolling around on the kitchen floor, making out and humping like two psychos. We were panting—we could hardly breathe.

"Ding-dong" – our party guests began arriving! What incredible shit timing! We stood, caught our breaths, and greeted dozens of our friends.

The party was legendary – it became our unofficial five year high school reunion. Friends caught up through a haze of pot, beer, and vodka. Lori's quiches were a huge hit. The whole night, she and I stayed on opposite sides of my apartment, staring at each other from afar. I told Steve and Dean what had briefly transpired. Dean said, "Really? That's cool. Make sure you fuck her tonight."

During the party, a former high school classmate was making moves on Lori, while she blatantly flirted back with him. At one point, I thought for sure I'd lost my shot. As the party was winding down, everyone began to leave, and even Lori was about to waltz out of my place with this dude. Surprising even myself (I was quite drunk,) I walked up, put my arm around her waist, and said to this putz, "Sorry, bro. Lori's mine tonight." One of the gutsiest things I'd ever done.

The apartment now empty, Lori threw me to the floor. We picked up exactly where we'd left off hours earlier. Shoes and clothes came flying off, in all directions. Everything was removed, however, except for her dark blue, one-piece danskin. Nude, I was puzzled. "Ah, are you gonna take that off, too?" I gently asked. "No, it stays on," she replied. "Well, uhm, Lori, I'd really like to have sex with you. I have condoms in the other room and everything." Lori: "Trust me, you won't need any condoms tonight. This danskin stays on."

Pure confusion. Was Lori a virgin? Was she afraid of having sex with me? Was she a cockteaser? Should I just get a knife and cut the damn thing off? I recalled what Ramona had taught me: "Just because a girl says 'no,' it doesn't mean it really means 'no.'" But since Lori's "no" left little room for debate, and with a raging hard on the size of Wisconsin, I decided to move forward, regardless.

I humped Lori in every possible position and orgasmed onto her danskin three times. I'm pretty sure Lori came too, if her panting, sweating, and moaning were any indication. Exhausted, we slept on the living room floor, under a blanket.

The next morning, I was infatuated. I asked Lori if we could get together that night for dinner. "Of course," she said, as she got into her car and drove off. A bit later, Dean called. "Fuck her?" Not wanting to sound like a total loser, I simply replied, "Three times." It was a partial truth – one that would surely keep severe humiliation at bay. "Good job."

Late that afternoon, I called Lori's house. Her mother answered. "Hey, Mrs. S., this is Lori's friend, Danny. She there? We're going out for dinner tonight." Her mom explained to me that Lori was on a date with "the son of one of my best friends. I've been wanting them to meet for years. He's a very wealthy young man, and Lori's very excited about meeting him." Blowing me off, the woman hung up.

I should have just torn that goddamned danskin off with my bare teeth.

Out of the blue, Brad called to say his mother had "the perfect girl for Danny." Her name was Emma, a short, chubby Jewess who came from an incredibly wealthy family. The only problem for me, though, was that she lived in Manhattan. I met Emma at a party Brad's mom threw, and we hit it off immediately. While she wasn't exactly a "beauty" by any stretch of the imagination, she did have a sweet smile and nice boobs. But the best thing about her was that she really seemed to dig me.

"We're gonna have a lot of fun together in the City," she promised. "Sounds good to me," I said. We snuck into the bathroom during the party and started making out. Suddenly, from nowhere, I had a sophisticated, rich new girlfriend, who lived on the Upper East Side of Manhattan.

New Year's Eve, Emma invited me to spend the holiday at her tiny apartment (the toilet and bathtub were in her kitchen, exposed.) I had about eighty bucks to my name but spent half of it on a bottle of Jouet champagne, with hand-painted flowers on its front. We downed the bottle in her candlelit bedroom, then made love two or three times. "Let's go take a coach ride through the park," she suggested.

The streets at 2 AM were pretty deserted as I recall, but a few couples were lining up at Central Park South and Fifth Avenue for horse and carriage rides. Emma and I hopped up into a carriage, the driver gave me a rose to hand her, and we started clip-clopping through the snowlaced park. Shivering, we sat huddled together under a blanket, Emma leaning her head against my shoulder. It was really quiet.

As we rode, I realized it was <u>exactly</u> two years earlier that I'd spent dancing with and kissing Kim at the Royal Manor. While that encounter was certainly magical, this moment in time, in Central Park with Emma, riding a horse and carriage into the new decade of the 1980s, seemed much more normal.

This "Carrot" seemed much more real.

CHAPTER ELEVEN

Sex In the City, Abe's "Ass Shorts" and Babysitting Brooke Shields

Emma and I were having sex. A LOT of sex. She was horny as hell, and simply "couldn't get enough." She also hated rubbers. "Know what that is?" she once asked, after casually tossing a diaphragm onto her bed. (It was the first time I'd ever seen that device.) I'd ride a bus into the City each Friday evening after work, and Emma and I would spent most of our time together in her lavender bedroom, a hair larger than a broom closet. She was in love with all things lavender, and was falling in love (pretty quickly) with me. A mutual Dan Fogelberg fan, she and I always had sex listening to his wonderfully romantic albums.

Emma's parents were "filthy New York rich," she once said. She took me to their penthouse one day – the place was like an enormous, Egyptian museum. I was afraid to touch anything. I asked, since her folks were so wealthy, why she lived in such a dumpy place. "I make my own way in life," she said proudly. "Just because they're loaded, doesn't mean I am."

Emma was the world's worst cook, but who cared? I had a place to hang out in the Big Apple, was getting massive amounts of sex, and could read the New York Times on Sunday mornings, in my pajamas. "Life doesn't get much better than this," I thought.

Alas, my days of Sex "In" the City with Emma were to be short-lived. Valentine Day's weekend. I was up at Em's place, and we were doing our usual NYC stuff—the holiday was the furthest thing from my mind. I'd never had a girlfriend during a V-Day holiday before and didn't think ahead to buy her a gift. Big fucking mistake.

All that weekend, Emma kept looking at me with mysterious eyes—I suppose she was trying to glean what I planned to give her. Sunday afternoon, Emma burst into her bedroom, and

THREW a wrapped gift package at me. "Happy Fucking Valentine's Day, Dick Head!" The package cut my face. I sheepishly opened it – she'd given me two beautiful dress shirts, before storming out of the apartment, crying.

Instead of doing THE RIGHT THING, which would have been to go after her, fall at her feet and beg forgiveness, I decided to catch an earlier bus back to the Jersey Shore. Arriving home hours earlier than expected, I was kinda proud of myself for having avoided the horrific fight that would have awaited me, had I stayed any longer.

I was 23 and unbelievably immature. Instead of apologizing, I fled for my life, avoiding any chance of reconciliation. I had no idea how to talk to women, nor any clue about what was important to them. As long as I was getting laid, nothing else really seemed to matter to me. Confrontation of any kind? Color me gone.

I never had the courage to call Emma afterward, and, as result, I never saw or heard from her again.

One good thing did result from the months I dated Emma, though. I fell in love with the wonders of Manhattan. As a kid, my family and I would occasionally visit relatives in Brooklyn, but now in my 20s, I got to experience New York City really for the first time… the smells, the excitement, the too many people. I was enthralled.

I had a one-week vacation from the Boater lined up, so I secretly decided to spend those precious days "pounding the pavement" in the Big Apple to pursue a job in communications. I had a few interviews with personnel agencies, but nothing came of them. On the last day of that week, I called a friend of mine, Stu, from B.U., who was now working at a movie company called Columbia Pictures. (I knew absolutely NOTHING WHATSOEVER about the entertainment industry. I could barely have named the three major television networks back then.) He'd just been promoted to Publicist and told me his old job as an assistant was available.

I arrived at Columbia Pictures within a half-hour. The building was a beautiful older one on Fifth Avenue, just a few blocks south of Central Park and the Plaza Hotel. Stu introduced me to Abe K., a legendary motion picture promotions guy who made Methuselah look like one of the Olsen twins. Abe had been in the movie business for about sixty years. He used to play golf with the Warner Brothers (the ACTUAL Warner Brothers,) escorted President Truman around Hollywood, and once dated Jane Russell. Looking up from his clutter filled desk, his eyes caught mine. Abe: "You as good as Stuart?" Me: "Uh, I don't know, maybe, I hope so." (I had NO IDEA WHO these people were or what they even did. Movie Publicity and Promotion? What the FUCK did that even mean? No fucking idea.) Abe: "Well, if Stuart likes you, then I guess I like you. When can you start?" Me: "Uh, uhm, ergh, two weeks?" Abe: "You're hired."

Stu led me to personnel, shook my hand, and said, "Welcome to Columbia Pictures. You're in the movie business now!"

Concurrent with scoring my new job, I had to move out of my West End apartment, after a dispute with my landlady. As Steve (and Steve 2) were now both back living with their parents, I had no other roommate option, and was forced to move into my mother's small, two-bedroom, post-divorce place, which she shared with my youngest brother, Michael, now in high school.

I began work at Columbia Pictures, and, ironically, had I not completely fouled things up with Emma a mere few weeks earlier, could most likely have lived with her, just a few blocks north of my new job. Instead, I had to commute by bus from my mother's place into the City. I rode that motherfucking bus for four hours a day (two hours each way,) five days a week for four months It was true hell.

I had no idea what I was doing at that job. Basically, Abe was in charge of "field promotions" in the New York City area. He was constantly coming up with zany ideas. To promote the crappy film *Used Cars*, Abe brought a huge trash bag filled with greasy spark plugs, fan belts, and engine parts to my desk. He told me to wrap them, one at a time, along with free screening passes, and messenger them off to local area film critics as gifts. There I was in a new suit and tie, gift wrapping disgusting, oily car parts, and tying them up in ribbons. "This is the movie business?" I asked myself.

To promote the film *The Hollywood Knights*, Abe had printed up little white short shorts—with flesh-color painted "ass cheeks" on the back. He asked me if I knew any beautiful young girls. I told him about some of the more recent Asbury Park boat show queens I'd met. He had me hire two of them to walk around Manhattan wearing these shorts, while handing out promotional materials for the film.

I hired a gorgeous blonde boat show queen, and her friend, a sweet brunette, both from New Jersey, to come into the City, and walk around with me. They were good sports about wearing Abe's "Ass Shorts." Construction workers hanging from steel girders in unfinished skyscrapers wolf whistled after them. That night, I took the brunette to see the just released movie, "Friday the 13th". Scared out of her mind, she threw up on my shoes in the theater, half-way through the film. Afterwards, she asked that I please never call her again.

During the time I worked at Columbia, the studio's biggest hit film was *The Blue Lagoon*, starring Brooke Shields, then a young teen. Brooke and her mother were constantly hanging out in the PR department. Brooke's mom was nicknamed "Terrible Teri" by my co-workers, all of whom were scared to death of her. But, for some reason, Teri seemed to like <u>me</u>. One day in a panic, Abe called me into his office. "Dan, I need you to babysit Brooke Shields and her mom. 'Terrible Teri' specifically asked if you could bring them up to the screening room, and tell them to run her movie, ok? They haven't seen the finished film yet." I took the two ladies upstairs to the beautiful private screening room at Columbia, where, together, the three of us watched *The Blue Lagoon*. It was the first time they had seen the film in its entirety. In the elevator back down to the PR offices, I said: "Brooke, you were terrific…a really talented actress." Brooke: "You really liked it? I thought it was embarrassing."

One day, while I was busy filing, with my back facing toward the front of my desk, I could sense the "presence" of someone powerful standing – in silence – behind me. Brooke Shield's charisma was literally magnetic – it "pulled" me to turn around. She was young and sweet, modest and electric at that time. I adored her.

Commuting by bus every day into Manhattan from the Jersey Shore was killing me. I began shaking and trembling, and my asthma (which I'd overcome from childhood,) was acting up by inhaling bus fumes. I felt exhausted and depressed. Although I was making good money, and was, technically speaking, in "showbiz," the effort was more than I could handle.

And to exacerbate matters, there was a beautiful woman who rode the same bus with me each morning. My age perhaps, dirty blonde hair, expensive business suit, briefcase – I imagined she was a lawyer. However, any time I glanced in her direction, she would deflect my gaze and look away. I never once was able to catch her eye. Several times, we were even forced to sit side by side, when no other seats were available. She became another "Long Red" to me – yet another elusive "Carrot." God forbid either of us could have, just once, broken the ice.

One day, Abe handed me a package. "These are film trailers for Brooklyn. They need to be put on the truck, today. It's important, OK? Take them down to the mail room." I completely fucked this assignment up, and had the trailers <u>mailed</u> instead of delivered by rush messenger. The next day Abe got a screaming phone call from the producer of one of our films. The trailers weren't showing in Brooklyn. Abe called me to his office. "You put those trailers on the truck yesterday, right?" Me: "Yeah, Abe, of course. The mail truck." Abe's face fell. "The MAIL truck? I wanted you to put them on the DELIVERY truck! They had to be there by last night!! Are you trying to get me fired??" He was beyond pissed. He was incredulous—the only time I'd ever seen him angry. He skulked away and closed the door in my face. I knew, at that moment, my job there was doomed.

I stayed at Columbia another three weeks after that disaster, but Abe barely spoke to me any longer. This screw up of mine, on top of my growing medical ailments, and the ice queen on the bus, were all conspiring against me. This job was much too hard for me to maintain. I simply couldn't do it. I asked the head of the PR department if she could please lay me off, so I could get unemployment benefits. Both she and Abe agreed.

At the end of my last day at Columbia Pictures, Abe said, "You're a good kid, Dan. You mean well. I'm sure you'll find something out there more suited to your personality." We shook hands. I left, feeling enormous relief, but, also, huge disappointment.

Had I blown my one big "show business" break?

Honestly, I couldn't have cared less. All I could think about, on that final bus ride home from Manhattan that night, in July 1980, was the serious amounts of sleep I needed to catch up on.

CHAPTER TWELVE

Hello N.J., My Old Friend

Now unemployed, living once again with my mother and little brother, Michael, really sucked. Growing up, we'd had a huge house with a massive yard. Post parents' divorce, the three of us (my brother Bobby was at college in Arizona) were now squished inside a small two-bedroom garden apartment, in which Michael and I had to share a bedroom. Within the complex, we had to share laundry facilities, fight for parking spaces, and listen to strange neighbors fighting, watching TV, or having sex. Without question, my parents' divorce had dramatically caused my family to "fall from grace." (Strapped for cash, my father was living in a miniscule beachfront apartment he called "the hovel.")

At this point, my mother, no longer able to find work as a schoolteacher, had earned a Masters degree, and was now a full time probation officer. Michael had become a local guitar hero with his own band. Steve kept pursuing his rock and roll dreams, Brad moved back to Boston. And Paul had become despondent, after his floozy, Megan, died of cancer.

I was a man without a country.

Fourth of July arrived. I had no plans. Neither did my mother. "Take me out on a date tonight. Let's go to the boardwalk for dinner and then we'll watch the fireworks," she suggested. I drove her to the Long Branch boardwalk. We ate and watched the holiday celebration in the sky. My mother put her arm through mine, as though we were actually "on a date." A shiver ran down my spine—this was getting a little too weird.

As we walked back to the car, I noticed all of the young couples everywhere, laughing, kissing and walking, arm in arm. These were my peers—my colleagues—all with loving, sexy partners. All enjoying their youth. Here I was, my MOTHER on my arm, with nothing resembling a girlfriend for miles in any direction. I suddenly became sickened—I almost threw up. "What's wrong?" she asked. "Let's get back home. I don't feel too well," I replied.

Desperate now for money, I went back to the Boater, tail between my legs.

I asked Tourettes Danny if he could re-hire me, but pay me under the table, so I could also collect unemployment benefits, and he agreed. Paul couldn't have been nicer – he felt pretty bad about my Columbia Pictures fiasco, and, surprisingly, never once rubbed in the fact that I'd blown such a major career opportunity.

Here I was in a dead-end job I'd already quit, living with my lonely mother and little brother in a small apartment, broke. My parents were divorced, my car was falling apart, I had no female companionship of any kind, and my closest friends were nowhere to be found.

(Note: The one thing that did keep me occupied during those few months was taking a first crack at writing *Carrots*. At that time, I wrote it up as a fictitious screenplay. It took me decades to finally realize *Carrots* should be a book, instead. Thus, the piece you are now reading took over 40 years to craft.)

One day, I came home early from the Boater to take a nap. My mother happened to be home and had left her bedroom door open. I went to say hi and caught a scene I've been trying to erase from memory ever since. Standing alone in her bedroom, the naked woman was plugging an enormous, vibrating, "massage wand" into a wall outlet. I froze in silence, then tiptoed backward very slowly, trying not to "creak" the floor. I knew she hadn't seen me, because if she had, she'd still be screaming, to this day.

Outside in the parking lot, I had a talk with myself: "You can't stay here anymore…it's time to do something new. Time to go somewhere else. You do <u>not belong here</u>! You need to find your destiny."

The problem was, I had absolutely no idea what—or where—that destiny was supposed to be.

Miraculously, my destiny called me by phone a few days later. Ronnie, a long-lost friend, rang to say he was now living in Los Angeles, and suggested that Steve and I swing out for a visit. I asked my dad, "You think I should visit him?" Dad: "Schmuck!! Don't just VISIT! MOVE there! That's where show business is, right? That's what you want to do. Sell off your stuff, pack up some clothes, buy a plane ticket, and MOVE to Los Angeles. That's the best advice I can give you."

I thought about it for about five seconds...maybe less. "OK, Dad, thanks. I guess I'll do that." (And thus, the future of my entire life was decided just that quickly.)

Concurrently, and by pure coincidence, a female singer from New York who was friends with Steve, had also recently moved to Los Angeles. She called to invite Steve and I to visit her and her new boyfriend there, as well.

Now, with absolutely zero advance notice of any kind, I became West Coast bound. Planning my relocation to Los Angeles gave me a new lease on life. Having never before been a fan, I bought The Beach Boy's "Greatest Hits" LP, and listened to it, over and over again. I bought a map of Southern California and studied it. I'd never heard of the Hollywood Bowl, the Walk of Fame, or even the Hollywood Sign. My knowledge of Los Angeles was only that it was far away, it was hot there, and the ocean was on the left-hand side.

Within about a month, I sold off my meager possessions (except my Bar Mitzvah drum set, which would remain in the basement of Steve's house for decades.) These items included my shitty old car, my furniture in storage, old record albums, and the one thing I owned of any real value—a coin collection my grandfather had left me. I raised exactly $2,000, an immense fortune.

The hardest part about moving to LA would be saying goodbye to my mother. While she'd just begun dating a nice guy named Jay (who my brother and I were convinced was gay,) she was still extremely sad about her divorce. She was raising Michael alone, and he was rarely even in the apartment. Mostly, he was out smoking pot or stealing beer. (He was actually arrested four times within the first year after I'd left New Jersey – a fact I didn't learn until 2022!)

After Steve and I purchased tickets to Los Angeles, I realized my mother's 46th birthday would be the day after I split. I arranged for a dozen roses to be delivered to her, in my absence. The morning of my flight: I hugged my mother goodbye, turned, and walked away. Smoking a cigarette behind my back, she said, "Fine, go to California. Leave me here all alone. See what I care."

Outside, Michael was waiting for the bus to take him to school. I hugged him goodbye as well and advised him to try to stay out of trouble. As I watched him pull away, I had a tear in my eye. About to leave the East Coast for the first time in my 24 years of life, I realized I was going to miss my baby brother – who I'd diapered when he was an infant – the most of all.

CHAPTER THIRTEEN

"Jersey to Jacuzzi:" The First "Carrots" of Los Angeles

During our first-ever, cross-country flight, the airline Steve and I flew served an all you can eat, buffet style lunch, which I'm sure, to this day, has never been repeated, anywhere. (My Bar Mitzvah had less food.) Landing at LAX, we were greeted by our mutual friend Ronnie and his girlfriend, who allowed us to crash at their large, two-bedroom apartment in Culver City. Adrienne was much younger than us – a busty redhead. She and Ronnie worked full time, so during the days, Steve and I were on our own. On our first afternoon in LA (it was October,) we went to Santa Monica beach in shorts, flip flops, and T-shirts, expecting 100 degrees, bikini girls everywhere, and The Beach Boys, themselves, actually performing on the sand. Instead, we froze our asses off. "This is Southern California?" Steve asked. "Where are all the half-naked chicks?"

In the early evenings, Steve, Ronnie, and I would lounge around in the outdoor Jacuzzi, located in the center of his apartment complex. Looking up at the stars at night and drinking a cold beer in a bubbling hot Jacuzzi, was a completely new experience. Ronnie said, "Hey Danny, if you ever write a book about your life, you should call it 'Jersey to Jacuzzi.'" Then, Steve and I would hear Ronnie and Adrienne screwing. Once again, I was confronted with the "Call of the Wild."

After three weeks, Steve's friend, Joanne the singer, insisted we next stay with her and her boyfriend at their apartment, on Venice Beach boardwalk (actually, a blacktop cement walk.) Feeling that we'd overstayed our welcome with Ronnie, Steve and I were glad to leave. John and Joanne (J&J) had a tiny, one bedroom place, but the location was terrific. Steve and I took turns sleeping on the couch and the floor. J&J toured us through Hollywood and the mansions of Bel Air, drove us to Disneyland and ferried us out to Catalina Island.

That Halloween, J&J took us to a costume party at Madame Wu's nightclub in Santa Monica – the place was packed. There, I met a very attractive blonde dressed as a fairy princess, all in white, with extended wings. Her name was Carole. She insisted on giving me her phone number, which I gladly accepted. "Looks like your luck's about to change," Steve noted.

After quick side trips together to San Francisco and San Diego, Steve was ready to return to New Jersey. We took a cab to the airport together, then approached the gate. "You need to smile more," he admonished. "You always look like the world's about to end. If you smile, you'll feel better, and people around you will want to get to know you. Try it sometime. Your life isn't so bad." Me: "Yeah sure, Steve, thanks. I'll do my best." (Neither of us realized at the time the depth of clinical depression in which I was immersed.) We hugged. He boarded. I watched his plane vanish.

Having been virtually co-joined for exactly 12 straight years, Steve and I were logistically breaking up. I no longer had a fall-back buddy to rely on. I didn't really know Joanne very well, had just met John, and my boyhood friend, Ronnie, was distracted by his girlfriend. Almost alone, now, in a vast, unknown new city, with no connections, no car, no job, no relatives, no girlfriends, and very little money left, I was three thousand miles away from everything and everyone I'd ever known in my life.

The only person who could bail me out of a problem, now, would be me.

John allowed me his car for my date with Carole, and I was incredibly excited. Here I was, about to experience my first date in California, convinced that my "Carrots" years were behind me. This was my clean slate – my fresh start with women. Carole was attractive, funny, and young. Surely, she'd be the girlfriend I'd been waiting for.

Arriving at her home, I found a note taped to the front door: "Dear Danny, I'm so sorry about this whole thing. I can't believe this has happened. One of my best friends was involved in a car accident, and her family is out of town. I have to go to the hospital to be with her. I'm so sorry to ruin your evening. Please call and let's try it again. Thanx (sic) for understanding—Carole." I called Carole again many, many times afterward, but no one ever answered the phone. Today, that note lives inside my "Carrots" scrapbook.

My very first girl in California = Brand New Carrot #1.

During the course of the first year I lived in LA, I had an assortment of temporary jobs, including selling women's clothes on Venice Beach, typing legal documents for a Korean law firm, typing TV scripts for the production company behind the TV show *Solid Gold*, and packing files into storage for an ad agency. My income was completely "cut and pasted" together, but since I didn't have to pay rent, nor cover car or health insurance, my only expense was food. I lived on coffee, pizza slices, ice cream, crackers and peanut butter, for months.

On the days I had no temp work lined up (and they were many,) I'd lounge around for hours on Venice Beach, sunbathing, reflecting, and writing poetry. (I refer to this now as my "Jim Morrison" period.) For the first time since early childhood, I felt peaceful and content. My only obligation was, simply, to stay alive. I didn't have to appease my parents, teachers, or our frightening Rabbi; wasn't fighting with my brothers, arguing with band mates, or dealing with deafening rock music; didn't hear "Call of the Wild" sex cries (I think J&J were asexual,) nor did I have to endure sexcapade tales from Steve or Paul. And best of all, I was no longer obsessed with the myriad of girls who'd come before. Surely, with all the millions of beautiful females in Southern California, God could spare JUST ONE for ME, eventually!

However, this footloose and fancy-free lifestyle did come with a price: After just a few months in LA, I had six dollars to my name. When I told my dad, he flew out, took me for a prime rib dinner, bought me $250 of groceries, and flew back to N.J. the next day. Talk about a superstar parent. My dad was my hero.

A few weeks after John Lennon was murdered, a remarkable thing happened. J&J told me that they were going to move back to New York to get married. I would be "inheriting" their apartment, and they would continue to pay one half of the rent. Between my temp work in LA, and the long-lost unemployment benefits from back East which had finally found me in California after many months of delay, I now had enough income to cover all expenses. After a solid year of living with others, I could now sleep in my own bed, eat from my own refrigerator, and shit in my own toilet, a view of the Pacific Ocean visible from my bathroom window.

Shortly after J&J left, I was sitting on a bus stop bench, waiting for a ride back to the apartment. I'd just picked up a few items at the grocery store and was enjoying incredible LA weather. A young brunette sat next to me. She was cute. I flirted with her. She flirted back. Her name was Patrice. She'd just broken up with her boyfriend and was going to Venice to get some last things from the apartment they'd shared. Coincidentally, that apartment was a block from mine. She also told me that her car's starter had died, and she needed the vehicle towed to a repair shop.

Having nothing better to do, I helped Patrice retrieve her clothes. I even called Triple A, and offered to pay for her car repairs. She was very grateful.

Patrice stayed with me for the next three days straight. We got high together, walked the Venice Boardwalk together, ate at the outdoor café together, and had sex. Not a lot of sex, but romantic, fun sex. No rubbers—she said she had an IUD.

I was 24, Patrice was 21. On our third day together, she confessed she had a baby son in the high desert, and that her mother was watching him. As soon as her car was ready, she'd be leaving to head back there. I knew Patrice wasn't girlfriend material, but nonetheless, I enjoyed helping out my little "damsel in distress."

Early on the morning of day four, Patrice split while I was asleep. She left a note: "Danny, thank you so very much for everything. You are truly my night (sic) in shiMing (sic) armor. Thanx (sic) for fixing the car. I have to get back to Jake. I'm sure my mother is going nuts. I'm SOOOOO glad we met. Love forever, "P."

The three days and nights with my gal-pal Patrice were wonderful. She didn't leave a phone number. I never saw her again.

After a week with Patrice, I realized how great it was to have a girl around the house, so I placed an ad in the Venice community paper. It read, "Female Roommate Wanted, to share small, one bedroom apartment with great guy. No smokers. Call Phone Number, etc." The ad had appeared for less than two weeks, when I got a knock one afternoon on my door. TWO AMAZONIAN GERMAN GIRLS IN BLACK DANSKINS ROLLER BLADED into my life. One, a dark-haired beauty, said, "I'm Insa. This is Irena." Irena was an equally impressive blonde. "We need a place to live. We are here from Germany. You are American?"

I had NO IDEA where I "was from" just then. I had visions of living the role of John Ritter from the TV show *Three's Company*. Two incredibly hot beauties wanted to live HERE with ME? You have got to be kidding…

"Yes, I'm American. Actually, I'm from New Jersey," I chuckled. No response—these chicks didn't know from "Jersey." Insa: "How much do you want for rent?" I told them I was only seeking one roommate. "Don't you want two cutie-pie girls to live with you?" Irena teased, leaning forward to stroke my hair. I was a goner. I instantly broke down and agreed. "So, where is OUR room?" Before I could respond, the girls skated into the bedroom. This was NOT my plan. I wanted to keep the bedroom for myself and was going to offer my new roommate the couch. Irena: "You sleep on the couch, yes, Danny boy?" My mouth was open. Their bodies were terrific. Both clad in very tight danskins and nylon stockings, their long hair and exposed cleavage were prominent. "Argh, uhm, yeah, sure, I'll sleep on the couch, no problem. You can take the bedroom." Done deal.

"Holy shit, Danny, are you fucking serious? You're living with those two amazing chicks?" Terry asked me the next day, as the Germans went rollerblading down Venice boardwalk. My next-door neighbor, Terry was a freakishly tall engineer my same age. We became instant friends and smoked a lot of weed on the beach. "Yeah, those are my new roommates," I snorted, in my best "Barney Fife" bragging impression. "Dude, you are so gonna be getting laid," he replied.

The Germans lived with me for four months. I NEVER ONCE TOUCHED EITHER OF THEM, EVER. They were the biggest slobs on the planet. They never washed dishes, left hair, pee, and shit all over my toilet, and would fling blood-stained panties across the bathroom floor. Insa was dating an American Indian – the two of them would come and go at all hours of the day and night (shades of Mike and Pam.) Irena and I would often sit together on the couch, watching TV. She'd stare at me and smile. I knew she was available for sex, and I often considered it, but her body odor wasn't pleasant, and I knew I'd never be able to get hard. And, after all, who needs that kind of pressure?

Late that summer, a friend of the Germans was in town visiting from the Motherland. Greta was taller than the other two, blonde, and had enormous tits. One day, Irena insisted I take Greta down to the beach. "Show her a good time, Danny boy," Irena winked. "I know she'll show you a good time, too." Greta and I laid out a large blanket on Venice Beach. "OK here for being topless?" she asked. "Ah, uhmn, yeah, sure why not," I replied. Off came the bikini top, and out popped her two wonderful German melons. Greta told me she was in Los Angeles "to have a sexual adventure." But because I'm a complete and utter loser in life, I did nothing to help her accomplish that goal. Greta was the friend of my roommates, I thought, and you should never "Shit where you Eat," (an expression I'd learned from Paul, years earlier.) After Greta returned to Germany, Irena asked, "Why didn't you give sex to my friend? She thought you were a cutie-pie." She giggled and walked away. I simply had no answer.

Early that summer, I got a full-time job as a gofer/office assistant for a brand new company in West Hollywood that had developed a new consumer product called "Video Discs" (a far-too-early predecessor of DVDs.) The pay was $165 a week, and the gig allowed me access to a brand new Toyota Corolla.

(SIDE STORY: One day during this time (1981) I was getting my boss' BMW cleaned at a West Hollywood car wash, and realized Jerry Seinfeld was standing next to me. I'd seen him perform two years earlier in New York, and thought he was hysterically funny. "Jerry Seinfeld? My name is Dan. I'm your biggest fan." He took a step back, mystified. Quite sincerely, he said, "Really? I didn't know I had ANY fans." Me: "Since we're both from back East, why don't we become friends?" Puzzled, he gave me the phone number of his agent, "in case you ever want to reach me." By coincidence, that same night, he made his debut on *The Tonight Show Starring Johnny Carson.* Twelve later, I ran into Jerry again: Startled, he said, "I remember YOU! YOU wanted to be my FRIEND!" then turned, and quickly scurried away in disgust. All I can think of now is that since we'd originally met in West Hollywood, he must have assumed I was gay.)

The female assistants who worked at the video disc company were all very attractive, and I had "Carrots" encounters with several of them. But my attention was focused on Erin, the CEO's secretary. About 10 years older, Erin was a soft, elegant, blonde beauty with a sad smile that melted my heart. With a blatantly obvious crush, I'd bring her flowers, and she'd write me thank you poems. We ate lunch together in a nearby park a few times, and I'd tell her how attracted I was to her. I so wanted us to become a couple.

"You'd be very disappointed if we ever made love," Erin said. I had no idea what that meant—Was she really a man? Did she have a penis? Was she frigid? I asked Erin if she'd honor me with her presence by having a dinner date with me on my 25th birthday. She agreed. But late that same afternoon, she panicked, and cancelled. I was crushed.

Driving home from work that night, I reviewed my life. At 25, I was decent looking, and had access to a brand new car and some cash, but nothing resembling a female companion. I was living platonically with two German babes and surrounded by very attractive women at work. Horny beyond words, something SIMPLY had to "give." My "life situation" was just completely unfair.

As I drove, I noticed a cluster of alluring whores in miniskirts, standing at the corner of Sunset and Laurel Canyon Blvds. In the early '80s, the cops had not yet eliminated this practice. Plus, the hookers who used to work Sunset Blvd. back then were mostly young (18-30,) blonde and white. Visions of the "Heather/Larry" excitement from two years earlier came flashing back. Having been rejected by Erin for a birthday dinner date at the last minute, I was fed up. "I deserve some sex," I told myself. "Why shouldn't I be getting laid? Today's my birthday. If Erin won't fuck me, I'll just pay for it myself."

I parked the car and approached the whore gaggle. A very busty, short and adorable blonde approached me. "Hey Honey, I'm Joanne…need a date tonight?" "It's my 25th birthday," I softly muttered.

Joanne got into my car and had me pull into a nearby motel. The drill was very similar to what I'd done with Heather/Larry back in New York. We approached the office clerk, I paid $25 for a room, and we went inside. I asked about her "fee." She told me she charged $50. A fortune, I figured I was a good person and deserved giving myself a $75 birthday present.

We took off our clothes, and Joanne lay on the bed. She whipped out a condom from nowhere and had it on my boner in seconds. "Fuck me, baby, please, please fuck me." OK, I can do this, I thought. There was no foreplay, no kissing, no oral interaction. Just straight, simple, direct fucking. "This is what I need right now," I said. "I deserve this."

I put myself inside her and it felt great. Really fucking great. I asked her to talk dirty some more. "Oh, baby, baby, fuck my tight wet pussy. Shove your big hard cock deep into my wet dripping hole. I love you baby. Fuck me hard and deep." Joanne was "reciting" the words, completely devoid of any feeling or emotion, whatsoever. I imagined that Johnny Carson's "cue card guy" was standing off to one side of our bed, holding up lines for her to read. Joanne's face was expressionless – there was no intimate connection between us, other than my hard, neglected cock, pounding away, deep inside her well-worn vagina.

I came. She sat up and smiled. "Well happy birthday, guy! I hope you enjoyed that as much as I did?" And the truth is, I LOVED IT. I loved it with ALL MY HEART. Fucking a pretty blonde girl without pretense of any kind was a gift. No small talk, no dating, no "My friend was in a car accident" notes on the front door bullshit. I didn't have to meet her parents, listen to "Moondance," drift through snowbanks, or bungle using a condom. This was a simple, straightforward business transaction. I needed my cock to be inside a pussy, and for a mere $75, that goal was achieved. This was the greatest discovery of my life. I should have been doing this since the age of 17.

After five months as the gofer for the video disc company, I had a falling out with my boss and quit. I next answered an ad for a typist/receptionist at an adult film company in Hollywood called "Swank" – they hired me on the spot. Swank distributed shitty, soft porn/hard "R" rated movies, with titles like "Hot T-Shirts," "The Yum Yum Girls," and "Car Wash Chicks." The top execs there were men, but every other employee was a woman. The assistant to the CEO was Bonita, a fiery tempered redhead. I sat at the front reception desk answering phones, while Bonita would sexually harass me. She'd stand behind me, rub her tits against the back of my head, and massage my shoulders. I'd get hard and try not to screw up the phone calls. She'd laugh, knowing full well she was torturing me.

Bonita asked me out to see the new movie *The French Lieutenant's Woman*, then lured me back to her apartment. Not wanting to fuck up my job, I just stared at her. She stared at me. I didn't make a move. Realizing after an uncomfortably long time nothing was gonna happen, she said, "Well, I guess you should get the fuck outta here now," and I split, greatly relieved.

One day, a stunning graphic artist came by the Swank offices to work on a film poster. She reminded me of Sophia Loren, with dark sultry hair and eyes, and very large breasts. She and I were flirting with each other, and I actually had the balls to ask for her number. A few nights later, she asked me to take her to see *The French Lieutenant's Woman* (God, how I grew to hate that fucking film.) Afterward, I walked her back to her garden apartment. She stared at me in the moonlight, waiting for a kiss. I knew that. I knew I could have kissed her, and maybe have even been invited inside her place. But, for GOD ONLY KNOWS WHAT REASON, I grabbed both of her enormous boobs and HONKED them, like horns. I'll repeat that. I actually HONKED this woman's breasts – I even said "Honk, Honk," out loud. She was dumbfounded. "Why would you DO THAT?" she shrieked. In retrospect, I honestly have no idea, but I did follow up with the brilliant, "Those things are just so freakin' big!" She almost pushed me over the railing of her second-story balcony.

The King of Self-Sabotage strikes again.

Early that fall, John and Joanne moved back to LA, married now, and gently suggested that they wanted the apartment back to themselves. (I'd kicked the Germans out months earlier.) I knocked on Terry's door: "Hey man—you wanna get out of this shit-hole building and be roommates someplace else?" He responded, "Sounds great. I don't think I can handle living with these guys much longer." I poked my head into his tiny studio apartment. Hundreds of cockroaches lined the walls and ceiling of his miniscule kitchen.

Terry and I quickly secured a good sized, two-bedroom apartment in the Mid-Wilshire area of LA. As I was still quite poor, he fronted the rent and security deposit. We moved in our meager possessions—a broken couch, stained mattresses, splintered dressers, and a tiny black and white TV with tinfoil on its rabbit ear antennae. Hey, at least we weren't overrun with insects anymore.

To celebrate our new place, my pal and I went to the infamous Barney's Beanery for some massive burgers and beer. I'd been striking out with women left and right, and he'd just broken up with his longtime girlfriend. Both feeling particularly down and out, we drank pitcher after pitcher. "God, I'm so horny," Terry confessed. "I wish there was something I could do about it." At this vulnerable point, I revealed to him my "birthday whore" encounter. "Man, there are really sexy hookers standing out on every street corner on Sunset Blvd.," I said. Toby's ears perked up: "I just got paid, and I've got a $100-bill burning a hole in my pocket. Let's go get laid!"

Terry had a decrepit, falling-apart Falcon. The glass panes in both the driver and passenger side doors would constantly fall down into the recessed holes. You'd have to pry them back up with your fingers. The seats were torn and tattered, the horn didn't work, and, if I recall correctly, the glove box would open and close by itself, as if a ghost was its operator. Since I no longer had the "gofer" job, I'd lost access to a car. For all its shittiness, Terry's Falcon was a Rolls Royce, as far as I was concerned.

We'd only been on Sunset Blvd. a few minutes, and were driving in an easterly direction, when I saw a blonde beauty on the opposite corner, in front of a liquor store. "Oh my God, Terry! I just saw a vision. A fucking goddess!" Terry glanced across the street, saw the woman, and, in a flash, made a 180-degree, totally illegal, U-turn, across four lanes of intense, on-coming, Hollywood traffic.

Instantaneously, we were now heading west. It's truly amazing we weren't killed—a moving van almost plowed into my side of the car. Miraculously, the Falcon stopped just exactly in front of our lovely blonde vision at the liquor store. The woman approached me. As I went to roll down the window (with a manual handle,) the glass pane fell, yet again. Horny guys in cars whizzing past us honked their horns, screaming, "I love you baby! Marry me!" to our "chosen one." She waved and smiled. This chick was way popular that night.

The whore poked her head into the car. "Hey there fellows, the two of you tonight? You both need some lovin'?" Me: "Yeah, we're pretty horny and you're so sexy. How much for my friend and I?" She inspected us, thought for a moment, then said, "You guys are kinda cute. I'll do ya both for a hundred bucks." We agreed, and Terry invited her in. Sitting between us, she smelled like cigarettes, stale perfume, and skin lotion. She put her hands on each of our thighs and giggled. I popped a boner in seconds.

Terry: "Where to sweetie?" I could tell he was really nervous. Whore: "There's a little place a few blocks from here, on Hollywood Blvd. Oh, by the way, I'm Beverly." Beverly the Whore then directed us to a small, hidden motel, where we parked. "So, which one of you fellows wants to go first?" Terry: "Take him – this was his idea." Beverly and I went up to the office clerk, and I paid $25 for a room. (I'd become an old pro at this ritual by now.) We went inside. Beverly stripped down in an instant and lay on the bed. Her body was amazing—to me, she was a Playboy model come to life. I took a pee, came back out, and saw Beverly masturbating. "Show me your dick, sweetie pie," she said. I kneeled over her face, and she began to blow me. It was great.

When I was good and ready, Beverly put a rubber in her mouth, then secured the rubber onto my dick, using only her oral skills. Now THAT was impressive. I entered her missionary style, and she grabbed my ass. She pulled me deep inside her. Her acting was quite good. "Make me cum, baby, I need it bad. I'm a bad, little whore. Fuck your little whore. Fuck me hard." I'd like to think we came together, or that she came at all, but who knows. I didn't last too long – a few minutes, max. This chick was awesome. "OK, tell your buddy it's his turn," Beverly ordered. "And remind him I want my money when he waltzes in here."

Terry smiled at me in the parking lot: "Dude, are you serious? Done already? What a loser!" We laughed, and then he went inside to take his turn. As I sat in the car, I recalled how Paul and Lloyd had waited for me at the Globe Hotel. Apparently, I was now a regular at this "paying for sex" game. Honestly, it didn't make me feel guilty or sad or shameful in the least. I felt elated.

A few days before Christmas, Terry and I decided we needed another Beverly the Whore "fix." She'd given us her number, so we called to arrange another session. "Good timing," she said, "I need some money to buy my daughter Xmas gifts." Terry had just gotten paid, and didn't mind treating me, yet again, to more adult entertainment. Beverly took a cab to our place, and this time Terry went first, walking her by the hand into his bedroom. The two played around in there for about half an hour, as I watched TV. Beverly finally came out, found me in the living room, and took me by the hand. Walking into my bedroom in silence, she turned off the lights, dropped to her knees, and made love to me with her mouth. 15 years later, I'd finally gotten my "7 Minutes in Heaven."

Car-less, Beverly requested a ride to the Hollywood bus station, because she needed to see her daughter, who lived in San Diego. Back in the shitty Falcon, Terry and I were giggling like schoolboys – our beautiful whore once again situated between us. Along the way, Terry's window fell into its hole, and he couldn't get it back up. It was freezing outside. I laughed my ass off.

We walked Beverly the Whore into the station. Everywhere we looked, disgusting, homeless men stained with puke were staring. Clearly a prostitute, Beverly paraded her two little "Johns" across the lobby, for all the miscreants of society to see. My pal and I watched her get on her bus. Like imbeciles, we smiled and waved goodbye, feeling we'd done a good deed.

Thanks to our pathetic, abject horniness, an abandoned little girl somewhere in San Diego would be getting her Christmas presents that year after all. And, in the bigger scheme of things, what's so wrong with that?

CHAPTER FOURTEEN

Eleven Years

The most famous nightclub in LA in the early '80s was "Chippendales," which featured waitresses in lingerie for the men, and half-naked, bow-tie clad, beefcake-muscled waiters for the women. Terry and I went there on New Year's Eve, 1982, to try to score with some babes.

After just a short time inside, an attractive black girl approached Terry and started licking his ear. I went to pee and returned. "Danny, I'm gonna take Latonya home now. I'll catch you later." It wasn't even 11 o'clock and I'd been abandoned. I recalled Steve's motto at "The Manor:" "If you're thinking too much, you're not drinking enough." I drank like a fish, then danced with at least a dozen girls in a row, striking out with each.

Shortly after midnight, I vowed that the VERY NEXT GIRL who walked through the front door would be mine. An adorable, curly-haired blonde, dressed head to toe in white, entered at that moment. The SECOND I first saw her, I distinctly recall thinking, "She reminds me of ME." We danced for a few songs, the first being "In the Mood."

After our last dance, she said "Thanks," and walked away. "What's your name?" I shouted. "Kim." Kim?????????????????????????????

I lunged at her and grabbed her arm. "Kim, please don't leave me," I insisted. I escorted her to a quiet place at the back of the club and we talked. The music was loud, but over the din, I was able to glean that she was a junior nurse in a hospital and had just turned 20. Now for those of you not yet keeping score, let me clarify this. Here I was:

** On a New Year's Eve, just around Midnight
** In a Nightclub
** With a Girl named Kim
** Blonde Hair
** Blue Eyes
** Just turned 20
** Who Worked as a Junior Nurse in a Hospital
** Whose Last Name included the Capital Letter "W"

I'd met my "first Kim" EXACTLY FOUR YEARS EARLIER. She had EXACTLY THE SAME FIRST NAME & LAST INITIAL, was the SAME AGE and had the SAME APPEARANCE & JOB, and had met me during EXACTLY THE SAME CIRCUMSTANCES! Instinctively, I knew that this "new Kim" would become the next love of my life—this was a blatantly obvious Karmic sign. I began calling her a few days into the new year – while she was always sweet on the phone, she kept telling me she had other plans. "I'll try to squeeze you into my schedule, but I just don't know when." I was not going to give up.

After countless phone calls, I wore her down, and Kim finally agreed to a date (although it was iffy there for a second, when I told her I didn't have a car.) Kim gallantly offered to drive us in her old Honda station wagon. On the night of our first date, she pulled up to my apartment, and when she got out of her car, I saw "stars" swirling about her head – they looked like special effects animation from a Walt Disney movie.

We had dinner at a cool place, then attended a taping of the ABC TV series *Taxi*, which shot on the Paramount Studios lot. A few minutes into the taping (during which time John Belushi made a surprise appearance,) we began kissing. The people behind us weren't too thrilled – a guy back there said, "Hey buddy, could you cool it?" "First date," I snapped back. (Belushi died six weeks later.)

On our second get together, we double-dated with friends, but afterward I couldn't reach her by phone for weeks. Finally managing a third date, we went to Grauman's Chinese Theater in Hollywood to see the new Coppola film, *One From the Heart*. It was Valentine's Day. We held hands during the film, and, while walking back to the car, started to kiss. "Why were you avoiding me these past weeks?" I asked. "I had to get rid of all the other guys who've been chasing after me," Kim replied. "I only want to be with you now."

After hot fudge sundaes, we went back to my place and made love for a few hours. Wonderful. She spent the night with me, and the next morning, I walked her to her car and watched her drive off. I looked up at the sun. "Thank you, God," I said.

Having been laid off from Swank due to budget cutbacks, I next landed a full-time job at the American Film Institute (AFI,) a renowned filmmaking college in Hollywood. The job (administrative assistant) allowed me access to free movie passes, which came in handy for cheap dates with Kim.

When we weren't at the movies, I'd watch Kim rollerblade at Santa Monica beach. One weekend, she insisted I try to skate. We met her best friend, Suzanne, and I rented a pair of skates. The two girls slowly held my hands, "gliding" me along. Scared to death, I imagined falling down and breaking my face. I gave up moments later.

Kim and I were spending a great deal of time together and having a lot of sex (I was the first guy she ever spent a full night with, much to the consternation of her stepfather.) Once, during our third month together, Kim and I were doing it doggie style. Next to my right knee, a condom was staring up at me, screaming, "Quick, put me on NOW, you fucking putz! Put me ON NOW! You're waiting too long.... what are you doing? PUT ME ON RIGHT FUCKING NOW, you STUPID IMBECILE!!!" Unfortunately, I didn't take my little friend's advice, and ejaculated inside her. Kim instantly turned around. "Did you use a condom, just then?" she asked, panicked. "Urhg, ahm, no, sorry, really sorry, I didn't." I showed her the little unopened guy, lying there in shame. "I meant to." Kim stared into my face. "I'm gonna get pregnant! You know that right?" Me: "No you won't. God wouldn't do that to us."

Three weeks later, Kim's mother, Mary, called: "Nice job, kiddo. So how were you planning to pay for this abortion?" Kim hadn't even broken the news to me yet; here was her mom taking command. "Abortion? Really…oh my God! I am so, so sorry. How much will that cost?" Mary explained that I'd need to come up with $400. She might just as well have said $4,000. Almost penniless, I'd miraculously just gotten my very first credit card. I tapped into it the same day it arrived in the mail.

Kim and I had our first, post-abortion date about a week later. I was consumed with guilt. She was philosophical: "We weren't ready for a kid! We're not married, and you don't even have a car." I was extremely grateful for her forgiveness. She'd come to my apartment to make breakfast. While setting the table, I quickly glanced up at Kim's face. In slow motion, she turned her head:

"WIFE"

At that second, I saw, in all capital letters, "W," "I," "F," "E," on her forehead, as bright as a sign in Times Square. I swear to God, this is true. It was there for maybe five-six seconds. Kim smiled. My heart skipped a beat. I looked out the window, just as two clouds parted above, sending a sunbeam through the glass. "OK, God, well, I guess that couldn't possibly have been any more obvious," I whispered to myself. I knew now what my next step would be.

I was gonna max out my credit card and buy Kim a diamond ring.

We had a picnic up in the Hollywood Hills. I'd placed the ring (without question the smallest diamond in the history of carbon,) in its tiny little box, underneath the blanket. All through lunch, my heart was racing. Finally, I said, "Hey, Kim, what's this?" and lifted the blanket. "What is that?" she asked, taken aback. I displayed the ring. Trembling: "Kim, I love you. Will you marry me?" Truly shocked, she stared at the ring, then into my face, then back at the ring. "Urh, ahm, ah…I don't know," she replied. Stunned silence filled the next 15 seconds. "Yes, OK, I'll marry you. Of course, I'll marry you."

Kim # 2 was going to be my wife!

Kim's family, and my family and friends were all pretty psyched about the news of my engagement. Not my father: "She's not Jewish," he moaned. I was hoping he'd come around eventually.

I was now spending a great deal of time at Kim's house in Santa Monica, with her incredibly non-Jewish parents. There were plenty of home-cooked dinners there, and I lived the "Good ham, Grammy" scene from Woody Allen's classic *Annie Hall*, many, many times in real life. Their house also had a terrific pool and a sculptured garden in the backyard. I was 26, dating a pretty blonde in Southern California, hanging out with her wealthy parents in their swimming pool, and having all the sex I wanted with a girl I loved. For me, life couldn't get much better than this.

Kim's aunt was a wealthy property owner in Santa Monica. As an engagement gift, she offered to rent us a little house she owned for a minimal sum. (Legend had it that Charlie Chaplin's servants had once lived there.) Telling Terry was tough. In the two years we'd known each other, we'd virtually become brothers. Once he accepted the fact that I was now engaged, and that he and I would be "breaking up," he was gracious enough to even help schlep Kim's possessions and mine into the new place.

That first night, Kim and I made love on the lawn in front of the "Little House," the only time in my life—ever, to this day—I've had sex outdoors.

Unbeknownst to Kim or her mother, however, Kim's stepfather, a noted attorney with a prestigious law firm, had recently embezzled over a million dollars. After he was caught, Kim's parents were forced to sell their home, and the resulting animosity led to their divorce. Kim and her mother were extremely close back then and were deeply distraught over this turn of events.

Kim's friend Suzanne had begun attending Bible study classes at this time and had suggested to Kim that they attend these classes together. "Maybe God can help you get through this shitty time with your parents," I advised. One night that spring, I was reading a newspaper on the couch, when Kim returned home from Bible study. She stood frozen in the living room, zombie-like. "Hey, how was class tonight?" I asked. "You're Jewish!" Me: "Huh?" Kim: "You're Jewish…you don't believe in Jesus Christ." Me: "Kim, I've been Jewish since the day we met. What are you talking about?" Kim: "Jews don't believe in Jesus Christ. Jews don't go to heaven, they go to Hell. I can't marry you, Danny. You're going to Hell."

I scanned the room for Allen Funt's *Candid Camera*. What on Earth was she talking about? She was JUST realizing we were of different religions? So what if I didn't believe in Jesus Christ? We were in love! Kim and I had already made extensive wedding plans at this point, and had placed deposits on the venue, the DJ, the wedding rings, and the photographer, and had even made arrangements with both a Rabbi and a Minister.

Kim: "We can't get married. I'm sorry. Plus, I can't sleep with you anymore. You'll have to stay in the other room now." She walked off into our bedroom, and gently closed the door. I remained seated, newspaper in hand. "Terrific," I thought, "My father's gonna LOVE this one."

A friend of mine from AFI with a huge apartment near Downtown LA suggested I room with him. The place was dirt cheap – probably because it was located in a drug-infested neighborhood where sleazy hookers and pathetic Vietnamese women would squat in the gutter, pissing and shitting. Still, to me, it was a better option than the "Bible-Belt" house in which I'd suddenly become an unexpected prisoner.

After hearing about the "Jews go to Hell" thing, my father went ballistic. "Find another girlfriend!! This girl is NOT for you! She hates Jews?? We're Jews!!! You can't possibly think you have a future with her, do you?" I was remarkably confused. A few days later, while visiting Kim at the little house, Mary said, "Kim, did you tell him the big news?" Kim: "Danny, my mother and I are moving to Boulder, Colorado. I'm gonna go back to college to finish my degree. But, we should stay in touch."

STAY IN TOUCH?? The woman I was MEANT to MARRY, who'd broken my heart, told me that I was going to go to Hell because I didn't believe in Jesus Christ, and kicked me out of our "love nest," was now moving states away?? How much did that suck? I went silent. "I just hope you find what you're looking for, Kim. I'll miss you," I finally replied. We hugged, and I headed back to my new shithole apartment in silence and despair.

The summer that Kim left LA, I'd gotten a new job with, ironically, The Playboy Channel, *Playboy Magazine's* just launched cable TV network. I became the very first publicist there. When I started, I envisioned that the employees would be walking around naked. In fact, it was just a regular, 9-6 working environment with normal people, who just happened to be focused on all things "tits" and "ass."

One day, Kim called from Colorado. "I need to tell you something." My heart stopped beating—she couldn't be pregnant again, we hadn't had sex in ages. "What?" Kim: "I met a guy named Jim at a party last night. We had sex. He's got a pretty big penis. I thought you should know. I hope that's OK?"

I couldn't talk. Here was an exact "life repeat" of my final phone call with Kim the First. "Gotta go Kim, we'll talk later, bye." I rushed her off the phone, and from that moment on – and for the next three weeks – I developed a STUTTER. Her lovely news triggered a speech impediment. I was so deeply upset, it changed the way I fucking spoke.

I relayed the news to my new roommate, Ron, who I'd befriended when we were both employees together up at the AFI Campus. Always one to make a joke about ANY and ALL situations, no matter how upsetting or painful (he even joked with me at <u>his father's funeral</u> years later!) Ron told me how I could get Kim to stop fucking Jim. "Buy her a giant dildo," he advised.

In those days, adult sex shops were much more taboo than they're considered today. We found "The Love Shack" store in Hollywood, and after quite a bit of embarrassment, I bought Kim an impressively large sex toy. Driving back to our apartment, Ron, brilliant in the writing of song parodies for any conceivable occasion, began to sing "The Dildo Song."

Set to the tune of "We're Off To See The Wizard:"

> "We're off to buy a dildo, a flexible dildo for Kim.
> We hope a stick, that's shaped like a prick,
> Will keep her from fucking Jim.
> A horse-cock, a moose-cock, a one-eyed snake…
> Should keep her from making the same mistake…
> The same mistake that she will surely MAKE.….
> If she decides to keep fucking Jim..
> Da-da-da-da-da-da-da-dah…
> We're off to buy a dildo, a flexible dildo for Kim"

I mailed the dildo to Kim. She loved it. And yes, believe it or not, she actually DID stop fucking Jim. (At least, that's what she later told me. Not sure I ever believed that, though.)

During the time Kim was in Colorado, I got a random call from Callie, a former neighbor of mine and Terry's. She'd somehow heard that Kim and I had broken up and invited me to a Dan Fogelberg concert. In the back of my mind, I seemed to recall that she used to stare at me a lot. (Kim once told me the previous year, "You know Callie's got a big crush on you, right? She wants to sleep with you, bad.")

After the song "Longer" finished, I glanced at Callie and said, "I want you to sleep with me tonight." "Yes, of course," she replied. Simplest "sex negotiation" I've ever made in my life. Callie spent the night, and we had sex three times. When she orgasmed, her whole body just shivered, from head to toe. She never said a word, never made a sound. The next morning, I took Callie back to her car and hugged her goodbye. "You'll call me soon, right?" she said. "Of course," I reassured her. As I had no feelings for Callie of any kind, I never called or saw her again.

After five months away, Kim rang. "I made a terrible mistake. I never should have moved here. My mother is driving me crazy, I hate school, and I'm over the whole 'Jesus' thing. I love you, I miss you, and I want to come home. Will you take me back?" This was the call I'd been hoping for. "Of course," I said. "I love you, too. Come back. We're meant to be together. God told me you're the girl I'm supposed to marry."

Kim lined up a job as a nursing aide at a major hospital in LA, and I helped her secure a new apartment. Back in LA by that New Year's Eve, we had our first real date in a very long time. However, as we were about to eat at a very nice restaurant, Kim turned ghostly white and said, "Something's wrong. I don't feel well. We need to leave...we need to leave RIGHT NOW." She ran from the restaurant. Although I was starving to death, I got up, flagged the waiter, and asked, "My fiancé's really sick…what should I do about the check?" "Forget it. It's New Year's Eve. Go be with her," he kindly answered.

I took Kim back to her place. She lay in bed, shaking and crying. "What's wrong?" I asked. "I don't know…I just don't feel well, at all. I feel really, really sick." I spent that New Year's Eve sitting on the floor in Kim's new apartment beside her bed, holding her hand, and watching her sleep. It had been exactly two years since we'd met. She was back in LA, we were reunited, and we were still in love. But something very unusual was happening. I recalled a lunch her mother and I had had the year before. "Keep an eye on Kim's health for me, Dan," Mary said. "She had a lot of strange medical problems as a child, and I'm afraid that someday all that weirdness may come back." Was Kim's New Year's Eve "mystery illness" just the tip of the iceberg her mother had warned me about? Was I in way over my head?

My position at The Playboy Channel came with an enormous office, on the top floor of the Playboy building in West Hollywood. The view to my right was of the gorgeous mansions of the Hollywood Hills, while the view to my left was of gorgeous Playboy models with "hills" of their own. The Playboy Modeling Agency was across the hall, and for a guy who'd been addicted to whacking off to naked girls in those very magazines for the previous 16 years, I was now in a position to actually meet these same babes in real life. I was in charge of writing up TV show "blurbs" that were listed within television program guides, and also producing photographs to illustrate each of those TV shows. My boss never asked to clear my ideas in advance, and no one was around to supervise me.

Autonomous, I reigned like Hugh Hefner, Junior.

I was also in charge of designing much of the promotional Playboy Channel "swag" – T-shirts, coffee mugs, baseball caps, etc. The models who would come and go across the hall became regular visitors to my office. Wearing skimpy, mini-outfits (nipples poking through) and cowboy-boots, long blonde hair flowing everywhere, they'd saddle up to me, cooing, "Oh, these new T-shirts are so sexy, Dan…can I have a few?" And really, who was I to say no?

One day, an extra voluptuous blonde Playmate walked right up to my desk and shook my hand. "Hey, I'm Lynda Weismeier…you're Dan? The other girls say you've got the coolest stuff." I was behind my desk. She leaned ALL THE WAY OVER from the front of my desk to shake my hand, purposely smushing her big, beautiful tits against the desktop. "I know who you are, Lynda," I said, staring into her massive cleavage. "I've studied your photos many, many times." Giggling, she then noticed behind me on the wall a photo of Kim and I, taken from a romantic trip a year earlier to the coast of Monterey. "Who's that?" she asked. "Oh, ah, uhm, that's Kim… my fiancé." "You're getting married? Why would you want to do that?" This perfect "10," clearly annoyed, was asking me WHY I wanted to marry my fiancé. "Because I love her?" I answered in question form. Lynda shrugged. "Too bad…we coulda had some fun. Ok, then, caio." She split. And while nothing would ever happen between us, Lynda would continue unabashedly flirting with me for the next year.

So now, while I was surrounded in real life by the fantasy girls I'd grown up lusting for on a daily basis, I was simply not in a position to even consider asking one for a date without breaking my commitment to Kim. Occasionally, I would produce photo sessions with bikini models at Mr. Hefner's legendary Playboy Mansion, and on more than one occasion, the man, himself, would wander around and watch the proceedings. Of course, he'd be in his red silk pajamas, smoking his pipe, drinking a Pepsi, and nodding his approval. I only ever spoke to him twice, but the fact that I was hangin' with "Hef" at the Playboy Mansion, surrounded by remarkably beautiful girls, was an adolescent dream come true. I was a kid in a candy store. But, since I'd sworn to myself that I would never cheat on my fiancé, I was more like a "diabetic" kid in that store.

When we'd first gotten engaged, Kim and I had originally planned a fairly elaborate wedding, since, at that time, her wealthy parents were still together. Now, 18 months later, we were completely on our own, financially. We decided to have a TINY wedding, outdoors, in Santa Barbara. We'd lined up a justice of the peace to officiate in the "sunken gardens," located in the backyard of the Santa Barbara Courthouse building. We only invited our immediate blood relatives and closest friends. The body count was 16 people, total.

October 28, 1984, saw a particularly beautiful, sunny day in Santa Barbara. All our guests had arrived on time, but Kim and I were nervous wrecks. I had a 1940s style tuxedo and had recently grown a mustache. Kim had a cute, white, lacey dress with gloves and a matching hat. It had rained the night before, so the ground was rather soggy, and the high heels of the women sank into the mud. Mere moments before the ceremony, I had a panic attack and a serious talk with myself: "Are you SURE about this? Is this really the woman you're supposed to be marrying, after her whole 'Jews in Hell' routine? What if 'Jesus Freak Kim' comes back? And what's going on with her health? Do you really know what the fuck you're doing, Dan?'"

With this tumorous mass of negativity swirling through my brain, the judge began the service. A ray of bright sunlight poked through some clouds just as the ceremony began, and I took that as a positive sign. But when Kim handed me my ring, we were both so nervous, it fell into the mud, below. I looked down – the ring looked up. My inner-panicked voice: "Oh my God—this relationship is doomed! My wedding ring just fell into the fucking MUD! That can't possibly be a good sign! Oh, fuck!" Regardless, I picked up the gold band, brushed it off, and placed it onto my own finger. Bada-bing, bada-boom, we were officially married.

After a lunch reception at the romantic El Encanto Hotel (which, remarkably, and much to my utter surprise, my father paid for,) our guests left to head back to LA. Kim and I said our goodbyes, and returned, emotionally drained, to our room. She immediately took off her dress, jumped into bed, and began shaking under the covers: "I feel sick," she said, shivering, "Really, really sick." Her facial color was a cross between yellow, green, and sky blue. I stood in front of her, still in my tuxedo, thinking, "Well, this should certainly be a sex marathon honeymoon."

We remained in Santa Barbara for three relatively calm days. During the afternoons, we walked slowly along the beach, went window shopping on main street, and ate at a variety of restaurants. I THINK Kim and I MIGHT have had sex ONCE, MAYBE, during the entire honeymoon, but I honestly can't remember. I don't think we did. But even if we did, it probably lasted about a minute and a half, just enough to get it out of the way. Mine simply had to be the least sex-filled honeymoon in the history of honeymoons.

As soon as we got back to LA, Kim's "I feel sick" situation got worse. Much worse. She crawled into bed at our new apartment (now in Hollywood,) where she would remain for the next four months, even missing Terry's wedding a few weeks after ours. Kim had low grade fevers, night sweats, uncontrollable shaking and trembling, dark black rings under her eyes, and a sore throat from hell. She looked really ill, and, on many days, could hardly make it from the bed to the bathroom. I managed to locate a doctor in Century City who specialized in what seemed to be a fairly new medical phenomenon among women at that time, Chronic Fatigue Syndrome. He told us she could be the poster child for CFS.

Mary and Kim's grandmother, Nana, took turns staying with us to help. For the months that Kim was sick immediately following my wedding, my life was truly a 180-degree dichotomy. At nights and on weekends, I was tending to a very sick young woman, helping her onto the toilet, and washing her body with a wet cloth, not to mention doing laundry or grocery-shopping. During the weekdays, though, I was spending hours and hours with the sexiest, most beautiful women in America, quite often while they were semi-clad. Several of them would blatantly flirt with me, winking, rubbing my shoulders and laughing. My cock would scream: "YES, YES, HOW I WANT YOU!" while my brain would counter: "TOUCH JUST ONE OF THESE ANGELS, AND GOD WILL SMITE THEE DOWN." This was the most dramatic "Carrots" dilemma imaginable.

Adding into the mix: The Playboy Channel had hired a very alluring, voluptuous British actress/model named Ava Cadell to star in their TV show called *Pillow Previews* – the show reviewed adult films, ala Siskel & Ebert. Ava was a redheaded bombshell and as I was now the publicist for her show, she and I became close and very quick friends. By pure coincidence, Ava lived directly across the street from Kim and I in Hollywood. During the months when Kim was deathly ill, I'd often go to Ava's apartment building to work out in her gym. Kim, her mother and her grandmother were convinced I was having an affair with Ava! While that never did happen, there were a few moments in time, during this era, when the idea did occur to me. (Ava was married to a gay man then. To this day, she and I have been, and have remained, good friends, for nearly 40 years.)

After many months in bed, Kim eventually felt better. She'd lost a bunch of weight and was now eating only healthy foods. One night, she told me she'd decided she no longer wanted to work "with sick people" as a junior nurse, but, instead, wanted to change her career path and become a travel agent. We took out a school loan, and she attended a nearby travel college. Within a few months, she got a job as a travel agent at a popular agency in West LA. I was ecstatic—my wife, who I loved very much, was finally healthy, happy, and gainfully employed. This was major progress.

A few weeks into the new job, Kim had to fly to Dallas for a few days of computer training with one of the airlines. Concurrently, I'd just done a photo shoot with a different Kim—actually Kym Malin – a recent Playboy centerfold girl. The shoot had to illustrate a Playboy TV show about Halloween, so Kym wore devil's horns and the tightest red bikini on the planet. She and I had chemistry—scary chemistry. After bonding during our photo session, Kym would swing by my office to get T-shirts for her friends. She'd sit on the couch in my office, crossing and uncrossing her legs, brushing her thick, curly blonde hair, while staring at me. I'd be engaging her in wildly flirtatious banter. Invariably, my pissed-off wife would call: "So, which Playmate is in your office with you right now, Miss May? Miss June?" Somehow my wife instinctively knew when to phone me EVERY SINGLE TIME.

Kim was on a plane to Dallas, when Playmate Kym came into my office to invite me to a Grammy Awards party. "Sure, sounds fun." Why shouldn't I go to a party with a hot girl? I thought. She gave me her address and asked that I pick her up. I arrived at Kym's apartment on Venice Beach, trembling. "What am I doing here?" She answered the door—a fucking vision, in a tight, black, cat suit. "I've been out in the sun all day...do I look OK?" she asked. My penis smiled. Her suntan was incredible – she was "glowing." "You look great—amazing," I managed to say. Kym finished smoking a reefer. "Wanna hit?" "No thanks, I'm cool," I said, high just from the sight of her.

We got into my WIFE's car (her mom had bought Kim a brand-new Volvo with her divorce money,) and headed off to the party. Kym immediately opened up the sun, or more appropriately now, MOON-roof, and popped a cassette tape into the stereo. As I drove, we heard Sadé sing the hit song, "Smooth Operator:"

"Smooth Operator. He's a Smooth Operator..."

And, as we all know, I am truly one of life's smoothest of operators.

Kym smiled, applied some lipstick, and then started "dancing" in her seat (she refused to buckle in,) swaying gently to the music.

Her hair was so long, some of it went flying thru the moon-roof. I was on a date with a vision. The conflict in my head was overwhelming: "You have GOT to fuck this girl. You can't possibly go the rest of your life without having fucked a Playboy Centerfold! You will NEVER EVER get a better chance than tonight. Imagine telling all of your friends back East you scored a Playmate!" Other half of brain: "Are you fucking kidding me? You're MARRIED, you stupid fuck head. You took vows to stay true to your wife, to love only her. If you even touch this chick, God will kill you…he will fucking hunt you down and slay you." This LOUD argument eclipsed all other thought for hours.

At the party, Kym and I danced a bit, but mostly we just talked quietly, in the corner, where she told me about problems with a recent boyfriend. I don't think she enjoyed the drooling stares she was getting from every other guy there, and, quite frankly, I was pretty uncomfortable, also. We were at the party for maybe two hours, till she said "You wanna go?"

The wild and crazy blonde bombshell I'd driven from her house to the party had become, on the drive back, serene and mellow. "You OK?" I asked. She told me she'd been drinking and smoking dope that whole day and had been lying on the beach for so many hours that her skin was now "on fire." I felt her shoulder—it was burning hot. She was crashing from a day-long high.

We arrived back at her apartment, and she quickly hopped out of the car. WHAT the FUCK do I do NOW?? These were the thoughts racing through my pea-brain:

** Tell her you need to use her bathroom – that gets you upstairs;
** Tell her you want to get high – that also gets you into her place;
** Walk her up to her front door, spin her around, and kiss her IMMEDIATELY. Do NOT think! Just DO!
** Kiss her BEFORE you even get near the entrance to the building!

We walked in silence to her front door. She unlocked it, took one step up, turned, and looked at me with a peculiar, quizzical expression. I was completely frozen. This was far beyond simple fear. I could not move, nor could I speak. This moment, here and now, made it look like I'd been George Clooney the time I sat next to "Long Red" at my college dorm.

A remarkably loud, inner-voice screamed: "IF YOU KISS THIS GIRL, GOD WILL NEVER FORGIVE YOU, EVER. YOU CAN NOT KISS HER. IT'S THE WRONG THING TO DO. YOU'RE MARRIED. YOU KNOW IT, AND I KNOW IT." This freeze-frame scene went on far too long, and I realized, after about 20-seconds, that I'd lost the moment. Then, thank God, she yawned. "I am so friggin' tired," she finally said. "Guess I'm off to sleep." "Good idea," I responded, "I had a lot of fun. Let's do it again sometime." Half-heartedly, I went in for a very quick kiss on the lips but got the cheek instead. We hugged. "Later, Dan," she said, walking up the stairs.

Back in my wife's car, I felt something weird on my forehead. A ZIT the size of a CALZONE had appeared from literally nowhere and was now prominently displayed in the middle of my fucking forehead – a puss-filled ZIT that had not been there just an hour earlier. Was this God's way of "Cock-Blocking" me? (I recalled having gotten a surprise zit just seconds before my aborted "Seven Minutes in Heaven" with Bonnie when I was 14.) I took this new zit as a very strong sign: I was ABSOLUTELY NOT to pursue this fantasy girl any further.

Back at my place, alone, I listened to my wife's message on the answering machine. She was doing well in Dallas. It was great to hear her voice. I tried to go to sleep, but "Mr. Johnson" in my underpants had other plans. "He" remembered that one of the Playboy VHS videotapes I owned included naked montages of various centerfold girls, one of whom was Kym. I popped the tape into my VCR, and watched as she frolicked naked in a bathtub, rubbing soapy bubbles all over her ass and tits. Having no choice but to masturbate, I figured it was a compromise. It was OK with God if I <u>imagined</u> fucking Kym. But absolutely NOT cool with him if I'd try to seal that deal in real life.

I wasn't making much money at Playboy, so through a friend, I met with the head of publicity for Columbia Pictures Television in Burbank. He told me that he needed a "male" publicist there, since he was surrounded by too many women. Before I knew it, I had a new job at twice my Playboy salary. I'd been assigned as the publicist for a new, nationally syndicated TV series called *The New Gidget*. The star of that show was an adorable, Jewish actress from New York named Caryn. I was smitten by her the second I first met her.

The show once shot a week's worth of episodes in Honolulu. I spent that week on one of the world's most beautiful beaches, watching Caryn and assorted, cute little teenage girls, cavorting in bikinis. I was always off a bit in the distance—there, but "not there" – part of the crew, but "not." A publicist is unique on any film or TV set. There is only one of him/her. The cast is comprised of many, the crew, many more. The publicist stands alone.

During that week in Hawaii, feeling remarkably lonely, I began fantasizing about what it would be like to be in love with Caryn. Of course, I couldn't ask her for a date, or touch her for many reasons, not the least of which was the fact that she was dating her co-star, I was married, and she wasn't the least bit interested in me.

Upon my return from Hawaii, I was elated to be back with my wife, where I belonged. However, just a very short time later, Kim's back went out. She was brushing her teeth one morning, while getting ready for work. Hunched over the sink, her back made a loud, "gushing" noise, and Kim was suddenly shaped like a question mark. She started to scream. I couldn't straighten her up – she could barely move. I called 911, and two men had to lift her onto a wooden plank and into their ambulance. The doctors weren't sure what was wrong.

Concurrent with my wife in the hospital, I had somehow pissed off an executive at Columbia Pictures TV (June '87) and got fired on my 31st birthday. I was stunned. I'd been there 19 months and was fired without explanation. (Fortunately, my medical insurance would continue to cover my wife and I for quite a while, so the hospital stay wouldn't be an issue.) Kim was in the hospital for two weeks, until her back finally straightened itself out, on its own.

Over the course of the next five years, Kim would experience many, many more bodily malfunctions and maladies. These would include: Knee Surgery, Hemorrhoid Surgery, an Impacted Colon, Carpal Tunnel Surgery, numerous Back Spasms, a "Mimicked" Stroke, various Heart Palpitations, and severe sore throats. (I'm sure I've forgotten a few.)

One night, Kim's stomach "exploded." I rushed her to Cedar's Sinai Hospital. Her gall bladder had ruptured, and she was in need of emergency surgery. In the ER around 3 AM, we looked up to see a surprisingly well-preserved Zsa Zsa Gabor. She held Kim's hand. "DAH-link," she said, "You are much too young to be in here! Get well soon and go home. You need to be with your handsome husband." That was kinda cool.

In between doctors' offices, emergency rooms, surgeries, and ambulances, Kim and I had decided we wanted to try to have a child. Shortly after leaving Columbia, I'd gotten a new job at a top entertainment public relations agency, during which time I would become Jay Leno's West Coast publicist (occasionally hanging out with him – in his underwear – backstage at *The Tonight Show.*) When Kim's health allowed, she had evolved her work skills, and became an in-house travel agent with ABC Television (booking trips for the cast members of *Dynasty*.) Between us, we were finally making some decent money. After a year of trying to conceive without success, Kim had a laparoscopy, to "blow out the dust" from her fallopian tubes. It worked. She got pregnant.

I took Kim to the hospital the morning we'd scheduled for a caesarian section (our son was expected to be large.) At the time, I was taking medication that made me especially queasy. When Kim's surgeon asked if I wanted to watch the birth of my son, my nausea became so intense, the hospital began "spinning" like I was drunk, and I almost fainted. The doctor became adamant: "Listen, pal, if you wanna see your kid being born, you better get your ass in here right now!"

When the doctors pulled an enormous, amorphous, white "blob" out from Kim's spread-eagle abdomen and into the air, I asked, "What the hell is THAT?" "THAT, my friend, is your SON," came the surgeon's snarky reply.

The second I looked into Jordan's face, the FIRST SECOND I ever saw it, I saw an apparition—a "ghost-like" vision of the face of my late Grandpa Joe (my father's father) "superimposed" over it. I cut my son's umbilical cord, picked him up, held him aloft, and began sobbing, uncontrollably. "Thank you, God," I said. "Thank you for my son." The nurse standing next to me wiped away a tear as well.

Kim and I were madly in love with Jordan - a great little kid. We found a new apartment near Sony Studios in Culver City and fixed up his room. It was the joy that parents everywhere, since the beginning of time, have experienced. Mine brought just one other thing, however. A complete and total end to my sex life. After Kim gave birth, I no longer saw her as a sexual being and lost all interest in her - the whole classic "Madonna/Whore" syndrome, I suppose. She quit her job to raise our son. My job was overwhelming. We were exhausted. Thank God for my downstairs closet.

I set up a "Whacking-Off Center" in a storage closet in our garage, near the trash dumpster. I had the only key—I never gave one to Kim. I had my girlie magazines spread out in there, with lotion and tissues at the ready. Whenever I took the trash downstairs, I'd steal an extra three minutes to pleasure myself in that little closet. This repetitive act would remain virtually the full extent of my sex life, for most of the next four years.

My dad came to visit his new grandson, and while walking together on Venice Boardwalk, he asked if I was happy. "I'm not sure," I replied, confessing doubts about the future of my marriage. "Whatever you do," he strongly advised, "Do NOT have another child." John Lennon once said, "Life's what happens to you while you're busy making other plans." I got Kim pregnant again a few days after my father's talk. What makes this particular "seed planting" truly extraordinary was that it happened during one of the three times we had had sex that ENTIRE YEAR. I was panicked when I realized what I'd done and became extremely depressed. (Fortunately, this would become my daughter, Anjuli, the most wonderful 'mistake' of my life!)

When my son was just under two, I was offered a higher paying job at a much bigger entertainment PR firm. Although the owner was a renowned asshole, I took it, and quickly began attracting clients of my own to his agency. During this second pregnancy, Kim's CFS returned, and she became bedridden for many weeks. I was doing PR for a TV show called *The New Lassie* at the time, and the star of that series, Dee Wallace (best known as the mother from *E.T.*) became a good friend. Since she, herself, had had a terrible time conceiving, Dee sympathized with my wife's plight, and, at her own expense, sent an acupuncturist to Kim's bedside for therapeutic treatments. They worked, and my wife was able to get out of bed after not too long. Dee's act would be the nicest thing any Hollywood celebrity would ever do for me.

My daughter was born in the spring. Her name, Anjuli, is a Hindu Indian word that means "to give" as in "to give an offering to God." While she was completely healthy, Anjuli decided she had no interest in sleeping a full night through for TWO YEARS. Kim and I took turns feeding, changing, and rocking her, literally every single night, for two years. We were beyond exhausted. Kim's dark rings returned under her eyes. I was incredibly irritable. We loved our two kids to death, but this extended, "no sleep" thing was torture above and beyond the call of duty.

Kim's health remained shaky at best, while my prick-head boss was constantly sending me to New York, Nashville, New Orleans, San Francisco, Houston, Las Vegas or Miami for business. He couldn't have cared less about my tenuous family situation. Kim's elderly grandmother, Nana, moved in with us again to help out. It was a team family effort, and it was actually working…until Kim's back went out, again.

I don't remember the exact circumstances (this period of my life was so horrific, I've managed to black most of it out,) but Kim returned to the hospital when my kids were three and one. However, this go-round, the doctors told us she'd need a serious operation on her vertebral discs.

Kim would remain in the hospital for nearly three months.

My boss kept throwing major projects at me, while my two little kids were fighting over their toys. Nana did her best to run the household, but the stress on her was more than she could handle.

One night after work, I came home to find an 82-year-old woman sobbing uncontrollably on the couch. "I can't do it anymore, Dan," Nana managed to say, in between body-heaving wails. "It's all too much. I'm an old woman…I can't do it…I just can't do this anymore." I held her and stared out the window, trying to be as encouraging as possible. We didn't have the money to hire a nanny. Nana was the only family member we had willing to pitch in.

I used to sing a Bruce Springsteen song, out loud to myself, everyday: "But Now I'm Trapped, Oh Yeah, Baby…I'm Trapped, Oh YEAH, YEAH…" I'd become a walking zombie man. Almost no sleep. Working my balls off for a total shit boss. Two babies to keep safe. An ancient woman nearing a complete nervous breakdown. And a wife in the hospital who couldn't walk. Not to mention the fact that I had NOTHING resembling romance, sex, or passion, anywhere. The only relief I had from my misery were fleeting seconds of pleasure inside my little whacking-off closet in the garage, next to a smelly, disgusting trash dumpster.

There had to be more to life than this. I was convinced God couldn't possibly hate me this much.

After the three longest months of my life, Kim finally returned home, her back now in rather good shape. The kids were ecstatic to see her. Unfortunately, because I'm a cock, I'd bottled up a ton of anger and frustration, silently directing that rage squarely at Kim. While her medical problems were not her fault, I couldn't help thinking I simply needed to escape from them—from her. I couldn't keep up with this massive amount of responsibility. I needed some female attention—a female partner.

WHAT ABOUT MY NEEDS??? WHAT ABOUT ME???

With Kim home, things settled down for a bit. I took Jordan to preschool each morning, while a nice Indian family down the street babysat for Anjuli. With her intermittent CFS, Kim still needed a great deal of rest, sleeping her afternoons away. She and I were civil to each other, but we didn't speak much...our relationship had become strictly platonic. Kim suggested we see a couples' therapist, and we did, maybe four times. All I recall of those sessions is that we talked about some of the small things we each did that annoyed the other. I played the good soldier, pretending our marriage was "pretty good." Sex, or my lack of interest therein, was never once discussed.

During one of these sessions, I decided I wanted to retain my own therapist, and without telling Kim, arranged to do so. My private therapist was an older woman—a hard-core "Freudian" type. During our first session, I gave her a big picture view of my life—she told me my mother was essentially to blame for every problem I had. But then, she asked me the million-dollar question: "Do you want to stay married?" Me: "Huh? What do you mean?" Dr. "It's an easy question—do you want to remain married to your wife?" I thought for about 10 seconds, and then said out loud, "No, I don't," truly surprising myself with that answer. I was dead set against divorce, having seen how it devastated the lives of my parents.

About a month later, a miracle happened. Kim approached me: "We need to get a divorce. You don't love me anymore, and I know that you need to be with other women. It's OK. The kids and I will move away and live on our own. My back is healed now and I feel much better. It'll all work out just fine."

I was speechless. I would NEVER, EVER, in a million years, have made this suggestion. I would have been the "brave soldier" for the rest of my life, suffering in silence—a robotron singing Bruce Springsteen's "Trapped" song to myself, and visiting the masturbation closet every night until my death.

A line from "Trapped" goes: "And I know someday soon that I will find the key." Here, now, my wife was offering me the key. The enormous question was: Should I take it? I broke down, sobbing. "Kim, I am so sorry," I wailed, hugging her tightly. "I never wanted this to happen. Can you forgive me?" Kim smiled. "It's OK, really, we'll be fine. You don't need to feel guilty. Our marriage is over. The kids and I need to go in a new direction. You didn't have that much sex before we met. So, go sew your wild oats – get that out of your system."

The physical pain that encapsulated my body at that moment was in direct conflict with my emotional jubilation. Kim was setting me free. Free to sleep, masturbate and come and go as I pleased while not constantly be rushed to and from hospitals. Free to pursue sex wherever and whenever I wanted, and to find as many young, available, beautiful women as possible, so I could bang all of their brains out.

Without telling me, Kim had already rented a large house in Lancaster, about a two-hour drive from where we'd been living. When I looked at a map, I freaked out. This new place was FAR away, and I was stuck driving Kim's creaky old Honda. We retained a mediator, and divided our meager property, such as it was. The kids would live with her, but we'd retain joint custody.

I moved Kim and my kids to the Lancaster house one September weekend. When it finally came time for me to leave that Sunday night, I fell to my knees on the kitchen floor, sobbing. My son, 4, said, "Don't cry, Daddy…we like this new house." My two-year old daughter kissed me on the cheek: "I love you, daddy. Bye." They went off to play in their new, toy-filled bedroom. I hugged Kim. "We'll be just fine out here, I promise," she assured me. "Go live your life."

Driving my 16-year-old, shit-box car back to LA from Lancaster in the pouring rain that night was the single most difficult thing I've EVER had to do in my life, to this day. I cried so hard, I couldn't see through the windshield, and strongly considered driving off the freeway and crashing into a canyon. Yet, I somehow made it back to my barren apartment, unscathed, the remnants of eleven years scattered everywhere. A major era in my life was over. I knew that I loved my children with all my heart, and that I would always be there for them, no matter what.

However, as I lay in bed alone that night, I had absolutely NO idea that hundreds of future "Carrot Ladies" lay-in-wait for me, in my not-so-distant future.

CHAPTER FIFTEEN

Really Bad Dates

For months, I sat on the floor of my tiny new apartment in Studio City, re-reading old love letters and poems Kim and I had written each other. We really had been in love in the early days, and I fought back many a tear.

The grief of not living with my kids was overwhelming. I'd work at my office (at a company I hated) till 6 o'clock on a Friday night, then dash out the door to retrieve them for the weekend. The drive to Kim's new house in Lancaster from my office would take three hours. I'd arrive, quickly shove the kids into their car seats, then drive another two hours back to my apartment, arriving after 11PM. The children were so excited to be at "Daddy's house," they'd be wide awake, and raring to "play toys." I had to pry my eyelids open with my fingers to indulge them.

I made this exhausting commute EVERY SINGLE FRIDAY NIGHT for the first five years after my divorce, never missing even one weekend.

I'd been assigned the publicity campaign for the grand opening of a NASA Space Museum in Houston. I had to take a three-day trip to Houston to coordinate media coverage of this new visitor center. Peter, a fellow publicist from our PR agency, flew with me, and we checked into adjacent rooms at a shit-hole motel. That night, we watched a presidential TV debate between George Bush, Sr., Bill Clinton, and Ross Perot.

Back in my room after the debate, I suddenly realized I'd not had sex in three and a half years. I flashed back to the excitement of Beverly the Whore and wondered if Houston had any "pay for play" women to offer. I looked through the yellow pages and found "Entertainers: Female."

Woman (on phone): "Sparkles Entertainment, can I help you?"

Me: "Uhm, ah, yeah, do you have women that make 'house calls'?"

Woman: "You mean outcall service? Yes, we do…what are you looking for tonight, honey?"

Me: "Ahh, do you have any beautiful women with long brown hair and nice large breasts?"

Woman: "We sure do. Where are you at?"

Me: "XYZ motel. How much do you charge?"

Woman: "Sweetheart, that's between you and the girl. But it'll be in the neighborhood of $100."

Me: "Uhm, ah, OK…when can she be here? I'm in room number 123."

Woman: "I'll have someone there within the hour. Have fun."

I had to be at the space museum the next morning early, and wondered: What if Peter woke up when my whore arrived? How could I possibly explain that to him? Would he tell everyone back at the office? Would I lose my job? I sat on the bed watching TV, a nervous wreck.

In under an hour, a tall, haggard looking woman in her early 40s, with long, fake brown hair but a decent figure, knocked. "I'm Gabriella, baby, how you doing tonight?" She looked really tired – attractive but worn out. "I'm OK, I guess," I responded. "So, how much are we talking about here?" "Well, darlin', it's seventy-five bucks for the company I work for, and then it depends on what kinda 'action' you're looking for. What did ya have in mind?" Me: "I really need to get laid, I guess." I was miserable, tired, and sick to my stomach. Here I was, the father of two kids just out of an eleven-year relationship, negotiating money once again with a whore. "Fucking me will be another $75 dollars," Gabriella said. $150 bucks! I was about to throw half my money on hand out the window. But then I looked at Gabriella's fishnet stockings and black leather miniskirt, and realized I was in too deep. I gave her the cash.

She laid on her back, hiked up her skirt, pulled down her panties, and said, "OK, baby, do it." This woman was all business. I quickly took off my clothes and popped an immediate boner. She took a rubber out of her little purse and quickly rolled it down me. Hungrily, I shoved myself inside her, and started pounding. She practically leapt off the bed, wincing in pain. "EASY BABY! You're killing me. Not so hard. That big fat cock of yours is ripping me apart. SLOW DOWN." It was the first time in my life a woman told me I was well endowed.

As I banged Gabriella, I noticed bruises on her neck and shoulders. Looking into her tired face, I could see that this woman had been a whore for a very long time, and appeared to have been "fucked out." While doing her, I looked into her eyes, desperate for affection, but saw only pain. "Fuck me baby, give it to me good, I'm a dirty, filthy whore who needs cock," she said, reciting by route. Surprisingly, I lasted a long time. Physically, it felt great. Psychologically, I honestly couldn't tell if I felt more pity for Gabriella or for myself.

Back home, I realized it was time for me to "get back on the horse," and start dating. The Gabriella incident re-ignited my sexual appetite, one that had been seriously sublimated during the last years of my nearly celibate marriage. In those days, long before the advent of the Internet or online dating, the *Los Angeles Times* featured a weekly section of personal ads called "Dateline." I placed an ad: "Funny, witty and warm. SWM, 36, Studio City, seeking attractive, fun, and successful woman for love and romance. I've got dark brown hair, hazel bedroom eyes and a good build. Please respond to XYZ."

Within the first weeks, I received at least 30 responses from woman as far south as San Diego and as far north as Santa Barbara. I was amazed by how impactful my stupid, free little ad had been. I dated from that ad for the next several months, but as I had my kids every single weekend, I was only available for dating during "school" nights.

Unfortunately, the women I met from my LA Times ad weren't exactly the most desirable of partners:

** "Tessa the Hut": A "very sexy redhead" who worked as a masseuse, and "gave the best massages in town" was the first to answer my ad. Intrigued, I lined up a date for Chinese food. As I stood in front of the restaurant awaiting her arrival, one incredibly good-looking couple after the next walked past me. Arriving about 15 minutes late, an ENORMOUS woman with very short, cropped red hair, waddled up to me. "Danny?" she smiled. "I'm Tessa." I quickly glanced at my car, thinking if I ran as fast as I possibly could, it might not be too embarrassing for either of us. "Yeah, I'm Danny." "Great, I'm starving,' said a woman who appeared to have already eaten Chinatown.

Tessa and I sat, ordered, and ate. Watching her devour a plate of spareribs, smearing sauce all over her massive lips and gums, was almost intolerable. I kept glancing at the other incredibly attractive couples gracing the place that night, while I sat with "Jabba the Hut." The check arrived. Tessa: "You wanna come back to my place? We can watch that funny, new TV show, 'STEIN-FIELD.' Have you seen it?"

After a long series of hems and haws, I managed the brilliant, "Uh, gee, Tessa, that's really nice of you, but, ah, uhm, I kinda have a pretty bad headache right now. Work was really a bitch today—can I get a raincheck?" The look of disappointment on her face was remarkable. For a split second, I felt sorry for her. She leaned closer to me: "I PROMISE that you'll leave my house with a smile on your face!" she implored.

As horny as I was, I simply couldn't make this comprise with my penis. (I'd sooner have made love to a corned beef sandwich.) "Sorry, no, I just can't." We stood, I paid, and she kissed me goodbye on my cheek. I raced back to my apartment, as quickly as the laws of physics would allow.

** The Aerobics Chick: An aerobics instructor at my local health club suggested I pick her up. I stood at her front door and heard, "Be right down." As I waited on her stoop, I noticed a prominent "humming" sound but couldn't determine what it was. Then, the noise became louder and louder, until it overtook me. A hornet's nest about the size of a large football was suspended mere inches above my head. Thousands of hornets were swirling about. Panicked, I flew off the stoop and ran into the street. My date appeared. "Sorry," she said, "Probably should have warned ya about those guys."

Aerobics Chick and I went to a classy restaurant. "Tell me about your life," I began. "Well, I make my living as an aerobics teacher now, but I used to be an actress in soft porn. You've probably seen me nude in some films – not that Glenn was too crazy about that." "Glenn?" I asked. "Yeah, we broke up about two months ago. We lived together for a while, but I told him I didn't love him anymore and made him move out. He's got a really bad temper. Sometimes he even stalks me. He sits in his car outside my place when I'm out on a date, waiting." "How does he know when you're on a date?" I inquired. "Oh, I tell him. He's gotta learn that my life goes on without him. In fact, I even told him about you tonight." I gulped. "Are you serious? Is he dangerous?" AC: "Well, he confronted one of my dates once – punched him in the nose. They settled out of court. He's a weightlifter, but, to me, he's really just a big pussy."

During my hours with this woman, I learned that she'd: been kidnapped by a man in a leather mask off a bus in Kansas (but was spared being raped because she was on her period;) been introduced to the joys of double-dong-dildo sex with women during an orgy in Miami; and was once picked up by a gorgeous redhead model in New York. "When that redhead orgasmed, oh my God! She squirt a ton of cum all over me. I was soaking wet. I clearly remember thinking, 'If I was a guy, I'd really be enjoying this right now.'"

My cock was doing push-ups in my underpants.

Sensing the mood was right, I bravely offered, "I have to admit, you're really turning me on right now," to which she responded: "Oh, I am SO SORRY! That was not my intention. I just recently decided that I've been too sexually promiscuous for far too long! I took a vow of celibacy about two weeks ago. In fact, I don't even masturbate anymore."

For cinephiles: I'd just lived the scene from the Woody Allen film *Play It Again, Sam,* when Woody is sitting on a couch next to a woman who's telling him she's an incurable nymphomaniac. Woody makes a move to kiss her, and she starts to scream: "What kind of woman do you take me for?" Fortunately, when I dropped my date off that night, neither Glenn, nor those five gazillion hornets, chose to kill me.

** The Laxative Queen: This well-built brunette and I decided to see a movie on our first date, and met in the theatre lobby. Attractive, with glasses, she had a nice smile. We each bought a bag of popcorn and took our seats.

Inside for maybe two minutes, she said, "Oh, shit. I've got a piece of popcorn stuck back here, near my molars." She opened her mouth, wide, and pointed out the criminal kernel to me. "Can you see it?" she asked. Me: "Urgh, uhm, oh yeah…looks like it's in there pretty good." "Damn," she continued, "This happened to me once before. I flossed like crazy for days, but the thing wouldn't budge. Finally, my dentist had to operate on me, sticking all kinds of tools back there—blood squirting everywhere, puss in my gums, you name it. A real mess."

I was queasy. I just wanted the fucking movie to start. Suddenly, she placed her popcorn tub on my lap and said, "Hey, can you watch this for me? I gotta hit the can! I took a laxative about an hour ago, and it just 'kicked in.'"

Laxative Queen missed the first 15 minutes of our film. When she came back to her seat, she whispered, "Got that son-of-a-bitch piece of corn outta my face AND took a major dump! I feel like a new person. What a relief." She beamed at me, elated.

I was nauseated for days.

** The Sneezer: A cute, husky lady with long, dark blonde, curly hair and big boobs, "The Sneezer" met me at a local bar for a drink. A photographer, she and I happened to have mutual friends. During our date, she kept staring at me. "Can I tell you a secret?" she asked. "Of course." "I saw a psychic the other day, and he told me that I would soon meet the man I was going to marry – his name would be 'Daniel.' Maybe it's YOU!"

Before I could even consider being flattered, she started to sneeze.

Not once. Not twice. Not three times.

My curly-haired date sneezed at least 40 times. So many times, in fact, that all other activity at the bar and in the restaurant adjacent came to a halt. The Maitre D' came to our table offering his aid, but there was really nothing anyone could do. Waiters, cocktail waitresses, and busboys stood at the ready, in case "The Sneezer," now turning shades of purple I'd never before seen in a human being, passed out.

"I'm so sorry about this!" she'd gasp, in between overwhelming, explosive bursts. "This hasn't happened to me since I was a child!"

** The Ketchup Mommy: A tall, lanky redhead told me she only dated guys that loved kids. I arranged a date at a nearby deli. Arriving early on a beautiful Southern California evening, I got a table on the outside patio, and was excited about this new possibility. About 20-minutes late, my date arrived, dragging her son, 5-year-old Chester, behind her. "I am SO sorry!" she announced. "My babysitter flaked at the last minute, and I really wanted to meet you. I hope you don't mind?" This woman had a very sweet smile and I could tell her story was legit. "No problem," I said, "I have small kids of my own."

The woman and her son sat opposite me. She and I tried desperately to have a normal conversation, but little Chester was impersonating "Dennis the Menace," throwing forks to the ground, spilling ice water, and pulling his mother's hair. "He's not usually quite this rambunctious," she said. "I'll bet he's just a little angel back home, eh?" I snarked.

The waiter brought our pastrami sandwiches and French fries. Chester started screaming, "Ketchup mommy! I want KETCHUP! I need KETCHUP for my French fries!" Chester reached across the table and went to grab for an open ketchup bottle just in front of me. It shot out of his hand, and a ton of ketchup flew all over my brand new, expensive, brown leather jacket. Incredulous, I looked into the eyes of my date, mid-pastrami bite. "Send me the bill," she sighed.

** The Lisp Lady: I met "The Lisp Lady" at a quiet, romantic restaurant in the Hollywood Hills. A former "C-level" movie actress, this woman had appeared in a number of shitty little horror films during the late '70's, but was still rather attractive. During dinner, I immediately noticed her lisp. My date simply could NOT pronounce the "ish" sound. Words with an "ish" ending sounded like "HISSSSSSS" – like the hissing of a snake. As we were eating dessert, she asked, "So tell me, Dan, are both of your parents 'Jew-HISSSSSS?'" And really, how could anyone honestly answer that question?

Escaping the pouring rain, we wound up back at my place and made out for close to an hour. Clearly aroused, she placed my hand inside her skirt and masturbated herself, cumming loudly. Excited,

I said, "That was really hot! I can't wait to fuck you," to which she replied, "Oh my God, you are so incredibly 'child-HISSSSSS!'"

Lisp Lady leapt to her feet, fled for the door, and stormed her way out of my life.

CHAPTER SIXTEEN

So This Is Sex ?!?!?

Uninspired by the women who were answering my LA Times ad, I gave up on that strategy, and invested in a dating service. I joined "Great Expectations," or, "GRAVE" Expectations, as I would mock it years later when I performed stand-up comedy at some of LA's top comedy clubs (1998-2001.) Members of Great Expectations had to go to their local office and review notebooks that contained photos and profiles of members of the opposite sex. (Was this the precursor to Mitt Romney's "binders of women" 2012 Presidential Debate remark??)

Of the many ladies I met this way, a few were certainly memorable:

Lynda was gorgeous. Older than me (40,) she was tall, with shoulder length blonde hair, killer green eyes, and a perfect figure. We met at a Thai food restaurant near her home in Woodland Hills. I was smitten the second I first saw her. She'd been married to a wealthy lawyer named Joel for many years, but he split unexpectedly. She also had a 21-year-old daughter living somewhere in Florida.

Lynda's eyes were as sad as she was beautiful. We covered a lot of ground during that first dinner date, and I realized she was the first person I opened up to, regarding the end of my marriage. "You're so green," Lynda said. "You need time to heal. I'm not sure you're ready to be dating anyone, just yet." I responded: "I was mourning the end of my marriage even when I was still married. The fact that I'm newly divorced doesn't change my being able to start a new relationship. I'm incredibly attracted to you, and I haven't felt this way about anyone in ages." "I'm hot, and you're just horny," she chuckled. "But you are kinda cute. Maybe I'll give you a shot."

We met in mid-November ('92,) and for the next six weeks straight, while almost inseparable, Lynda simply would NOT let me kiss her or sleep with her. "Be patient," she'd say when I made a move. "I'm not ready, and you're not ready. Please don't rush me." We went out to dinners and movies, holding hands like teenagers. She even gave me a sexy, 8X10 photo of her from her days as a model, and actually said, "Since we're not having sex, if you wanna pleasure yourself to my picture, that's OK with me. I wouldn't be offended."

With the Xmas and New Year's holidays fast approaching, Lynda was particularly sad because she hated to be alone. While I was going to spend Xmas with my kids, I told her I'd love to be with her on New Year's Eve. Much to my surprise, she said, "Let's do it! I'll cook you a fantastic dinner. You bring the wine. You've been really patient with me...maybe you'll even get lucky."

New Year's Eve: I entered Lynda's magnificent condo, courtesy of her wealthy ex-husband. She'd lit perhaps 30 white candles throughout the house—a fire was roaring in the fireplace. This scene couldn't possibly have been any more romantic. In the kitchen, I spun Lynda around and tried to kiss her. "Uh-uhn, not yet. I'm not ready, sorry." "Time to drink" I said aloud. Lynda and I had a great dinner in her upstairs kitchen with the lights off – the luminescence from the downstairs candles penetrated the room. At the end of the meal, I couldn't stand the anticipation another second. I grabbed Lynda by the waist, pulled her into me, hard, and pushed her up against the kitchen wall. We started kissing wildly, tongues everywhere. My chest was hard against her gorgeous, perfect breasts. I was in heaven. This was the moment I'd imagined for weeks.

Just then, the motherfucking telephone rang.

"Don't answer that!" I implored. "Please do NOT answer that God damn phone!" My penis was throbbing. Lynda pried herself from my death grip. "I have to...it might be my daughter. She took the call, walking the long cord into the adjoining dining room.

Moments later, she returned to the kitchen. "We've been invited to my friend Robbie's house for a party. You'll like him. I've gotta go get dressed. Can you clean up?"

I didn't want to go out! I had the perfect arrangement right there. Clearly left with no choice, I drove Lynda's brand-new Jeep Cherokee to the party, about 20 minutes away. We walked in, hand in hand, to her friend's place. There were about 30 people there, a few couples, and one or two very attractive women who seemed single. Robbie grabbed Lynda almost immediately and whisked her away. "Be right back," she winked, just as a striking brunette approached me: "Can you get me some champagne?" I wasn't sure what was happening, but this woman was cute. "Sure, why not."

During the course of the party, I got so drunk, I was guzzling champagne directly from the bottle, along with beers, martinis, and random other lipstick-stained drinks left scattered about the place. Some of the couples were smoking pot, and a few of the men were kissing other men (something I'd never seen before.) The brunette lured me into the hallway, shoved her tongue down my throat, and began dry humping me. While she was certainly pretty, she wasn't Lynda, and besides, she tasted like cigarettes. I felt queasy. "Wait a second. I'm not feeling too good right now," I said, extracting myself from her embrace. "Let's go watch TV. It's almost time for the ball to drop."

We sat on the couch, watching a pre-stroke-victim Dick Clark broadcasting live from Times Square. Robbie and Lynda returned to the living room, laughing. Lynda walked directly toward the couch, saw the brunette, and brusquely said, "Outta the way, bitch, he's MY date." Lynda collapsed onto my lap, curled up into a fetal position. "She took a few Quaaludes. She always gets like this," Robbie informed me. Then, he smiled, grabbed the brunette's arm, and walked away.

I had the feeling that Lynda and Robbie had been lovers but couldn't be sure. I was so drunk, in fact, I couldn't even remember what digits the new year was gonna be. Dick Clark did his countdown and a few folks blew noisemakers. Robbie was outside with the brunette, and I'd have to guess that, since I could see them through a screen door, he was getting the blowjob that could have been mine just moments earlier.

Perhaps around 1:30 AM, the party guests vanished. Lynda was still curled in my lap, snoring, and drooling onto my pants. Robbie tossed me some keys. "Dude, these are Lynda's. I think you better get her home." I froze. Me, drive a car, NOW? I was so fucking wasted, I couldn't see. How in the fuck was I gonna drive Lynda's brand new, beautiful car back to her place? Everyone knows the cops are out en masse on NY Eve, just waiting to bust drunk drivers. But Robbie, holding hands with the brunette, was insistent: "Seriously, guy, I need you two to leave. NOW!"

Somehow, I managed to rouse Lynda. Slurring her words, I'm not sure she was speaking English. As drunk as I was, I still managed to tap into my inherent sense of responsibility and drove to Lynda's place safely, without getting arrested or killed. (I prayed to God for help.) Back at her condo, we walked in silence to her living room. She went directly to her fireplace, placed a few fresh logs in there, and lit a fire. The depth of sadness and sorrow on her face overwhelmed me. I stood a few feet behind her, just watching in silence.

Lynda stood, turned, and looked right through me. As though a scene from a movie, she effortlessly stepped out of her clothes, laid down on the thick, beautiful white carpet, spread her legs, and motioned for me to have sex with her. The moment I'd been fantasizing about every second for the past six weeks had arrived. In a flash, I removed my clothes, and positioned myself on top of her. We resumed our make-out session from hours previous. She was, without question, one of the best kissers in the history of my life. I hadn't felt this turned on in years. I sucked her perfect breasts, fingered her pussy, and stroked her long hair. "Do it. Stick it in me. I want it now!" she commanded.

I had a few condoms in my pocket, but my pants were across the room. I had a panic moment: "To stick it in, or not to stick it in? That is the question." I didn't want to lose any of this spontaneity, but I also didn't want another kid walking the planet. Confused, drunk, and beyond horny, I decided NOTHING was worth interrupting this magical moment for.

Lynda spread her legs wider apart and stared into my eyes. "Fuck me, JOEL! Do it NOW!" I was stunned. JOEL??!! Hearing the name of her ex-husband at that second was equivalent to taking the ANTIDOTE to Viagra. Here was a goddess, the woman of my dreams, begging me to fuck her. All systems were go. She was completely nude on the floor in front of a roaring fire. It was New Year's Eve, and we were both wasted out of our minds.

Realizing my moment had arrived ("Joel/Schmoel,") I got onto my knees, and positioned myself for intercourse. Just then, the "Carrots Curse" kicked in, big time, baby. I hadn't noticed, but my cock was completely and totally limp – 100% soft, numb, and devoid of all purpose. It was, to borrow a phrase from Howard Stern, "the size of a mushroom cap." Hours earlier, when that brunette was mauling me at the party, I almost shot a load in my underwear. Here I was now, just a short time later, less a man than a 5th grade schoolboy.

Lynda looked into my face. "What's happening?" She was NOT happy. "Urh, ah, uhm, there seems to be a little problem down here," I whispered. Lynda glanced at "The Incredible Mr. Limpitt," and said, ANGRILY, in a sentence that's haunted me for decades: "I'm FINALLY ready to FUCK YOU, and you CAN'T EVEN DO IT?? JESUS FUCKING CHRIST, MAN!!"

COMPLETELY DISGUSTED, Lynda got off the floor, stormed upstairs into her bedroom, and slammed the door, HARD, aurally illustrating her rage. I remained seated on the living room floor, in front of the fire, naked and dejected. Recalling a similar incident I'd had with Claudia 16 years earlier, I once again had a "Man to Dick" talk: "All the times you've made me play with you, and THIS

IS HOW YOU REPAY ME? You are a fucking piece of SHIT, do you know that, cock? A USELESS FUCKING PIECE OF SHIT that just happens to be attached to my body. I HATE YOU. I hate you with ALL OF MY HEART. You should only burn in Hell for eternity."

Some time later, I slipped into Lynda's bed – she was sound asleep, snoring, her two, massive, Siamese cats sitting atop her legs. Still nude, I stealthily slid under the covers and tried to sleep but couldn't. The entire evening had been so incredibly bizarre—a complete and utter mishmash of alcohol, sexuality, and confusion.

I awoke hours later with a hard-on the size of Kentucky. It was, possibly, the strongest boner I'd ever had in my life. I turned and saw my beautiful, "sorta girlfriend" snoring. Her cats looked at me with hatred. "Get the FUCK outta here!" I hissed. They fled for their lives, sensing the fact that I could have easily slaughtered them by simply swinging my enormous Johnson across their stupid Siamese heads. I got onto my knees and slowly pulled back the covers. Lynda was wearing a pink teddy, with no panties. I positioned myself over her, and slowly spread her legs. Her beautiful, wonderful vagina, exposed to me once again in all its glory, whispered: "Danny, fuck me… fuck me…I want you…I need you…I forgive you for last night. Please, please make love to me."

My cock was rock hard and throbbing. My dream girl was lying there, naked and unconscious—a perfect combination. Here was my miraculous, second chance at making up for the FIASCO that had taken place just a few hours previous. I was gonna shove my big, fat, hard weiner deep inside Lynda, pound her with all of my might, and give her a screaming orgasm in her sleep.

"Lynda," I boasted, my cock perhaps three inches away from her promised land, "I have a PRESENT for you!"

Her head still on the pillow, Lynda opened one eye, and looked up at my face. She then glanced down, saw my enormous tree trunk, and said, "Oh, that's nice." I aimed myself at her feminine opening, like a Space Shuttle astronaut lining up the retrieval of an errant satellite for a docking. "Here it comes!" I said. Lynda spread her legs even further. My Johnson was now less than two inches from Lynda's sweet spot. Her smile, and her eyes, grew wider.

SUDDENLY, UNPROVOKED, and with ZERO STIMULATION OF ANY KIND, my giant penis EXPLODED, in the most powerful, and messy, orgasm I've ever had in my entire life, before or since. I NEVER entered her vagina. Sperm shot all over Lynda's thighs, pubic hair, belly, and bed sheets. I was suddenly trying to maneuver an out-of-control fire hose, spraying its payload everywhere but the one place for which it was intended.

I have never seen anything like it in the history of my life. I went silent. Lynda shot me the most incredible look of disgust in the history of disgust. "There's a <u>towel</u> in the <u>bathroom</u>, James Bond," she scolded, before rolling over and going back to sleep. In the bathroom, I realized I was covered with enough semen to float Shamu, the killer whale at Sea World, for a week. I glanced at my reflection in the mirror—the loser looking back at me was stupefied.

After mopping up Lynda's body with a wet cloth, I returned to sleep. I arose around noon, got dressed, and found Lynda downstairs drinking coffee. She was quiet. "It would probably be best if you went home now," she said, softly. She walked me to the door. I went to kiss her goodbye, but she completely pulled away. "Take care," she said, "Happy New Year," all but slamming the door in my face.

I stood still on her front porch for a few minutes. It would be a long, quiet drive back to my apartment that afternoon. Although we spoke by phone a few times after that night, and even after I explained numerous times "I've never had those problems before," Lynda refused to see me again.

Following that holiday weekend, I relayed my tales to my friend Peter (long married,) who'd been even more excited about the possibility of me scoring with Lynda than I was. "Take a seat," I said, and closed my office door. I described, on a blow-by-blow basis, every single detail of the New Year's Eve debacle between Lynda and myself. When I recounted the "Lynda, I have a present for you" line, Peter fell off his chair, and onto the floor, laughing so hard, tears streamed down his face. He was punching the ground. "A present? I've got a PRESENT for you?? You actually said those words? What could <u>possibly</u> be <u>cockier</u> than that? <u>So unbelievably inappropriate</u>!" Hysterical laughter, rolling on the floor. (I joined him.)

When we had spare time during our lunch hours, Peter and I would write sexually inappropriate songs together. The Lynda incident inspired this one, set to the tune of "My Eyes Adored You:"

"I had your pillow…
Though I never was inside of you, I had your bed sheets.
Like a million miles away from you, I never was in your vagina.
Your mattress – must be thrown away.
About your lamp shade…
Though I never shoved my cock in you…
I had your nightstand…
From across the room, my penis sensed the time had come
To soil your night shirt…
Your hand-towels, must be thrown away.
Sorry 'bout your mirror…
Though I really meant to make you cum,
I had your carpet.
While your cats were laughing on the floor, I sprayed your Head-board.
Your alarm clock, must be thrown away…"

I was attracted to Candy immediately. At first sight, she reminded me of a younger version of actress Mary McDonnell (*Battlestar Gallactica.*) She worked in the accounting division of a leading aerospace manufacturing company. Never married, Candy had beauty, charm, grace, and a terrific sense of humor. At the end of our first date, I hugged her goodbye, and asked if I could call her again. "You better," she said.

It was easy with Candy—she didn't sit around and brood like Lynda. No regrets about ex-spouses, starring off into space, or drowning her sorrows with Quaaludes. Candy was just a great, honest, straight-forward woman –everything I'd been seeking. Toward the end of dinner on our third date, she leaned across the table, took hold of my hands, and said, "Let's forget about that movie. Let's go to Tower Records and buy some really great 'Fuck' music!" I was amazed. Here was a woman completely in command of her own sexuality, who simply wanted to get laid. Candy was the first woman I ever knew as horny as I was, and not the least bit embarrassed to admit it.

We bought a Kenny G. CD, and went to my little apartment, where we had sex all night long. It was fantastic. We were incredibly in tune with each others' bodies, and our orgasms were truly powerful.

Candy and I were smitten with each other. Having been separated from my wife at this point for six months, I'd not yet introduced my children to any other woman. "Let's take them to the beach," she suggested. My children connected with Candy instantly. We spent a long, wonderfully sunny day at Manhattan Beach. Candy wore a tight, black and white, one-piece swimsuit. Her body turned me on like crazy, in spite of her fake boobs, which bore the scars of numerous, botched, plastic surgery efforts.

Candy and I continued to deepen our connection. I would give her lots of oral sex (an act my wife abhorred) and she would moan with joy. While I'd be driving, she'd take my right hand and masturbate herself with it in the passenger seat. She was, without question, the most robust sex partner I'd ever had.

Then came a big problem. I'd asked Candy what she wanted to do for her birthday. "Bring me to the sleaziest hotel you can find. I want you to ravage me—tie me up, blindfold me, and fuck my brains out." We found a tiny place in a beach community, and checked in as "Mr. and Mrs." We went to our room upstairs – "Don't turn on the lights. Just fuck me hard, right now." I pushed Candy against the wall, lifting her dress, pulling down her panties, and shoving myself deep inside her. We fucked standing up. Her orgasm was so powerful, she began panting. Hard. Too hard.

"Oh my God," she gasped. "I can't breathe." Candy started turning sheet white, and her knees buckled. She collapsed. "Oh shit. I've literally fucked this woman to death," I thought. I lifted her off the floor and carried her onto the bed. "My medicine," she whispered, "Quick – my heart medicine. It's in my bag." Panicked, I rummaged through her purse, and found a prescription bottle. Sweat poured down poor Candy's face as she downed a few pills. Still struggling to breathe, she looked into my eyes as if to say, "I am SO, SO SORRY about this! Please forgive me!"

Unfortunately, during this episode, I began flashing back to the countless times when my wife had suddenly become ill, or had fainted, or had been in overwhelming pain. I remembered having to call "911" for an ambulance, later spending hours (or days or months) at her bedside, in various ERs and hospital rooms. While Candy's medication began kicking in, I'd already begun to mentally "un-couple" myself from her. I took a few steps back, stared at her stricken condition, and flipped my mental "kill switch" to the "off" position.

About an hour later, Candy's color returned, and she appeared normal again. She confessed that she had some kind of heart condition that, only rarely, flared up. She asked that I hold her while she slept. The next morning, I awoke to the sight of Candy sucking my cock, underneath the covers, the blanket bobbing up and down. Clearly trying to make up for the disaster the night before, Candy went to town on my Johnson with fervor. After I came, she looked up from under the covers, laughing.

"Good morning, Mr. Sunshine!" she said. This was the Candy I knew, the happy, confident, non-deathly girlfriend I'd just spend the past five months bonding with. "Feeling better now?" I asked. "I thought I was gonna lose you last night." Candy apologized profusely: "I haven't had an attack like that in years! It must be because you're such an amazing lover."

Candy and I had breakfast that morning, but instinctively, she must have known something was wrong. She kept looking into my eyes, but an imaginary sign over my head read: "Sorry, darling, you're a great girl, but I'm so outta here." I drove Candy back to the parking lot where she'd left her car. "Thanks for the wonderful birthday, Danny boy," she said, "I love you." "Me, too, kiddo," I lied. Candy must have felt like she was kissing a ghost. The look on her face said, "Oh My God! I've LOST YOU, haven't I?" That look haunts me still.

Candy and I drove off, in separate cars, in separate directions. She waved "goodbye" to me as she split, but I can't recall if I waved back or not. Because I'm the world's biggest and most insensitive shithead, I never called lovely, wonderful Candy again. Of the hundreds of times I've fucked up relationships because of self-sabotage, this one remains particularly painful.

A line from a Steely Dan song, goes: "Well, you wouldn't even know a diamond if you held it in your hand." Poor, sweet Candy was, for me, one of those diamonds.

This story "looms large in my legend:" A very pretty blonde had agreed to meet me for dinner. We had a great time talking. Recently divorced, she had two kids who were with their dad that weekend, and just wanted to have "fun with a new guy." Afterward holding hands, we walked past a movie theatre, located just next door. "Let's see something," she said. We checked the marquee – the ONLY film that had a starting time that made sense to us at that moment was *Schindler's List*, which had debuted that day.

"I want to see *Schindler's List*, blondie said. "Are you kidding?" I responded. "Do you know what that film is about? Jews getting cooked in ovens. That is absolutely NOT a DATE movie! I'll take you to any other movie on the planet, but NOT *Schindler's List!*" "No, no, no," she insisted, "I really want to see that. I read about it…it sounds fascinating. Take me inside." "Are you SURE?" I asked again. "Yes."

We took our seats in the theatre and held hands. The SECOND the film began, my gal pal JUMPED INTO MY LAP, and began molesting me. She was kissing me hard, rubbing my chest and my crotch, and thrusting her terrific breasts against me. I was overwhelmed with both lust and guilt: Here I was, a Jew, watching a film about the Holocaust, in a movie theatre in Southern California, with a blonde Shiksa goddess who was practically raping me with my clothes on. Compared to my poor Jewish ancestors depicted on the screen, I felt my situation was morally reprehensible. Yet, there I was, making out with this sex-starved woman for the first 10-minutes of a movie I've yet to see in full.

After the film ended, we went back to her house, and continued our kissing session. Clothes flew across the room, and just when I was about to "do" her, she began to cry. "No, no, Please don't fuck me, PLEASE DON'T!" she insisted, sobbing. I was on my knees on her couch – she was on her back, totally nude, legs spread wide. My cock was pointing at her pussy like a guided missile. "What's the story here?" I asked. "I can't, I just can't," she pleaded. "I haven't had sex with a man other than my husband in 14 years. I changed my mind…I can't do it. PLEASE don't stick that thing inside of me!"

Once again, I was caught between a "do the right thing" or a "fuck her—fuck her brains out" moment. I recalled Lynda's "I'm finally ready to fuck you, and you can't even do it," Jane's "please, please don't," and Ramona's admonishing me that "girls say no when they mean yes." Confused beyond reason, I remained kneeling and upright, my cock throbbing and ready, for about two minutes. Blondie's body was screaming, "Fuck me! Fuck me! Fuck me!" but her eyes were too sad, and I just couldn't. I may well be the world's horniest man, but I'm simply not a rapist.

"I'm really sorry...I thought I could. I'm really attracted to you, but I'm just not ready yet," she said.

My next move was thoughtful, tender and loving: "Ya got any LUBE at least?" I asked in disgust. She gave me a puzzled look: "Well, there's some baby lotion in the bathroom." Completely pissed-off, I insisted that this woman jerk me off. A bit repulsed, she did as I instructed, and I shot my love juice all over the cover of her brand-new *TV Guide Magazine*. I split from her house, and because I'm such a patient, kind-hearted soul, ripped her phone number into shreds, tossing them from my car on my drive back home.

Now: The Best Part of this story:

About three months after this event, the TV series *Seinfeld* had an episode in which Jerry Seinfeld takes a good-looking woman on a date to see *Schindler's List* in a movie theatre. I was watching this episode from my apartment, alone. Instead of watching their film, though, Jerry and his date start making out in their seats – a date that had happened to me IN REAL LIFE, just a few months previous! HOW ON EARTH did the creators and writers of *Seinfeld* know to re-create an event that had happened to ME? To this day, I am convinced that someone from the show (Larry David?) was sitting behind me in that movie theatre in Marina del Rey, on that very same February night in 1994.)

A very cute, young, and just slightly "meaty" blonde, Amy (who I'd met when she briefly worked at my same PR agency – and who told me she had a major crush on me,) was next employed as a secretary at a very popular, "rock and roll" hotel on Sunset Blvd. Her apartment was just blocks from mine, and after our first dinner date, she invited me there. Inside, she took me by the hand, and walked me straight into her bedroom. We sat on her bed. She lit some candles and put on some music. "I really want to kiss you," she said, and we made out for a long time. It was really, really great – passionate and romantic. Fifteen years my junior, Amy made me feel like I was in high school.

"You're turning me on so much—I think we should have sex," I suggested. "Sure…do you have protection?" she asked. And, of course, being prepared at all times, I said, "No, but I wish I did." We stopped kissing. "Well, this sucks," she said. "We could go to a drug store," I suggested. Amy: "Wait, I might have a condom in the bathroom." We went "exploring," and found, under the sink, a condom that had likely been stuck behind a drainpipe since the Carter Administration.

Back in Amy's bedroom, clothes came off, we got under the covers, and resumed our kissing session. Naked, her body was far sexier than I'd imagined. When we were ready to go all the way, I opened the condom packet – it burst into a mushroom cloud of dust. We looked at each other, laughing. "Next time," Amy said, "We'll be much better prepared."

Amy and I dated for the next five months. At the time, I was almost 38 and she was 23. Being with her made me feel young and strong and alive. She turned me on to her music – my new favorite song, which I often found myself singing out loud, became "Found Out About You" by The Gin Blossoms:

"Whispers at the bus stop…
I heard about nights out in the school yard…
I found out about you…found out about you…."

One night Amy insisted that I watch her "favorite movie ever," an old Nicholas Cage film called *Vampire's Kiss*. We watched that film on VHS, sitting naked on my living room floor under a blanket, eating cherries and drinking wine. Amy fell asleep on my shoulder. I picked her up, carried her into my bed, tucked her in, and watched her sleep. It was one of the most romantic moments of my life.

Sex with Amy was fun, lighthearted and pressure free. She had orgasms freely, so making her cum was never a chore. One time she gave me a terrific blowjob, and I orgasmed in a matter of minutes. In a childlike voice, she innocently remarked: "Gee, guys really seem to like that, don't they?" I adored her.

My birthday was fast-approaching and we'd planned a romantic evening to mark the occasion. However, I awoke that morning and couldn't stop swallowing. I went to a doctor – he said my uvula (that little "punching bag" thing in the back of the throat,) was inflamed, infected and enormous and "should probably be removed VERY soon." He gave me two injections, which made me feel incredibly nauseous and irritable.

Back at work a few hours later, someone called out: "Hey everybody! OJ's on the run!" My 38th birthday was the day OJ Simpson decided to elude the Los Angeles police department on national television. Work stopped for us all, as we watched the proceedings with mind-numbing fascination.

That night, I picked Amy up, and we went to a candle lit restaurant. I handed her flowers, and we sat in the restaurant's backyard patio, where TV screens replayed the OJ chase scene, ad infinitum. "You brought ME flowers on YOUR birthday?" she said. "That is without a doubt the most romantic thing any guy has ever done for me." We kissed. Amy was dressed to kill in a black sexy dress that showed off her cleavage. She was all over me, and only wanted to show me a good time. But, between the shots I'd gotten that morning, and the confusion surrounding the OJ debacle, I felt so sick and confused, it was all I could do not to throw up during dinner.

I drove Amy home. We sat in the car. "Can you sleep over?" she asked in her little girl voice. As tempting as that offer was, I thought I was going to faint. "Amy, I'd love to spend the night with you, but I feel so shitty right now, I just have to go home. I'm really sorry." The look on her face was profound. "Are you sure?" she said. (All the times in my life I'd waited for moments like this one. Here it was, and I couldn't do anything about it.) "Yeah, sorry, I just don't feel well."

Home alone, I took some Motrin, and sat up in bed, watching the news. There was OJ, once again, driving the LA freeways, as people held up signs cheering on a psychotic butcher.

The day had been such an extraordinarily confusing mess. The phone rang. "You OK?" Amy asked. "I feel like total shit," I said. "You want me to come over there and make you feel better? I miss you." Lost in depression, I said, "I really appreciate that. But no, not tonight. Sorry. I just can't."

At work the next day, I told Peter about my birthday date, then confessed: "I think I'm in love with Amy." My buddy encouraged me to share that news with her as soon as possible. I drove to the hotel where she worked and called Amy from a phone in the lobby. "I need to speak with you right now. It's important. Can you come downstairs?" Amy: "I'm kinda busy…but I'll meet you in the bar in a few minutes."

"What's wrong?" Amy asked, as she sat opposite me. I held her hands and stared deep into her eyes. "I've made a lot of mistakes with other women in my life, Amy," I said slowly, "But I really don't want to make another one with you. I've fallen in love with you, Amy…I love you, and I just wanted you to know how I feel."

The look on Amy's face could only be described as abject terror. She stood so quickly her chair shot backwards behind her about four feet. "Oh, my God!" she cried. "Are you kidding me? I can't believe you just said that! What were you thinking??" I had no idea what was happening.

And then, a truly classic "Carrots" line: "If I fell in love with YOU, I wouldn't have any love left over for MY MOTHER!"

Pale and shaking, Amy turned and ran away. Literally ran. I sat there, looking around the room once again for Allen Funt. "Huh?" Even the bartender shot me a look of incredulity. Anyone I've ever told the "Amy Story" to has found it simply remarkable. Common responses:

"Never heard anything like it;" "Really? She's a freak," and even, "Tell her to marry her mommy."

Although we went out to a few movies "as friends" afterward, Amy and I never dated again. She tried to explain that after her father had died prematurely when she was quite young, she'd promised her mother that she wouldn't fall in love with any guy until after she turned 30.

"Nothing personal, Danny," she offered. "It's just a commitment I made to my mother a long time ago. After all, a promise is a promise."

If anyone out there can figure this one out, please let me know.

CHAPTER SEVENTEEN

"Whack Shacks," Massage Parlors, Strippers and Las Vegas Call Girls

After Amy dumped me, I stopped dating for two years. My job was more than demanding, and the weekends with my kids, truly the only joyous moments of my life, were exhausting and expensive. Since I didn't have to deal with their homework, or take them to doctors, or meet their teachers, I was "Fun Guy," the divorced dad who takes his kids to every movie, theme park, bowling alley, playground, pizza shop, miniature train ride, kiddie museum, beach and toy store in Southern California. I was completely and totally in love with my children, and, to paraphrase Amy, simply "had no love left over for anyone else."

However, while my weekdays were consumed by work, and my weekends action-packed with kids, my throbbing penis was not to be ignored. He'd scream at me on weeknights: "Hey asshole! Remember me? Your dick? What about MY needs, buddy? What about ME? You can run, you can hide…but you can NEVER, EVER forget that I exist!" His demands became more and more impossible to ignore, and my nightly masturbation routine to the same old *Playboy Magazines* was no longer keeping the little guy (my "third child") at bay.

I had precious little time to myself every Monday-Thursday evening, after working and inhaling fast food for dinner. These were the hours when my hormonal urges would simply overwhelm me. I hadn't paid for a prostitute in years and had no interest in doing so again. I began to wonder if there might be other, "alternative" means out there by which to satisfy my schlong's relentless appetite.

Some research led to my discovery of a variety of "pay-for-play" sex parlors scattered about Los Angeles that appeared to offer meaningless pleasure, fairly inexpensively.

"Venus Faire" was an adult bookstore in N. Hollywood that advertised "Live Girls." Apprehensive, I entered for the first time, and asked the enormous, tattooed woman at the register what to do. "They're in the back, buddy" she said. "Ten bucks admission." I paid and walked through a beaded curtain. There, I found a large, circular area, comprised of a dozen little rooms, each featuring a glass door behind which lingerie-clad models of every size, shape, and color would stand. Attached to these little rooms were closets into which men could walk, slip a $20 bill into an ATM-type machine, and then watch, as a dark black curtain would rise, granting direct, line-of-sight access to these women through a glass partition that co-joined the two rooms.

Both repulsed and fascinated, I walked the circular pathway countless times, observing how my fellow horn-dogs, primarily Hispanic gardeners and blue-collar workers, would check out the merchandise, make a visual "connection" with one of the women, and then proceed into a tiny closet. I poked my head into one such closet, and saw inside only a stool, a small trash can, a phone, an ATM machine, and a roll of toilet paper. The smell of semen was over-powering.

Seconds away from leaving, one of the women, a fairly sexy Mexican girl with very long black hair, beckoned me. "First time?" she asked through her glass door. "I'm Sasha. Don't be shy. Come in and visit. I'll give you a good show."

Curious, I entered the coffin shaped "Whack Shack," and bolt-locked the door. Trembling, I slid a crisp $20 bill into the cash machine and watched as the black curtain between our two rooms rose. Sasha, now topless, was dancing for me on the other side of the glass, smiling and winking. Completely and totally in a daze, I wasn't sure if I had the nerve to jerk myself off, so I sat on the stool, frozen. Sasha called me on the phone: "Hey baby," she said, "You gonna show me your beautiful big dick? Why don't you look at my big tits and play with yourself. I love watching guys jack off their cocks."

Now well inspired, and hard as a rock, I pulled down my pants, stood, and masturbated. Sasha removed her panties, pressed her tits up against the glass, sucked her fingers, and, with her other hand, furiously rubbed her privates. This was, perhaps, the hottest thing I'd ever seen in real life. After a few minutes, the black curtain started to slide back down – I frantically slid another twenty bucks into the ATM slot and kept stroking. Moments later, I shot my load all over the glass window. Sasha laughed, applauded, then waved goodbye, just as the curtain separating us once again began to lower.

Breathless, I pulled up my pants, took some toilet paper, and wiped away the evidence. Gathering my composure, I closed my eyes for a second, collected my thoughts, took a few deep breaths, and came back to reality. As I walked off, Sasha, now re-dressed, waved goodbye and blew me a kiss. Leaving the store, the tattooed woman called out: "So, buddy, how was your first time?" "I'll be back," I replied, impersonating Arnold Schwarzenegger.

I became completely and totally addicted to the Venus Faire "Whack Shack" experience. As the place happened to be located along the route between my office and retrieving my kids, I began making regular pit-stops there on Friday nights. For a mere $50, I could have "hot, dirty, filthy, make-believe, fantasy sex" with naked women, whose sole purpose in life was to flirt with me while I masturbated. This was a whole new world of sex —no strings, no dates, no boring conversations. Just quick, cheap, erotic cumming, whenever a guy needed a little "stress relief."

After months of jerking off behind glass, I had a revelation: "What would it be like to actually get jerked off by one of these sluts for real?" After I'd attended a singles party in Santa Monica (and was drunk off my ass,) I walked into an "Oriental Massage" parlor. A sweet, older Asian woman greeted me at the door. "Hello, sir, you like sexy massage?" Me: "Yes, I really would." Woman: "OK, please for fifty-dollar. Then you go in back and meet beautiful girl, OK?" I gave the lady the money, and she ushered me down a tiny hallway, and into a small room with a massage table, chair, nightstand, and table lamp with a red-light bulb. "Wait here—I send in girl for you."

I had NO idea what to expect, but was so fucking drunk, didn't really care. A few minutes later, a beautiful Korean girl, about 22, entered. "Hi, my name Pretty. You like?" She slowly spun around, so I could see her perfect body. "Yes, I like," I said, "I'm Danny." "Danny, you so sexy," she giggled. "You take off clothes and Pretty give massage, OK?" In a flash, I was naked, and on my belly. Pretty also disrobed, then hopped atop the table and kneeled over me. She poured baby lotion into her hands and massaged my entire backside (including the crack of my ass.) It was heaven. "You like Pretty?" she asked. "Yes, I really do. I like Pretty very much," I whispered in ecstasy. (I'd never had a massage in my life.) Pretty make you very, very happy, Danny, but need money first," she explained. Me: "How much money?"

Pretty got off the table and stood before me—I sat up. "You want this," she said, demonstrating jerking-off with her hands, "I charge $25 dollar. You like this," sucking an imaginary penis, "You give me $50 dollar. Or, you like to have this," she said, thrusting her pussy back and forth, "I need one hundred dollar. What you like for tonight, my sexy Danny?"

While I wasn't planning to get laid just then, I did have enough cash for any option. My Johnson was ecstatic. "You have such nice, big hard cock for Pretty!" she laughed, applauding. I was way conflicted—I couldn't decide between a hand job, a blow-job, or a fuck. They all sounded equally great. "How about you do this?" I asked, indicating a blow-job. In a second, Pretty kneeled beside me, cock in mouth, balls in hand. She closed her eyes, and entertained me with long, slow, sensuous "sucks," giving me extraordinarily wonderful pleasure. Since I was drunk, I lasted a pretty long time, and, when I finally exploded, my eyes rolled back into my head.

"Oh, my God, Pretty," I said. "Thank you so much. That was amazing." She smiled, then held out her hand. "Please for fifty dollar now, OK, Danny?" I paid her the cash, plus an extra ten dollar tip. She kissed me on the cheek, opened the door and said, "You nice guy, Danny, you come see Pretty again soon, OK?" She vanished before I finished getting re-dressed.

Like the vaudeville performer who used to spin plates on long sticks on the old *Ed Sullivan Show*, I was now juggling my job, my kids, and visits to whack shacks and Korean massage parlors on a regular basis. I only needed a bit of advance planning to ensure that I had enough time, and money, to pull off these pathetic sexcapades properly.

Now a full-fledged "cum-a-holic," I continued to expand my repertoire of stimulating new "girly houses" in further exploration of my newfound "hobby." I'd heard about "Déjà vu Show Girls," and went to check it out. This place had extremely beautiful girls, professional model-level, many with enormous, plastic-surgery enhanced tits. I'd "upped my game," and was now willing to invest more of my hard-earned money to experience simulated sex with Playboy level fantasy girlfriends.

At "Déjà vu," each dancer stripped for a few songs, then, re-dressed in lingerie and high heels, would walk around the bar area, approaching drunk, pathetic losers like me. These women would ask patrons if they'd like to have a "private show in the back." Once I was drunk enough, I'd approach the most alluring woman possible and ask for a "date." As two enormous male bouncers watched, a drop-dead sexy woman would lead me by the hand to the back-room, where a variety of themed dens of iniquity were located. The ones I recall were the "Hawaiian Vacation" room, the

"New Orleans Jazz" room, the "African tiger hunt" room, and the "50s" room." As each woman and I would walk past, I could see a variety of my fellow desperados lying on their backs, as goddess-level girls rode them like bucking bronchos, grinding their panty-clad crotches against pants-restrained hard-ons.

Each of these rooms had beaded curtains, so tree-trunk sized bouncers could ensure that no "real sex" was taking place. I'd be on my back, with the sexiest women I'd seen since my days at the Playboy Mansion, astride me, grinding away. Fake moaning, they'd say, "Oh, baby, fuck me hard…fuck me baby, rub your big hard dick against my wet clit…make me cum for you, darling, shoot your big hot load all over me." While I left these sessions every time with a huge smile, it was rather embarrassing trying to hide the massive, "Scarlet Letter" cum stains prominent on the front of my jeans.

I often had to attend trade shows in Las Vegas, where I represented various clients demonstrating new technology systems for the entertainment industry. On a few of these trips, I extended my "hobby" into the world of Las Vegas call girls. I almost always stayed at The Mirage Hotel, and after dinner with clients, would return to my room, desperately horny. Recalling "Gabriella" in Houston, I'd, once again, leaf through the local Yellow Pages, find the "Female Entertainers" section, and make a few calls. I always requested the same thing: "I want a gorgeous woman, in her 20s or 30s, with big tits, a perfect body, a beautiful face, and long straight hair." The voice on the other end: "That's fine…we'll send someone up to your room within the hour."

The first time I treated myself in Vegas, a woman resembling Suzanne Somers from her *Three's Company* TV show era, knocked on my door. She was perfect. "Hi, honey," she said. "You're cute.

What did you have in mind for tonight?" Since I honestly had no idea what kind of money was involved at this level, I said, "Well, you're really beautiful, I'd really like to be inside you. How much would that cost me?" She sat on the edge of my bed. "Well, for starters, I need you to give me $250 for the company I work for." "That's fine," I said, "I can do that. Does that get me laid?" "Oh no, silly boy," my vision said, "That's for THEM. If you want to fuck me, MY FEE is $350."

I was floored. SIX HUNDRED DOLLARS for one fuck? Wow! That's a fortune. Even though I had the dough, and was in a drunken stupor, I still had a hard time justifying the spending of that kind of money. "That's A LOT," I said to blondie-locks. "I wasn't planning to spend that much. I'm really sorry." The two of us sat, side by side, at the foot of my bed, in silence. "Listen, you're a sweet guy. How much can you pay me?" I looked her up and down—this woman was as beautiful as any I'd ever seen in real life. "How about $200? That's $450 total." The woman stood. "You're gonna pay me LESS than what my company charges? That's kind of insulting, don't you think?" She walked toward the door. "Wait!" I said. "I'll give you $250. That's five hundred dollars. Please—I really want you, but I honestly can't spend any more than that."

My blonde goddess looked me up and down. "You seem like a good guy," she finally said. "Alright, I'll let you fuck this tight pussy for $250." She slipped off her shoes, hopped cross-legged onto the bed, and put out her palm. "Pay me."

I opened my wallet and saw that I only had about $300. "Urh, ahm, ah, I don't have enough cash right now. What should I do?" "There's an ATM in the lobby," my whore advised. "Go downstairs, get what you need, and hurry back, OK? I've got other clients to see tonight besides just you, ya know?"

At the door, I realized I was leaving a complete stranger alone in my room. "Listen," I said to this vision, "Please don't steal any of my possessions while I'm gone. These are brand new suits, and I honestly don't think they'd look that good on you." She chuckled, "Trust me, honey, I'm rich. I don't need ANYTHING you've got in this room. Now go bring me my money!"

A hypnotized zombie, I hit the lobby, found an ATM machine, and pulled out hundreds of dollars. As I re-approached the elevator banks, FIVE OF MY CLIENTS were about to walk past me. It was 2 in the morning. I was drunk off my ass wearing pajamas and had five hundred dollars in cash sticking out of my hands in all directions. If they'd seen me, and wanted to have a little chat, concocting a cover story on the fly would have been tough. Panicked, I crouched down and hid behind one of the tall potted plants next to the elevators. Fortunately, they walked past me, clearly drunk themselves, and continued on into the casino.

Back in my room, I fully expected my suits and brand-new Movado watch to be long gone. Instead, I found the most beautiful naked woman I'd ever seen, under the covers of my bed, reading a Cosmo, and smoking. "That's a good little boy," she said, as she snuffed out the ciggy. I fanned out her five hundred dollars, and she quickly stuffed the bills into her tiny purse. She took out a condom and said, "Let's see what we're working with here." I stripped down in seconds, popped a big fat boner, and watched as she quickly installed the rubber onto my shaft.

Laying back on the bed, she said, "OK, I'm ready now. Do what you need to do. But don't take all night." I got on my knees, and hovered over her perfect body, visually "drinking her in." I imagined she was a 3D Playboy centerfold hologram. Slowly, I put myself inside her, and began to thrust. However, blondie's head faced away from me – I could tell she wanted absolutely NOTHING to do with this transaction, whatsoever. I was about to fuck her body, but NOT HER.

While thrusting, I had mixed emotions. I knew this woman was the first "10" I'd ever had, but it felt like cheating. She wasn't really "there." I could have been fucking a blowup doll at this point.

"Honey, can you please look at me, at least? I'd love to see your eyes." Begrudgingly, she turned her head and shot me an evil, almost demonic look, as if to say, "Happy now, you fucking asshole?" While nothing short of an earthquake could have slowed down my humping at that point, it was a far cry from any kind of turn-on.

"Can you talk dirty to me?" I gently requested, and then heard perhaps the most classic line in the history of my sex life: "That'll cost extra."

The excitement of finally fucking a perfect blonde fantasy girl finally made me cum, which was even more amazing considering I'd masturbated both that morning and the night before. The SECOND I was finished, this woman slipped off the rubber, held it up to the light, and said, "Wow, what a big load! I have to say I am VERY impressed!"

In a flash, my whore was redressed. She stood at the door. "You're a nice guy. Keep my number, and the next time you're in town, let me know. I wouldn't mind playing with you again." A wink, a quick smile, and my Las Vegas "10" strutted out of my life, forever. (I never got her name.)

During another visit to Vegas, I bumped into my cousin Franz, a renowned magician, at the Luxor Hotel. He was there pitching a TV show idea about "Magic Around the World." We ended up eating dinner together, and then walked into the casino to play blackjack. We sat on stools, and after a few hands, two very attractive brunettes approached us. "Hi, boys," said one. "Need some company?" asked the other.

My cousin laughed, stood, and said, "Danny, I'm married. They're all yours!" He briskly walked away. Drunk, I invited the ladies to sit beside me and play. "But we need money!" said one. "Wait here a second, be right back," I slurred, walking off to the cashier's desk and returning with hundreds of dollars. The three of us played cards for a while, but once I'd blown through about six hundred bucks, I knew enough to quit. "Girls, I'm not a rich man.

I'm done. Nice meeting you." As I walked away, they said, "You're gonna buy us drinks at least, right?" My ears perked up, and now these two lovelies, one on each arm, escorted me into the bar.

Sometime after 2 AM, I realized I needed to get some sleep. "It's been a lotta fun, but I'm going back to my room now," I informed them. "We're coming with you," said one. "Yeah, you're really sexy—we're not gonna let you slip away that easily." I drunk "sleep-walked" through the lobby of the Luxor Hotel, a sexy brunette on each arm, hailed a taxi, and wound up back at The Mirage. My two new girlfriends escorted me to my room and sat on my bed. I hid in the bathroom. Looking at myself in the mirror—I was bleary-eyed and pale, nauseous and dizzy.

I peed, splashed my face, and could only think about the early client meeting I had in the morning, and the sweet call of sleep.

Out from the bathroom, I saw the two girls sitting topless on my bed, kissing each other. "You like this?" asked one. "Yes, of course," I said, frozen. "Sit here," motioned the other, and I sat between them. "Wanna fuck us both?" they asked. "Sure, that would be great," I said yawning, not knowing if I'd even be able to get hard.

The girls then stood, thrusting their tits in my face. "That'll be four hundred dollars," said one. "Apiece," added the other.

I've been "taken" several times in my life, but, perhaps, never as badly as at this moment. To say I was the world's biggest putz—having NO IDEA these women were hookers—would be a fair assessment. "Are you serious?" I asked. I kept glancing at my hotel pillow: "Danny...come rest your weary head...get rid of these bimbos and get some sleep." But then my little buddy in my underpants woke up, and realized this opportunity represented a possible "three-way" first. Exhausted, defeated, and disgusted, I said, "Wait here. Once again, I hit the ATM in the hotel lobby, returned with a big wad of bills, and angrily threw them at these two, young scam artists.

"Here, take it all, see if I care," I scolded. They took to the dough like birds to breadcrumbs, then stripped, then stripped me. I was all but asleep as one, then the other, took turns sucking me and playing with my balls. My eyes were closed and I was partially dreaming – even my semi-flaccid cock was almost asleep. All I could think was, "I just spent EIGHT HUNDRED DOLLARS for THIS?" Miraculously, after some serious "suckage," my cock got fairly hard, and the better-looking woman slipped on a rubber, mounted me, and began to ride.

"Fuck me, baby, "she said, "But don't come inside...I want to watch you shoot onto my girlfriend's tits." Banging a hot woman while you're asleep is interesting, but, for me, not exactly the biggest turn on in the world. (The second woman was lying beside the two of us, fondling my nutsack.) Of course, I shot my load while she rode me, not giving her "pull out" request a moment's thought. As soon as I came, I began snoring. The girls vanished.

I never caught their names. And, quite honestly, I couldn't recognize them today in a police lineup if my life depended on it.

The third and final time I engaged the services of a Las Vegas call girl was perhaps the most memorable. After a full day with clients, I was back in my hotel room when I remembered a flyer my Middle Eastern taxi driver had given me that morning. "If you're lonely tonight," he said, "This place provides the hottest women in town at very reasonable pricing. Just tell them Amir sent you."

Taking the guy at his word, I called the number and requested a "killer hot redhead, around 40." Instead, an hour later, the woman who knocked on my door LOOKED EXACTLY LIKE BRITNEY SPEARS, but with much larger breasts. I was so attracted to this young blonde vision, I gasped.

"Hey sugar pie," the Southern belle drawled. "You're cute as a button. You like what you're seeing here?" Beyond bedazzled, I said, "Yeah, you're not too shabby." She giggled. "Guys seem to like me…

must be that whole 'Britney' thing, I suppose." My whore walked right up to me, put her arms around my neck and started French kissing me. My heart raced. "So what do ya think now?" she asked. "I want you like you couldn't possibly imagine," I said. "Then, let's talk turkey, handsome. Do you want me to suck your cock? fuck you? or jerk you off onto these bad boys?" she asked, smushing her tits together. "It's up to you, sugar bear, I'm a full-service kinda gal." To be propositioned by a girl who looked like Britney's (bigger busted) twin was an opportunity I knew I simply could NOT pass up. "Well, I don't think I could live with myself the rest of my life if I didn't fuck you…so, how much?"

The next words that came out of her mouth were, to me, literally unbelievable: "Honey pie, that's gonna cost ya fifteen hundred dollars."

I wanted to kill Amir!

"Fifteen hundred dollars is simply out of the question. I won't do that…it's just NOT going to happen. I'm really sorry," I forcefully explained. Britney opened her shirt, removed her bra, pressed the most incredibly beautiful tits I'd ever seen against my chest, and stuck her tongue down my throat. "Don't you want to grab onto these beauties while you're pounding me doggie style?" she cooed. "They're real by the way!" My cock, once again my evil nemesis and lifelong betrayer, screamed: "Schmuck! If you don't fuck this girl, I WILL NEVER SPEAK TO YOU AGAIN IN YOUR LIFE! What is money but to be spent?"

Realizing I could max out two credit cards to raise the cash, I said, "What the fuck. OK, I HAVE to have you, screw the cost. Can you wait here? I'll go get your money." Britney: "Don't you buy a girl a drink before you fuck her?" she giggled. My voluptuous whore and I then went down into the casino, arm in arm. Guys' heads were turning – they all knew I was the biggest "John" in the room, but I simply didn't care. At the cashier's window, I maxed out my cards, and in an act of pure self-loathing, handed her the fortune, not thinking for a second how easy it would have been for her to simply run away right then and there, ripping me off blind.

We drank shots of Jack Daniels, and she told me a quick version of her life story: Model in Alabama as a teenager, abused by her stepfather, ran away from home at 15 to come to Vegas, began sucking guys off for money, fell in love with her best friend (another model), etc. Stuff you'd hear on Howard Stern's radio show was now being presented to me in real, "make-believe Las Vegas," life.

After the drinks, Britney said, "Darling, I am so wet for you! Let's go fuck the sheets off your bed!"

The sex I enjoyed that night with Britney Spears' doppelganger was so exhilarating, I have no words to describe it. Fucking a woman who looked like this was, for me, the ultimate "revenge" against all of the thousands of times I'd masturbated, alone, to perfect women in magazines. We finished off our session doggie-style, with me holding onto her "bad boys" for dear life. I cried real tears of joy when we were done. In fact, Britney even held me tenderly, while I sobbed.

Back in LA, I continued visiting my whack shacks and cum-parlors as often as circumstance would allow. I memorized the schedules of my favorite "cum sluts," and allocated a certain amount of masturbation money each week to be included within my overall budget. I knew the momentary pleasure I was paying for was completely meaningless, vapid, and devoid of any real emotion.

As Woody Allen so famously said in *Annie Hall*, "And what's wrong with masturbation? It's sex with someone I love."

Ditto.

CHAPTER EIGHTEEN

The Miracle of Prozac

Approaching my 40th birthday, I took a "life assessment." I realized I had two children who I loved and adored. I had a steady, full-time job in the entertainment industry, as well as my own PR clients under the table, and was finally making a good amount of money. I had my own apartment (a larger one now) filled with brand new furniture, a new car, and a bunch of good friends. My parents, brothers, and their families, were all healthy and alive. And, although not presently blessed with a "real life" relationship, I had access to an infinite number of fantasy cum sluts to keep me sexually satiated.

There was only one real problem in my life—I was unable to smile. I simply could not do it.

As though discovering fire, I said to myself: "You should probably go see a psychiatrist." I recalled, for the first time, that my mother had sent me to a shrink when I was a college freshman, but I'd rejected him, due to my distain of drugs. Perhaps now, lo these many years later, it was time to consult a medical doctor with a fresh perspective.

I glanced through my ever-trustworthy Yellow Pages, and chose a shrink completely at random. During my one and only session with this man, he asked, "So, why are you here?" I explained to him that I was unable to smile, and that it was almost impossible to ever feel joy or happiness (or much of anything,) with just two exceptions: Watching my children laugh and during an orgasm.

"Tell me about your family history," came the next question. I relayed the stories of my mother's "break with reality," my grandfather's history of insanity and incestuous interactions, my grandmother's time in and out of mental hospitals, and the depression that ran throughout my mother's family, including her older sister, my youngest brother and my nephew.

"How do you see yourself?" came next. I told him that since about the age of 15, I'd "heard" an endless, internal, reel-to-reel type, audio tape recording that played in the back of my brain. The tape says, "You're no good…No one loves you…Girls don't like you…You're a big loser…You're not good looking…You stupid pathetic loser…No one wants you," etc.

The shrink was furiously taking down notes, as I stared around the room. "How's your sex life?" he next asked. I told him that I loved sex, but rarely got enough "from actual women I didn't have to pay." I confessed that I hadn't made love to a normal woman in two years, had visited many a prostitute, and masturbated at whack shacks or nightly, at home alone, to magazines, so I could go to sleep in peace.

He paused for a moment, reviewing his notes. He then took off his glasses, leaned closer to me and said, "I am so impressed with you!"

"What do you mean?"

Doc: "You've had <u>a severe case of clinical, chemical depression</u> for at least 25 years! Your brain doesn't make enough serotonin. It couldn't possibly be any more obvious. The reason you love sex so much, and masturbate so often, is to trigger serotonin—an endorphin—into your brain. That's what makes you feel peaceful and calm. It's a drug you've become addicted to. Your family history of depression and mental illness clearly indicates you've inherited this disease. It's nothing you could possibly have prevented."

"But why are you impressed?"

"Look at all you've accomplished without any medication your entire life," my shrink continued. "You graduated from both high school and college, you have two children. You're successful in your profession. You were married and have had sexual relationships with a number of other women you were attracted to over the years.

You finally came to recognize that something was wrong, and you found me today."

Then came the big sentence, "*You're like a seriously ill diabetic who's never taken insulin!* You've become a high-functioning depressive, in spite of the overwhelming affliction you've endured since you were a teenager. That's quite remarkable. And that's why I'm impressed with you." The man wrote me a prescription for prozac, and wished me well.

Less than two weeks later, my life would change, forever.

I remember it distinctly: I awoke and sat up in my bed. The reel-to-reel audiotape recording that I'd been "listening" to every single day of my life since 1971 had STOPPED PLAYING. It was gone. The inner voice telling me what a fucking piece of shit loser I was HAD TURNED ITSELF OFF. I looked around, wondering "what was different?" The world had changed…but I couldn't figure out why. I stood, walked around my apartment, and happened to see my reflection in a mirror. I was smiling. For no apparent reason, I was smiling, naturally, for the first time I could remember since I was a young kid.

"Wow," I said aloud. "Thank you God."

My shrink had given me the name of a female therapist he highly recommended, suggesting I visit her at least once a week, to further explore the roots of my depression, my family history, my relationships with women, all things sex, and the whole idea behind the "Carrots Curse." The woman he introduced me to happened to be a very attractive blonde, slightly older than me, who would become, in a sense, the first in a series of "next generation" fantasy figures.

Dr. C. became the first woman I ever confided to in my life about my fascination with "all things penis." Sometimes trembling, sometimes crying, my cheeks often red with shame, I revealed to her details from the history of my sex life: The "Dustin incident" when I was 12, hearing my parents' screw in the room next to mine, the girls in high school and college I could barely talk to, the disaster that had been my marriage, and my extensive masturbation hobby – the whack shacks, call girls, massage parlors, etc. All of it.

Neither embarrassed, disgusted or shocked, Dr. C. was incredibly supportive. We explored my earliest days with my mother, and when we both realized that that bond had never been properly established, she said, "Well, it appears to me that you've been looking for your 'mommy' your entire adult life. In your case, you've come to equate a lost 'mommy' as an intense emptiness that expresses itself through your heightened sexuality. And coupled with your medical depression, your low levels of serotonin, and the warm, loving feeling you get when you ejaculate, it's no wonder your penis has been your special friend for such a long time."

My eyes were opened by Dr. C., and the months we spent together felt like re-learning to read English. I began to understand for the first time, ever, the psychology behind my hungers, and the rationale behind my frantic efforts to feed them. Unfortunately, less than one year into my therapy, Dr. C. and her husband moved to Hawaii. She suggested a colleague of hers as a replacement.

I was surprised to learn that my next therapist would also be a very attractive blonde, this time one 10 years younger than me. Most of our sessions were comprised of me regaling her with tales of my sexual misadventures, while she'd either furiously scribble down notes, or laugh hysterically. This woman LOVED my stories and treated me like I was a comedian – I began to feel as though I was there to "entertain" her. She dripped sexuality and always wore tight jeans. After each session with her, I'd have to race home to masturbate, her stunning appearance glued to my cerebral cortex.

After a year of seeing this woman, I realized I wasn't getting anything more from these sessions, so I sought a new therapist. Now using the Internet for my research, I selected yet another attractive blonde, this one based in Beverly Hills, and saw her for the next year. I would continue this pattern for years in succession, each time securing for myself women who were not only professional confidantes, but also gals who could provide me with fresh, fantasy sex partner material.

It took me a very long time to understand the genesis behind this behavior. I suppose it was to relive the fantasies I'd experienced in early adolescence, when I had secret crushes on my mother's attractive blonde friends, imagining the revelation of my sexual arrival to them. The relationships I was now having with an endless series of hot, blonde therapists had enabled this fantasy to come to life.

While in a session with yet another therapist (a woman who resembled actress Olivia Wilde,) I told her that during a recent, one night stand, I'd had some trouble getting a strong hard on. "So, then I started thinking about YOU," I confessed, "And I became so turned on, I was able to finish the job. I hope you don't mind." Calmly, she smiled. "Well, I'm very flattered. I'm glad I was able to 'help you out' in that situation. As long as they don't hurt anyone, sexual fantasizes are healthy and fine. Feel free to use 'fantasy me' whenever you want," she laughed.

My therapy sessions with "Olivia" turned me on so much, it was all I could do not to jerk off in my car while driving home. I was talking—in great detail—about every aspect of my sex life with yet another very attractive woman. But, I needed a pay-off. I needed a powerful cum explosion to conclude each experience and bring me back down to reality.

This phenomenon triggered my discovery of phone sex. In the back of a hardcore porno magazine, I found dozens of ads for cheap phone sex, and after a series of trials and errors, developed a "relationship" with Shannon, a self proclaimed "Mastur-Batrix" from Canada.

Shannon and I would enjoy a long-distance telephone fucking relationship for years. Her service was the least expensive, and most erotic, one I could find.

I became completely and totally addicted to jerking off for Shannon once a week, as soon as I arrived home from therapy. I would describe to her, in graphic detail, everything I'd just told one of my therapists. Shannon would then, in turn, tell me about her latest sexual exploits: the men she'd met and fucked that week in nightclubs; the men at her day job (she was a secretary at a warehouse) who made her so horny, she had to masturbate in the women's bathroom stall; the married couple next door who engaged her every Friday night in three-way orgy sessions, and the times she and her twin sister used to fuck each other with double-dong dildos, when they were teenagers.

Working in tandem, my "normal" therapy sessions, combined with my phone sex "fantasy therapy" sessions, completely helped focus, center, and relax me. And now, coupled with the wondrous effects of Prozac, both my sexual appetites and overall feelings of self-confidence had been elevated to new levels of satisfaction and elation.

I was still working for a prick boss – a Napoleonic little fucker who owned a very successful PR firm. But now Prozac-laden, I learned to laugh in his face whenever he yelled and screamed at me. Standing up to a bully always seems to work.

He and I were meeting with two executives from a local TV channel, seeking PR representation for their evening news cast. For what seemed like the one-millionth time, I had to listen to my short squat boss pontificate about his life story, his years on Wall Street, how he was "discovered" by some major Hollywood big shot, etc. I could have recounted his life story myself, as every time he told it, it was the same exact recitation, verbatim.

As I sat at this stifling meeting, in my suit and neck-constraining tie, I "heard a heavenly voice" emanating from the enormous chandelier hanging above us in the restaurant at the Beverly Hills Four Seasons Hotel. The "voice" called unto me: "START YOUR OWN BUSINESS."

"Huh?" The others at the table looked at me. "Oh, sorry," I said, "I just remembered something."

My boss continued his masturbatory self-aggrandizing, as my heart began to race. "Oh my," I said to myself, "I've just had a revelation from God." Pretending to take notes during the meeting, I had now been "spun off" into an entirely new direction. I turned my notepad to a clean page and began writing down all of the clients that I was representing, and what they were paying Mr. Cock Boss to be represented—by ME—through his agency. I realized immediately that if I simply represented these same clients FROM MY HOME, I could more than triple my income overnight.

The next day, I called each client I'd been representing. Every single one of them told me they would continue to utilize my services, regardless of where I was based. Said one: "I'd follow you to Batswana." I also lined up two business partners, one who provided start up cash, the other an office building in Hollywood, along with phone lines and a computer system. In less than 48 hours, I'd conceived, and was ready to launch, a brand-new company.

When my partners asked what I wanted to name this new entity, I said: "I grew up in Asbury Park, New Jersey. I'm gonna call it, 'Asbury Communications.'"

About to earn 100% (instead of 10%) of the same money that had been going to an asshole boss for close to a decade, I now stood at the cusp of earning well over seven times the annual salary that my father—a genius who invented technology preventing World War III—ever made in his best year.

CHAPTER NINETEEN

Ellen & Sharon

Launching my own business marked the most exciting era of my professional life. For 25 years, I'd been an employed "captive," having held a procession of demeaning jobs since the age of 15. Now, overnight, I was the owner of a corporation. I hired four fellow publicists and two assistants and also lined up an accountant, a lawyer, and a tax specialist. My company was housed inside a bungalow, just blocks south of the famed Hollywood Sign. My diverse range of clients produced digital, makeup, and special effects, animated TV shows, designed theme parks, edited TV commercials, wrote music for feature films and TV specials, created broadcast-designed graphics for CBS, ABC, and HBO, and were launching film festivals.

The instant success of my new company was overwhelming. I was being pulled in three hundred different directions at once, while concurrently learning how to use a computer for the first time. I had no idea what it meant to "go online," "Google something," or how to send an "E-mail." I had to keep pinching myself to ensure I wasn't dreaming.

Shortly after hanging my shingle, I was invited to a private party, an event marking the first social occasion I'd attended in my new prozac-laced body. I danced with a number of women, and realized I was smiling. Feeling elated after a few green apple martinis, the last woman I danced with that night I will call Ellen. About my age, Ellen had shoulder-length, dark brown hair, a very sensual face, and a slim figure. She told me she was a professional photographer who also had her own ceramics business. After we met, we stood outside on a fire escape, exchanging phone numbers.

Ellen and I began to date. I was in a "happy place" for the first time in my adult life and felt ready to commit to an exciting new relationship. Going out for dinners and movies, we'd return to her West Hollywood apartment, where we would tenderly make out. But we weren't having sex. At the end of our fourth date, during coffee, I asked her, "So, um, err, Ellen, do you happen to like sex, by any chance?" Deadly serious, she replied, "I LOVE sex—you have no idea how much. But, I'm almost 40. So, if I happen to get pregnant, ABORTION IS NOT AN OPTION!" She was adamant. "Well, I suppose I could use two condoms at the same time," I joked. "You don't have to over-react – but just know that if you get me pregnant, I'm gonna have your baby, and you're gonna have to deal with the consequences. Still wanna fuck me?"

For the next four months, Ellen and I barely got out of bed. Our first few attempts at sex were unbelievably awkward. I would accidentally pull her hair, or elbow her in the eye, while she would pull my weiner too hard, or inadvertently knee me in the groin. "We suck at this!" I said. "I know. This is gonna take some serious practice," Ellen answered. After perhaps our fifth go-round, synchronicity kicked-in, and our love making became extraordinarily powerful, lusty, and fun.

When we had sex in her apartment, Ellen liked to keep her bedroom windows open for the breeze – we both became overheated. Each time she would orgasm, she'd scream, "No! No! No! Oh my God, NO!" very loudly. Since this was only two years after OJ Simpson had decapitated his wife, I often imagined that Ellen's neighbors would call "911," police would come crashing through the door, and I'd be arrested for murder.

Ellen and I developed a powerful sexual chemistry. I'd be at work, and she'd call to say, "Come home RIGHT NOW. I need to suck your cock." Only Candy, years earlier, had been as horny for me. Ellen and I double-dated with friends, went dancing and had quiet, candlelit evenings together. She was a classy woman, confident, talented and successful in her own right.

Unfortunately, this relationship was to be short-lived:

** The nightly phone calls: Each night, I would call my ex-wife to ask how the children were doing. While I was on the phone, Ellen would shoot me a look to kill. "Why don't you just get back together with HER?" she'd shout in a clearly jealous rage. She'd then storm out of the apartment, slam the door, and go for a run, returning hours later.

** The inappropriate remark: In clothes, Ellen had a fine figure. Naked, her breasts sagged against her body like flap jacks. One night after sex, I happened to lift them up. "Ever think about having a boob job?" I innocently asked. Ellen became furious. "I would NEVER butcher my body like that!" she screamed. "If you don't like my tits, you don't have to fuck me anymore!"

The next night after work, Ellen greeted me at her door: "I read your hidden screenplay, *'Carrots.'* I think we're done. We just don't have a future. We need to go our separate ways. I thought maybe I was gonna marry you, but I can see you're not the guy I was looking for."

I was hurt, but not terribly surprised. I liked Ellen a lot and had solid feelings for her. I also knew I'd never marry her, because her rage could surge at the drop of a hat. In silence, I packed the few things of mine I kept at her place and stood at the door. "Wait a minute," she said. Ellen got on her knees, unzipped my pants, and sucked me off. "I wanted to give you something to remember me by."

Ellen got married shortly thereafter. I never saw her again.

My friend Ray, a noted Hollywood journalist and author, called. "Hey Dan," he said, "I've got a girl for you." Both recently divorced men with kids, Ray and I had bonded a few years previous, discussing the hazards of dating in Hollywood. My workload was mind-boggling, but, ever on the prowl for a potential girlfriend, I said, "OK, I've got three minutes. Tell me about her."

Sharon (not her real name) was a publicist for a popular children's TV series. Ray informed me she had a "killer body, nice, red hair, and a great, outgoing personality." For our first date, I met Sharon at my favorite Mexican food restaurant in Beverly Hills. She was tall and striking, had a great smile, and intrigued me immediately. We had a quiet dinner and drinks, talking mostly about the PR business in Hollywood.

After dinner, we walked a few blocks, and wound up at a coffee and pastry shop for desert. I suddenly became overwhelmed with a desire to kiss her and did so. She responded. We kissed for a short while. "Where did that come from?" she asked. "I have no idea. I'm sorry. It was just something I <u>had</u> to do. I couldn't help it," I whispered.

("Pre-Prozac" me would never have made such a move.)

I walked Sharon back to her car, parked a few blocks away. While stopped at a crosswalk, I began shaking—almost violently – from head to toe. "What's going on?" Sharon asked. Me: "I have absolutely no idea…This has never happened to me before in my life. I think we might be onto something here."

For the next full year, Sharon and I had the most powerful, passionate, and troubled relationship I've ever had with any woman. I came to believe Sharon was the love of my life, and the woman destined to become my second wife. Unfortunately, the circumstances of our lives never fully gelled, and, quite frankly, we just couldn't get our shit together.

The first few weeks Sharon and I dated were magical. We had so much fun cooking dinner for each other, going to the movies, drinking, partying with friends, and or just watching TV. On our fourth date, I wrote her a song (I'd bought myself a guitar) and sang it for her at her apartment:

"When I look into your eyes…Just imagine my surprise.

I have waited oh, so long…For someone to inspire a song.

Chorus: It's in your eyes. In your eyes. You're my girl. It's in your eyes"

Flattered, Sharon initiated sex for the first time. After that night, we made love fairly often, and the sex was fun, but she seemed distant and removed from the action. Eventually, she confessed that she could only orgasm if she got stoned first—I didn't mind.

"I need your help," Sharon called one Saturday afternoon. "I'm painting my bedroom, and can't do it alone." We removed the furniture from her bedroom and began painting the walls with extended roller brushes. Alanis Morrisette's CD "Jagged Little Pill" had been recently released, and Sharon was blasting it. As we painted, we accidentally splashed the blood red paint all over both the drop cloth and ourselves. We laughed so hard, we fell to the floor, and made love, rolling around in splotches of that dark liquid.

This was another of the most romantic moments of my life.

My mother came to LA for Thanksgiving. Sharon spent hours in the kitchen, while concurrently holding a very long conversation with my mom. My kids and I were playing board games on the living room floor, not far away. "Danny, come here a minute, I want to talk with you," my mother said. The two of us left the apartment and took a short walk outside. "This is THE girl for you!" my mother shrilled into my face. "She's beautiful, smart, and she loves you. So, I just want to say…" My mother got about two inches from my face, and pointed her finger up – and almost into – my nose: "IF YOU FUCK THIS ONE UP, I"LL FUCKING KILL YOU!"

The woman had a way with words.

Sharon presented the turkey feast, then began to cry. She dashed into my bedroom and shut the door. Hours later, she emerged, after my kids and mom were gone. She told me that when she was seven, her parents had had a huge fight. Thanksgiving was the same day her father left her family behind, traumatizing her for life.

One night, Sharon invited my kids and I to her place for dinner. As a child, my son was an incredibly fussy eater, and would only eat hamburgers, ravioli, or submarine sandwiches. Sharon had prepared some kind of lamb – something he would not have eaten in two hundred years. "Daddy, what is this?" Jordan asked, with an expression of utter disgust. "It's lamb," Sharon snorted. "Eat it…it's good for you." My son: "No, I don't like this, Daddy, it smells funny." Then, looking up at her heartbroken face, he said, "Sharon, do you have any cheeseburgers?"

Holding a glass of wine, Sharon left the table, went into her bedroom, and quietly closed the door. The tug of war I would consistently experience between Sharon and my son would endure throughout the course of our relationship. She never liked him, was unable to embrace him, and found him to be little more than a complete nuisance.

Jordan became our Berlin Wall.

Sharon's parents invited us to spend Christmas weekend at their house near San Diego. After Xmas dinner, her stepfather took me aside. "She'd probably kill me if she knew I was saying this to you," he said, "But we've never seen Sharon so in love before. So, I just wanted to say, welcome to the family, Dan." His words meant a lot.

My business was booming, and I decided to throw a New Year's Eve party for my clients and friends. Sharon embraced the idea (at first,) and, together, we bought a ton of liquor and food for the big shindig. We were expecting about 30 people. Just moments before the party was to begin, however, Sharon had another panic attack.

"I don't want to do this!" she announced. "Let's get out of here and go see a movie. Please?" Me: "What are you talking about?" I'd just spend hundreds of dollars for this event and had a whole bunch of important clients about to walk through my door. I couldn't have been any more confused.

The guests arrived, and everyone had a great time except Sharon, who spent the entire evening alone, on my balcony, smoking cigarettes. "What's wrong with your girlfriend?" a number of my guests asked. "She's got a migraine, that's all. She'll be fine," I meekly responded.

My father came to the La Jolla, CA, area, in search of a new home in which to retire. My kids, Sharon, and I met him for dinner at a restaurant near Sharon's parents' house in San Diego. The waitress delivered my son's hamburger. "Daddy, it's burnt," he said, "I can't eat this." Sharon (to my son): "You wanted a well-done hamburger. So now you just need to eat it. Don't complain about it." My son gave her a "Huh?" expression. "See—it's black," Jordan said in self-defense, lifting the top of the bun. "That's OK, we'll get a new one," I said, motioning for the waitress. Steam began seeping out of Sharon's ears. She leaned into me. "You're spoiling him," she whispered. "You should just make him eat that one." "Why?" I replied. "I can afford a new one. Why should my son eat something he doesn't want?" The look of anger in Sharon's eyes was remarkable, but, to her credit, she dropped the argument when she noticed my father's concern.

After the meal, goodbyes were said, and Sharon, my children, and I got into her car for the (long) ride back to my place. Hyper-ventilating the entire time, she blasted the radio LOUD, and drove at least 80 miles an hour, with the windows wide open. My poor children in the backseat were almost blown out of the car. "Daddy, can Sharon close the windows?" my seven year old daughter asked. I had to—gently but firmly – insist that she do so.

I'd arranged a surprise Valentine's Day getaway for Sharon at a beautiful, Santa Monica hotel suite. She'd just come back to LA from a New York business trip – I picked her up from LAX, took her to the suite, and let her nap. While she slept, I took a shower, and much to my surprise, a naked Sharon walked in. This was the only time I've ever had "shower sex."

The next morning, as we were about to leave the hotel to walk along the beach, the topic of my son's "burnt hamburger" unexpectedly came me up in conversation. In the flash of seconds, Sharon became "Mr. Hyde." She flew into a rage.

"My father would have MADE ME eat that fucking hamburger!" she screamed. "You are spoiling that boy rotten. He needs to learn about discipline. YOU need to keep that little brat in line!" I was expecting Sharon's head to start spinning like Linda Blair's from "The Exorcist."

"What difference does it make? Why on earth should my son, who I love, eat something he doesn't want to eat?" I argued back. For at least half an hour, Sharon and I had the worst fight of our relationship. All I was able to glean from it, when it ended, was that Sharon's biological father, a former military officer, had been a prick tyrant to his three daughters. They truly feared him during most of their early childhoods.

"I'm outta here," Sharon said. In silence, I drove her to her car. She got out, tossed her suitcase in there, and approached me. "I love you," she said, "But you and I—together—it doesn't work. We're done. I can't see you anymore." We kissed, passionately, and then Sharon drove off. "Happy Valentines Day?" I shouted after her.

As had now become routine, Sharon called a few days later to apologize and to say she missed me. I realized that, since we'd met, we tended to have at least one major battle every four-six weeks almost like clockwork. Sharon revealed that she was manic depressive and had been on anti-depressant medication since the age of 15. I admitted my depression to her as well, and told her about my 25 years of mental illness and how prozac had changed my life. During this same conversation, we also discussed for the first-time previous relationships and the history of our sex lives. Sharon went to her closet and took out a notebook. Inside, she had a section chronicling the names, dates and locations and "notes" about every man she'd ever had sex with.

"Congratulations," she told me, "You're number 50," adding my name to her list.

Sharon was only the 10th woman I'd ever slept with. The fact that she'd had so many more lovers than I'd had made me feel kinda nauseous.

For her birthday, Sharon and I spent close to a week in Santa Barbara, staying at the same romantic hotel I'd stayed at 13 years earlier with Kim during our honeymoon. We rented a large, private suite, separated from the rest of the hotel, where we drank, smoked pot, and had a tremendous amount of sex. One night we got stoned and went to "Brophy's" Seafood Restaurant on the pier for dinner. Before our table was ready, we sat at the bar having drinks. I looked into Sharon's eyes, and, overwhelmed by emotion, began to cry. "God, I love you so fucking much," I said. "I really love you too," she replied. I came THISCLOSE to asking Sharon to marry me at that very second. But just then, our waitress called our names, and led us to our dinner table.

Sharon was visiting my apartment one Sunday afternoon – my kids were there as well. Lying on my couch, me at the other end, she said, "Danny…rub my feet." As I massaged her toes, my son, holding his favorite book, came up to me: "Daddy, can you please read me a story?" Never more conflicted in my life, I looked at Sharon's face, which basically screamed, "DON'T YOU EVEN THINK ABOUT LEAVING ME RIGHT NOW FOR HIM!" and my son's angelic little face, which said, "Daddy, I'm lonely for you. Please spend some time with me too." I glanced at Sharon and to Jordan, again at Sharon, again to Jordan. Finally making an executive decision, I said, "Sharon, I'm gonna read him a story. Give me 15 minutes. I'll be right back, and then 'll massage your whole body, I promise." As Jordan and I walked toward his bedroom, we heard the front door of my apartment SLAM closed. Moments later, Sharon's car burned rubber as it screeched away from my building. "I think Sharon's angry again at you again," my son said. "Yeah, I think you're right," I replied.

For my birthday, Kim kept the kids that weekend so I could solely focus on Sharon. I stayed at her apartment. After morning sex, we walked a few blocks to a nearby cafe. During my birthday brunch, Sharon started crying. "What's wrong?" I asked, sure I'd said or done something to upset her. "I'm very sad," she said, "Because, even though I really do love you, and I always will, I know, in my heart, that I'm never, ever going to marry you." This one was a heart-stopper, because I was THISCLOSE, once again, to asking Sharon to marry me. I suppose, instinctively, she knew.

"Your kids are your world, and I know how much you love them," she said, "But I really don't want to be their step-mommy. Your daughter is a love-bug, but I don't have the patience for your son. I want children of my own. If you didn't have kids, I'd marry you tomorrow. I know you're thinking about asking me, so PLEASE DON'T. It would break both of our hearts."

Sharon and I stared at each other for a while, tears rolling down both our cheeks. We finished the brunch in silence. Happy Birthday to me.

I officially declared the end of our relationship the night of Halloween. Sharon called me about 2 in the morning, drunk off her ass – she'd lost her house keys. "Danny," she slurred, "I'm really drunk…I can't get into my house…come save me." I hopped into my car in my PJs, and drove like a madman to her apartment. There, I found Sharon, fully clothed in a witch's costume, sprawled out on the front lawn of her building, sprinklers dousing her with water. She was a complete and total disaster.

"Danny! My Danny!" she screamed like a drunken sailor. "I knew you'd rescue me!" I'd never seen Sharon so incredibly fucked up—this was a different person. I put her arm around my neck, and slowly waltzed her up the steep flight of stairs that led to her apartment. I had my own set of her keys, so I unlocked her door, and walked her into her bedroom. "You're a mess," I said, truly annoyed. I dried her off, helped her into her PJs, and tucked her in.

"I'm horny!" she drunk-yelled as I was leaving the room. "Fuck me Danny! I miss you!" I stood at her bedroom door and froze. The woman I truly loved wanted sex. But, this same woman was impossible to please, would never marry me, and, most importantly, would never, ever, open her heart to my son.

"Sorry, kiddo, I'm out…I'm done," I said, making a momentous decision on the spot. "I'm leaving your keys on your coffee table. I love you, but I can't date a Yo-Yo anymore. Starting right now, we're just friends. I'll call you tomorrow."

Shortly thereafter, Sharon attended a weekend-long seminar called "The Forum," after which she quit her job, and spent a month in Greece. Upon her return to the U.S., she bought four cats, and moved to San Francisco, where she decided to study interior design. She later married a millionaire software computer genius and moved back to Los Angeles.

In touch just twice (lunches) since we split in 1997, Sharon and I represent a classic line from the comedy film *Galaxy Quest*, about people who "Never Give in, Never Give Up, and Never Surrender."

PHOTOS

Photos: 1956–2022

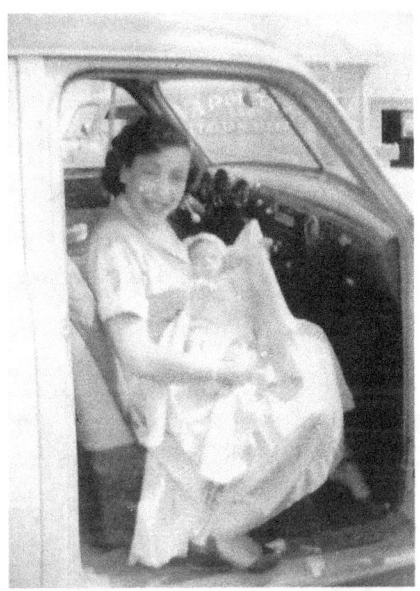

My Mommy, Joan the Carrot, Neptune, NJ, 1956

With Donna, Next Door Neighbor, Neptune, NJ, 1959

School Girls - Top Row Left to Right Wendy, 3rd Grade, Joanne, 6th Grade, Jamie, 7th Grade, Bottom Row Left to Right Janet, 8th Grade, Bonnie, 8th Grade, Cheryl from High School - Photos are 1965-1974

Long Red, Rutgers University, New Brunswick, NJ, 1974

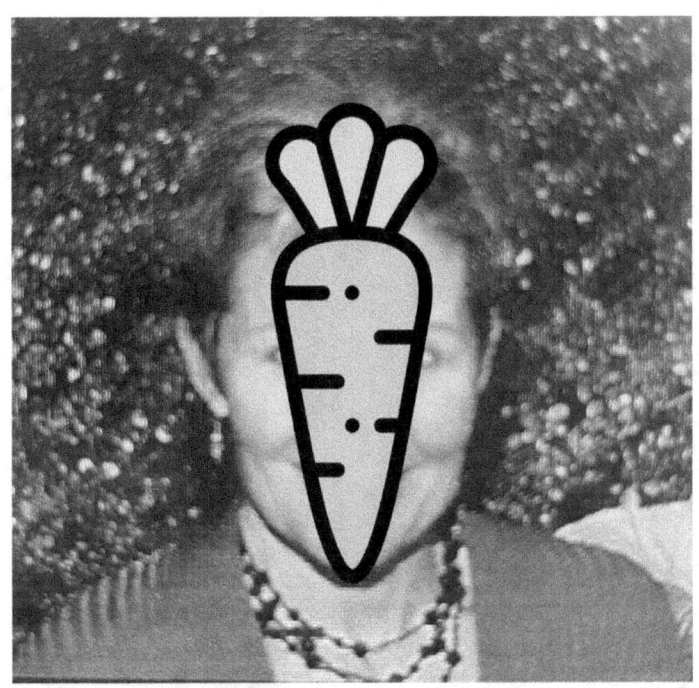
Morgan, Boston University, 1975

Randi, Deal, New Jersey, 1977

With Kim 1 in Boston, MA, 1978

Kim 1 in Boston, MA, 1978

Candy, Belmar, NJ, 1979

With She Who Deserves No Name, Asbury Park, NJ, Boat Show, 1979

Danskin Lori, Long Branch, NJ, 1979

With Emma, New York City, 1980

With Two Models Promoting Columbia Pictures Movie *The Hollywood Knights*, New York City, Summer, 1980

> 11/80
>
> 7:30
>
> Dear Danny,
>   I'm so sorry about this whole thing, I can't believe this has happened. One of my best friends was involved in a car accident and her family is out of town. I have to go to the hospital to be with her.
>   I'm so sorry to ruin your evening, please call and let's try it again.
>   Thanx for understanding
>   Carole

Author's "First Date" in Los Angeles, Nov. 1980

Patrice, Venice Beach, CA, 1981

With German Roommates Insa (right) and Irena, Venice Beach, CA, 1981

Erin from VHD, West Hollywood, CA, 1981

With Beverly The Whore, Los Angeles, CA 1981

Early Date with Kim, Motion Picture Academy Theater,
Beverly Hills, CA, 1982

One Night Stand Callie (with Unknown Baby,) Santa Monica, CA, 1983

Wedding to Kim, Santa Barbara, CA, 1984

Honeymoon with Kim, Santa Barbara, CA, 1984

With Playboy Playmate Lynda Weismeier, West Hollywood, CA, 1984

Actress Ava Cadell, My Next Door Neighbor, West Hollywood, CA, 1984

With Playboy Playmate Kym Malin, West Hollywood, CA, 1985

Out on the Town with Kim, Hollywood, 1985

With Kim at Brother Mike's College Graduation, Long Beach, CA, 1986

With Actress Caryn Richman on-set of *The New Gidget*
TV Show, Burbank, CA, 1986

With Candy, Manhattan Beach, CA, 1993

Amy, Studio City, CA, 1994

With Ellen, Downtown Los Angeles, CA, 1996

With Sharon, Santa Barbara, CA, 1997

With Dina, Center, and Friends, Xmas Party, Los Feliz, CA, 1997

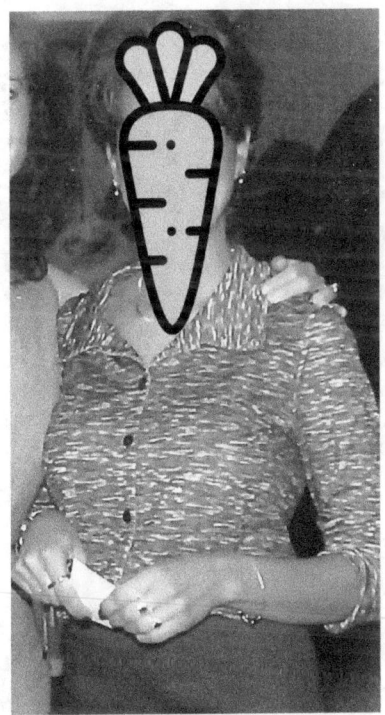

Rosie, Valencia, CA, 1999

With Sarah, Studio City, CA, New Year's Eve, 1998/1999

With Jeri, Santa Monica, CA, 2002

With Jennifer The Trainer, Santa Monica, CA, 2001

With Ruthie, Catalina Island, NY Eve, 2000/2001

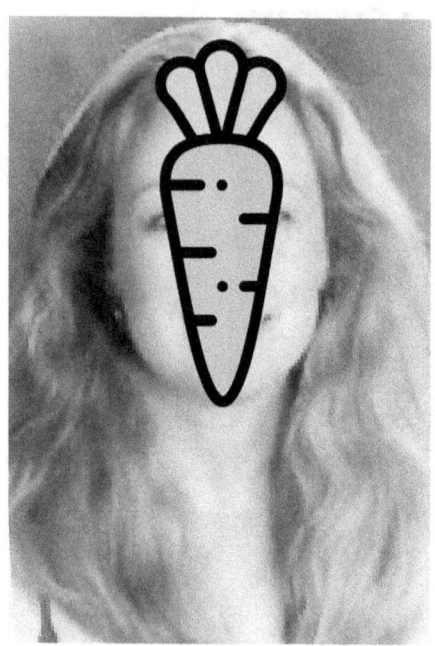

Zappy, Santa Monica, CA, 2002

With The Chubster, My 50th Birthday, West LA, 2006

With The Ten, Hollywood, CA, Xmas Party, 2004

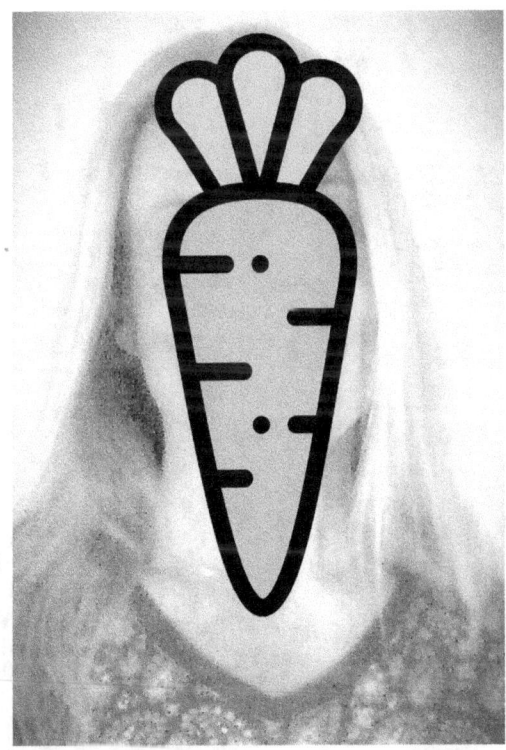

With Frenchy, Beverly Hills, CA, 2004

With Manny, Hollywood, CA, Party, 2005

With Bella, Santa Barbara, CA, NY Eve, 2002/2003

With Marti, Santa Monica, CA, NY Eve, 2003/2004

The Bikini Model, Hollywood, CA, 2007

With Bethany, Hollywood, CA, 2008

With The Soap Star, Hollywood, CA, Party, 2009

CARROTS • 209

J the Call Girl, Van Nuys, CA, 2009

Sher the Call Girl, Beverly Hills, CA, 2010

Kamila the Call Girl, Beverly Hills, CA, 2011

With Supermodel Amber Smith, Glamourcon,
LAX Hilton, Los Angeles, CA, 2009

Z the Dominatrix, Beverly Hills, CA, 2012

With Z the Dominatrix, Beverly Hills, CA, 2012

With Willow, Studio City, CA, 2013

With A, Beverly Hills, CA, 2016

With Kayla, Hollywood, CA, 2017

With Penny, West Hollywood, CA, 2019

Reunion with Danskin Lori, Vics Pizza, Bradley Beach, NJ, 2021

With Beloved Daughter Anjuli, Factors Deli, Beverly Hills, CA, 2022

CHAPTER TWENTY

Attack of the Nymphos

After the demise of my love affair with Sharon, I was desperate to just date an attractive woman who was "normal." I'd had enough drama for a while. However, during the course of the following couple of years, I experienced five women in a row who I can only describe now as sex-starved "nymphos." They were Remy, Andrea, Dina, Rosie and Drea.

Remy was the head of marketing for one of my ex-boss's clients. We'd flirted with each other during PR meetings and lunches, until one day, when I walked her to her car, she said, "So when are you going to ask me out? You know we can have a lot of fun together." Her intent was obvious, so we arranged a date for the following week. (This happened just before I'd left my job to launch my own PR company.)

The MORNING of our date, Remy walked into a solid glass wall at her office and broke her nose! I was convinced she was a victim of the "Carrots Curse." Regardless, I took her out for dinner (trying to ignore the looks of my fellow diners at the restaurant staring at her bandaged nose.) We went back to her place and had mind-blowing sex.

Remy LOVED sex, perhaps even more than me. She taught me a few tricks and made it clear that this was going to be a sex-driven relationship, only. Foolishly, one morning I asked her if she'd like to spend the day with me and my kids, as my birthday was fast approaching. She leaped out of bed, put on her clothes, and said, "Kids? What are you talking about? No, I can't meet your kids!" With that, she took off and fled out of my apartment.

(About a year later, I saw Remy one last time at my company's offices in Hollywood. I think we had dinner but can't remember. She remained a lot of fun, and I always enjoyed being with her. Remy was a "Carrot" who simply did not want to be plucked from the ground and harvested.)

During the first year I had my own agency, I'd developed a reputation within Hollywood as "THE PR GUY" to be hired by Visual Effects companies. At one time, I was probably repping a dozen of the leading VFX houses in show business, each competing with the other, and none caring, because these company owners knew I had a knack for getting their projects written about in important newspapers, websites and trade magazines.

Among my clients at this time was the visual effects company behind the hit TV shows *Hercules* and *Xena: Warrior Princess*. One day, I was early to a meeting with the owners of this company, and I met Andrea, the receptionist, while I was waiting.

Andrea was shamelessly flirting with me as I sat. Seated behind her reception desk, I noticed that she had a cute face, long red hair and big boobies. After the meeting, I was heading out the door. Andrea said, "When can I see you again?" accompanied by a big smile. I headed back to her desk, leaned over and said, "Let's have dinner sometime. What's your number?" It happened in a flash – quick and easy.

I'd arranged to meet Andrea a few nights later at a restaurant in Studio City. I was early, got a table, and was already working on my first green apple martini, when she arrived. I'd never seen her STANDING before, and when she walked into the room, I noticed that the TOP and the BOTTOM HALVES of this girl's body were two completely different things. It appeared as though God himself – drunk as a fuck during her physical construction—had "cut and pasted" two different people together.

Andrea's ASS was the size of a CAR TIRE. No exaggeration. It simply was NOT meant to be attached to her upper half, which was not only "normal," but rather attractive.

Andrea sat across from me at the table. We ordered drinks and dinner, and she told me her life story, none of which I remember. I was so obsessed and consumed with thoughts of her ENORMOUS BUTT, I was distracted and confused. I probably had at least three martinis, and, quite possibly, four.

Now clearly drunk, all I wanted to do was wind up this date as politely as I could, since she worked for one of my biggest clients. I didn't want to do anything to insult or humiliate her. I just needed to go home, masturbate, and go to sleep.

Andrea: "Don't you live nearby here?" she asked. "Yeah, actually, like half a mile straight up Laurel Canyon," I replied, pointing out the window. "So, you gonna invite me back to your place, or what?" Andrea asked. I was taken aback. "My place? Why would you want to go there?" I said. Andrea: "I think you're really sexy, and I had a fantasy. I want you to take me back to your place. Then, I'm gonna take off your clothes, and blindfold you, and have you lay down on your bed. I'm going to pleasure you, over and over again. All you need to do is relax.

How's that sound?"

BIG ASS, BIG SCHMASS, WHO CARES?? Andrea and I drove our two cars out of the restaurant parking lot and into my driveway, arriving minutes later. My cock was about to leap out of my pants. I'd never had a woman tell me that all she wanted to do was "pleasure me, over and over again," without any effort on my part. This sounded like a gift. The fact that Andrea's ass was bigger than South Dakota no longer concerned me.

We arrived at my place. "Got any neckties?" she asked. I gave her an assortment. She tied one around my eyes, pushed me back onto my bed, and said, "Now stay there and be quiet. Don't say a word." Doing as instructed, I was on my bed, as Andrea removed all of my clothes in a flash. I then heard her clothes coming off, quickly. The next thing I knew, Andrea was furiously sucking my cock like a wildebeest. I'd never been blindfolded before, nor had any woman ever suggested that to me. Cumming that way, especially drunk off my ass, was incredibly powerful. I loved it.

Andrea removed my blindfold. "How was that?" she asked. "Amazing," I said, "That felt absolutely incredible." I saw Andrea's large, voluptuous tits and was mesmerized by her long red hair. I distinctly recall telling myself "DO NOT LOOK AT THE ASS… WHATEVER YOU DO, DO NOT LOOK AT THAT ASS!"

After I came, Andrea lay beside me for a few minutes. "Mind if I masturbate?" she asked. "No, of course, not…show me how you do it." Andrea played with herself for a while, really working those fingers in and out of herself, and rubbing her clit frantically with the other hand. She came loud and hard and was staring deep into my eyes as she climaxed. "God, I needed that," she said.

Watching this scene turned me on so much, I was rock hard, once again, moments later. "Andrea, I've got a present for you," I said (recalling my legendary screw up with Lynda.) She smiled. "Fuck my tits." She lay on her back, and I positioned myself over her. She "smushed" her giant tits together, and I fucked them fast and with purpose. "Oh baby, you are turning me on so much," she said, "I'm watching your big cock fucking these big, huge titties." It didn't take long until I came a second time.

Now exhausted, I lay again on my back, panting. "Wow, you're a lot of fun," I said. Andrea laughed. We stayed in my bed for perhaps another hour, talking about our sex lives, past lovers, masturbation, and every other sex subject under the sun. It was fun, it was carefree and it was hot.

An hour passed. My cock was hard AGAIN. "I have got to have that beautiful cock inside of me this time," Andrea said. She got on her hands and knees, and said, "Fuck me doggie style, Danny boy. Shove that big beautiful hard cock into me now." When I saw the full scope and actual girth of Andrea's extraordinarily large ass, I realized I was gonna have a problem. My cock was still hard and throbbing, but, as I tried to maneuver it to reach inside her vagina, I realized that there was simply no way that that was going to happen.

My cock would have had to be the length of a stepladder to reach past the supernatural depth of Andrea's ass checks. Although I am, without question, well-endowed, I never even came close to entering her reproductive system.

"Urh, ahh, uhm, I can't get in there, sorry, kid," I said to her. She turned back around. "That's OK,,,alotta guys can't. I thought maybe you'd be the exception." Clearly in touch with her own "ass-fliction," I admired Andrea even more at that moment.

"How about I'll just jerk you off all over my face?" Andrea asked. "Sure, why not, enjoy yourself," I said, laying back down. She did all the work, once again, and made me shoot a third load all over her cheeks. She gave me a huge smile. "Thanks," she said, "That was hot."

I watched Andrea drive home that night, in the rain, and thought, "What the FUCK was that all about?" Clearly she was sex-crazed but was also completely uninhibited about her sexual desires. Although her ass had presented itself as a minor obstacle, I still planned to have a million more "Andrea Sessions" in the weeks and months ahead.

That next Monday at work, I got a phone call from the wife of one of the owners of the visual effects company for which Andrea worked. "I understand you and Andrea had a date the other night," she said. "That's fine, dear, but I don't think you should see her anymore. She's like a daughter to us, and she's so much younger than you are…we don't think it would be a good idea for you to see her again. I hope you understand?" Not wanting to do anything to lose a client that was paying me $3,000 a month at the time, I said, "Oh, of course, no problem! She and I had a lot of fun talking at dinner, but, you're right, she's much too young for me! We're just friends!" I never saw Andrea again. She actually got fired from that job, about two months later. I never heard why – but I hope it wasn't because of me.

My new business partner, Steve, had asked me to hire his brother-in-law, Mike (I called him Mikey) to work for me in starting up my new company. Mikey had long been an English teacher for years in Beverly Hills, but wanted to switch gears, and become involved in the entertainment industry. He and I became immediate and very close friends, and I taught him how to work as a publicist. I hired him full-time and paid him an excellent salary with full medical benefits. He became my right-hand man, and together, when we weren't scoring a ton of new business, we'd be rolling around on the floor, making very crude jokes about people and clients we knew and simply laughing hysterically for hours.

A few weeks after I'd ended things with Sharon, Mikey realized I was pretty bummed. "Dude, you want to meet a really hot brunette?" he asked. "Let me think…uhm, yes?" I replied sarcastically. He told me that a divorced, very attractive woman named Dina was on his wife's bowling team. I spoke with Mikey's wife, Kim, phone, and she told me that Dina was "a lot of fun, very outgoing, and seems to be on the prowl for a guy."

A few nights later, I called Dina, to set up a date. We spoke for at least an hour or more, covering all the usual stuff—being divorced, raising kids alone, working full time, dating, dating idiots, latest movies, favorite TV shows, etc., etc., etc. At the end, we'd arranged a restaurant date for the end of that same week.

About two hours later, as I was about to go to bed, my phone rang. "Danny?" a female voice said. "It's Dina." "What's wrong?" I asked. "Nothing…I don't know how to say this to you, but your voice was so incredibly sexy on the phone earlier, that I've been masturbating, just thinking about you, since we hung up. Will you talk with me now, so I can cum for you on the phone?"

This was simply unheard of in my life. A woman who was SO HORNY FOR ME, a guy she'd never even MET, that she was masturbating for hours JUST THINKING ABOUT MY VOICE? Clearly, I was in new waters here.

Having had some occasional experience with the phone sex phenomenon, I had a basic sense of what to say. I listened as Dina fucked her favorite dildo and made herself cum for me, I think twice. I was so charged up by the end of the call, I told her I needed "some relief also."

She said, "Oh baby, jerk off your big hard cock, just for me." It didn't take long for me to finish up.

Dina and I dated for about four months. We had a usual routine. We'd go out for dinner, where she would talk for HOURS ON END about the various TAX FORMS that she was using during her workday. She was an accountant. During our dates, for whatever reason, all she would ever talk about was her INCREDIBLY BORING JOB. She'd bitch and moan to me that her boss was using "the wrong forms" for the tax returns for one of her clients. I had no idea what she was talking about, nor ANY interest, whatsoever. I'd be glancing around the room of the various restaurants in which we'd be eating, observing other couples having "normal" conversations, in which the men, clearly, weren't planning their own suicides.

But as soon as we'd get back to my apartment, clothes would come flying off, and world class fucking and sucking would ensue. Hour after hour after hour, Dina was a sex champion, a thoroughbred fuck animal that simply could NOT EVER get enough. To this day, I've never seen another woman cum so many times, over and over again. She deserved many a standing ovation.

Dina and I did the usual movies, dinners, parties, hanging with friends, stuff, etc. One night, while I was working late at my office, she called. "What are you doing?" she asked. "Working…I'll be here for hours, I've got a new business proposal I have to finish by tomorrow morning," I said. "I need your cock in my mouth," Dina purred. "I've been thinking about you all day, and I simply HAVE to suck your cock, or else I'll never be able to get to sleep. Can I come by your office right now, please? I won't stay long." Me: "Oh, alright, if you must." What a cocky bastard, eh?

Dina drove about 50 minutes out of her way to come to my office around 10:30 at night. I opened my office door and motioned for her not to say a word. I sat on my couch and pulled down my pants. Dina, on her knees, sucked me off like a vacuum cleaner. I came, she smiled. "Thank you," she whispered, as I all but kicked her out my office door immediately afterwards.

After about the fourth month of dating Dina, and even though sex with her was beyond incredible, she was BORING ME TO TEARS. I simply could no longer LISTEN to her talking. She would repeat the same endless work stories about tax forms, ad infinitum. It got to the point when I realized I'd have way more fun fucking a bagel than having to listen to her talk for even just one more minute.

On the last date we had together, Dina and I had dinner and ended up, once again, back at my apartment. We fucked in my overstuffed chair, on the kitchen floor, and then, for a third time, on my coffee table. Cum, rubbers and panties were all over my apartment. She was smiling, sweaty and breathless. I finally decided I'd have enough.

"Dina," I said, after I'd just finished fucking her THREE TIMES IN A ROW, "I don't think this relationship is working out for me. We don't have any kind of future together. You're a really great chick, and I like you very much, but I need to keep looking for someone else. I'd rather not date you anymore. I'm really sorry."

Stunned, crushed, and completely heart-broken, Dina stopped getting dressed, standing topless before me, and said, "Oh God, please NO! I need you! I need your cock! It's OK if we don't date anymore, that's fine. But can I please just keep coming over here and fucking you? Please? I can't live without our sex." She actually had tears in her eyes.

Once again, being the most ridiculous idiot on the planet Earth, I said, "Dina, I'm not trying to hurt your feelings, but we're done. We're over. I don't want to see you anymore. Sorry. Goodbye." I walked her out of my apartment, all but slamming the door closed behind her.

Update: Ten years later, while cleaning out a closet, I happened to find Dina's phone number. I called her, we had dinner together, and ended up making out in my car for about an hour. I told her I wanted to fuck her again.

She said, "Not tonight…but your offer sounds pretty good. Let me think about." However, a few days later, she changed her mind. "You really hurt me last time," she explained.

In 1997, my ex-wife and kids moved from incredibly-far-away Lancaster, CA, to a city much closer to LA, called Valencia. This made my "picking up the kids" drives so much easier, allowing me many more hours of "Daddy time" with them on weekends. However, quite often, especially during the summer months, I would also stay at Kim's apartment, in my son's room or on the couch, so my kids and I could lounge around in the complex's swimming pool.

During one sunny summer afternoon at Kim's pool, she and I were sitting on chaise lounge chairs talking, as our kids were splashing about in the pool. A petite, well-built woman, Rosie, came by to watch her kid in the pool as well, and ended up sitting next to us. "Danny, this is my friend and neighbor, Rosie," Kim said. We shook hands. At this point, Kim and I had already been divorced close to seven years, and I had no qualms about blatantly flirting with another woman in her presence.

"Rosie, you're pretty hot…you single?" I asked, as the two women both laughed. Rosie: "Yeah, actually, I am. I'm divorced…

so what are YOU gonna do about it?" She and Kim laughed again. Kim: "You two should date each other. Rosie loves sex as much as you do, Dan." More laughter. Rosie handed me her phone number literally over Kim's body, as Kim was laying in her chaise lounge chair. (Kinda weird…)

I called Rosie a few nights later, to make a date. "What kind of food do you like?" I asked her, trying to determine the best plan for a restaurant. Rosie: "Listen, we don't have to go out to eat, see a movie, have an actual 'date,' or anything. I'm just really horny and I haven't been laid in a while. You wanna fuck me?" Taken aback, I said, "Oh, ahm, sure. You have a killer body. I'd love to fuck you!" Rosie: "OK, but I need you to fulfill a fantasy. I want you to come to my place tomorrow night at 10 PM – I'll have my front door open and unlocked. Walk up the stairs to my bedroom, quietly, so you don't wake my son. I'll be ready for you in my bed, but I don't want you to talk or say a word to me. Just come in, close my bedroom door, spread my legs, and fuck me, hard. After you cum, put $100 cash on my nightstand, because I'm a dirty, filthy whore. Then I want you to leave. Can you deal with all that?"

My cock was so hard as I was talking with Rosie on the phone that night, I thought it would break my zipper and burst through my jeans.

That Friday night went almost exactly as Rosie had outlined it on the phone. When I walked into her bedroom, I found her naked, with a gag in her mouth, and her hands handcuffed to her bedpost. Our first fuck session was so powerful, that, after I came, she insisted I stay. We fucked another two times that first night in various positions. Rosie came so loud each time, I feared that her young, little son, was going to walk in and catch mommy and some "perv guy" in the act.

After our sex was done, Rosie, exhausted, said, "OK, I need you to get the fuck outta here. I'm done being your whore. Where's my money?" I left five, twenty-dollar bills on her nightstand and drove home in silence. It was a hot, yet disconcerting, fantasy relationship.

I saw Rosie two more times after our first night of sexual perversion. The second time we were together was similar to the first, although Rosie only let me fuck her twice. ("You're cock is so big, it makes my pussy sore," she said). The third time, Rosie was having her period. "I'm gonna suck your cock, and then I'll jerk you off and make you cum on my face." And she did. Dirty, wrong and perverted. Everything I love in a woman.

After our third session, I'd become "addicted" to Rosie, and kept calling her. "When can I see you again? I need to be with you." Rosie's sexual fantasies had so enticed me that I felt I couldn't be without her. My new compulsion worked against me, apparently, and I so turned her off that my EX-WIFE actually had to call me to say, "Rosie doesn't want to date you anymore. She asked ME to tell you. She thinks you're being too 'clingy' and 'needy.' Sorry!"

I simply have to wonder, to this day: did Rosie ever told Kim the actual details of our sexual perversions??

I'd heard of "Speed Dating" a few years after I'd gotten divorced and decided to give it a try. "Speed Dating" involves about 20 men sitting at small tables inside the foyer of a restaurant or hotel lobby, while an equal number of women within a similar age range sit with the men, in a "round-robin" fashion. Each of the women gets about six minutes to "date" the man seated there, before a little bell rings. The women then rotate to the next, adjacent table.

During the very first time I "Speed Dated," I met Drea and was drawn to her instantly for one reason alone: She reminded me of a younger, thinner, sexier version of my ex-wife, Kim.

Drea had a great body, shaggy-longish blonde hair and doe-like, dark blue eyes. She had a terrific smile, an outgoing personality, and just seemed warm, cheerful and friendly. Plus, at 24 years old, she was 20 years my junior, and made me feel "alive" just by her presence.

Drea and I had a few dinner dates, where we did all the usual "Where you from? What do you do for a living?" stuff. I can honestly say I remember absolutely NOTHING of those talks. For some reason, those dates have been erased from my brain.

But I do remember two evenings with Drea that have been ingrained into my pathetic, sexual psyche, ever since. After perhaps our fourth "normal" date, I managed to lure her back to my apartment so we could watch TV. She sat to my immediate left on the couch, and we watched her favorite show, *ER*. During each and every commercial break from *ER*, I put my left arm around her back, and leaned in for a kiss.

"DO NOT KISS ME!" she sharply admonished. "I AM NOT READY TO KISS YOU NOW!"

"Wow!" I thought. "This chick's cold."

We watched another 15 minutes of *ER*, and, me being me, I tried again.

"WHAT DID I TELL YOU BEFORE?" she almost yelled. "DO NOT KISS ME! I DO NOT WANT TO KISS YOU. WHAT'S WRONG WITH YOU?"

Me (to myself): "It's gonna be a long night, here, brother."

Third *ER* commercial break, I actually tried one more time to kiss her.

"WHAT ARE YOU DOING? ARE YOU A PSYCHO? DO NOT KISS ME. DO YOU UNDERSTAND ENGLISH?"

Me (to myself): "Fine, whatever, I give up. I'll kick this chick out the door as soon as her stupid TV show's over."

ER finally ended. Just as I was about to stand up, Drea did so first.

"Where's your bedroom?" she asked. I pointed toward the other room. "Make a right at the hallway," I said. Drea: "Give me five minutes, and then come in there. Wait five minutes, first. You got that?" Me: "Yeah, sure, whatever." I had NO IDEA what this chick was doing.

Exactly five minutes later, I walked into my bedroom, to find it the scene from a porn film. She'd lit about five candles, had screwed a red lightbulb into one of my lamps, and had pulled the covers off my bed. She was laying totally nude on my bed, her legs spread apart, and was furiously masturbating her clit.

I stood a few feet before her, completely and totally stunned.

"Fuck this hot, wet pussy right now, pathetic bitch!" she demanded. "Show me your big fat fucking cock and fuck the shit out of me. What are you waiting for, loser? FUCK THIS CUNT! I'm a whore who needs to FUCK!"

I don't become speechless very often. But I certainly was that night.

I took off my clothes and joined in on the bed. Drea was staring at my cock, and then looked up at my face. "What's the story?" she asked. I hadn't noticed, but my cock was the size of a pea. Completely soft and hidden, my penis was doing an impersonation of a shy turtle. "You gonna fuck me, bitch? Or what?" she demanded, as she kept shoving half a hand inside her pussy.

"Of course, I want to fuck you," I said, meekly. I was suddenly "The Girl." There had been NO KISSING, NO FOREPLAY, NO WARMING UP, nothing. Two minutes earlier, she was screaming at me, "Do not kiss me," and now, here was the same woman, cursing me for not shoving my cock up her "tight, pink pussy hole."

Clearly, I'd discovered the female "Jekyll and Hyde."

I tried playing with myself, even squeezing my balls (with usually works), but nothing helped. "Hey, can you suck me a little bit, in your mouth?" I gently asked. "Ewww, gross!" she said. "That would give me germs. I don't put strange dicks into my mouth! Who do you think I am? You're not my boyfriend. Cocks are only meant to be inside pussy holes."

"Good tip," I said.

I tried, and tried, and tried to make myself hard, but it wasn't gonna happen. I started fantasizing about other women I'd been with, pages from my various *Playboy Magazines* that turned me on, and even my favorite scenes from the porno VHS tapes I'd practically worn thin.

Nothing, absolutely nothing, was gonna make me hard that night.

Drea stopped masturbating and sat up. Me: "I'm really sorry, kiddo. I would LOVE to fuck your brains out right now. You have no idea how much I want to fuck you. I think you're one of the sexiest chicks I've ever known, but it's just NOT gonna happen tonight. Sorry. I can't get hard right now. This has NEVER happened to be before in my life."

Of course, if you've read *Carrots* up till this point, you'll recall that I had had this problem twice before, and both times with women that also "demanded" my cock to perform on cue. They were Claudia (when I was 19), and Lynda (shortly after my divorce).

Drea stood quietly and replaced her bra and panties. "I need to use the bathroom," she said, calmly. When she returned, she was fully dressed. "Walk me to my car?" she asked. "Of course," I said.

She got inside her car and rolled down her driver's window. "Listen," I said. "I really like you, a lot, and I'm very attracted to you. I NEVER have this kind of problem. I need you to give me another chance, OK? PROMISE me that you'll give me another chance." Drea: "Sure OK, I promise. No big deal. I've heard that this can happen TO OLDER MEN." She drove off.

"OLDER MEN!" Ouch…now that hurt.

Surprisingly, Drea was good to her word and did, in fact, grant me "another chance," about two weeks later. She invited me to her house in Pasadena. We first went out to see a comedy show, had a few drinks and dinner, and ended up back at her house for some wine. We watched TV together, and this time she let me put my arm around her. She seemed much more relaxed and less intense.

Trying desperately to "psych myself up," a million thoughts were swirling through my mind: "You're with a very sexy, hot blonde, young girl. You are gonna fuck her brains out tonight. She wants you to fuck her. She's a dirty, filthy whore, the kind of woman that you love to have sex with. You're cock is gonna get so big and strong and hard, you are going to fuck her to death. She'll be out of breath when you're done fucking her. Now go in there, and GET THIS JOB DONE!" I stood up, took her by the arm, and said, "Come on, kiddo, show me your bedroom. I need to fuck you right now!" "Great," she said, giggling. Arm in arm, we walked into her room, she lit some candles and incense and put on some fuck music. We both instantly took off our clothes, threw off the covers, and hopped onto the bed.

Drea had dropped her dirty filty whore persona this time, and appeared to be a "kinder, gentler" woman. "Danny, please fuck me, baby, please? I'm a bad, bad girl that needs to be punished. Will you punish me tonight, big, hard Daddy?" Her legs spread, Drea was playing with her left tit with one hand, and sucking the fingers of the other. I'd rarely, in my entire life, seen a sexier scene in which I was supposed to have been a major participant.

I kneeled before her eager pussy and grabbed my crotch to get things ready. Once again, I was 100% completely and totally flaccid. I had NO FEELING down there AT ALL. My Benedict Arnold cock had fled, leaving behind, in his place, a veiny, flesh-colored imposter.

"Drea," I said, "I don't even know how to tell you this, but I'm having a problem again." She looked down at my cock and balls and became completely annoyed and disappointed. "That's terrific," she said, as she hopped out of the bed, put on a bathrobe, and left the room.

It was about 3 AM at this point, and I was exhausted and sad. I'd had quite a few drinks, and all I wanted to do now was fall asleep.

I continued laying on her bed, my head on her pillow, eyes closed. She came back into the room. "What are you doing?" she asked, totally pissed. Said I: "I'm so incredibly tired right now, I really just need to sleep. I'll leave first thing in the morning, OK? I promise." "Absolutely NOT!" she shrieked. "I need you to get out of here RIGHT NOW! You can't stay with me tonight. I NEVER let guys sleep over in my bed. YOU NEED TO GO HOME!"

There was no "wiggle room" here—no time for negotiation. Drea was madder than mad, and wanted absolutely NOTHING to do with me any longer. I managed to hustle up the remaining two ounces of energy I had left, got re-dressed, and walked out to my car. "Later, dude," she called out to me from her house, as she practically slammed the door behind me.

It was a long, lonely, drive back home from Pasadena that night, and, of course, you already know that I never saw—or heard from—Drea again.

CHAPTER TWENTY-ONE

The Very Close Call

Making more money than ever, I rented a huge house in Encino built in the 1950s. As moving men were schlepping my stuff out from my Studio City apartment, I spoke with my neighbor, Sarah, out walking her dog, Maestro (an ancient, one-eyed cocker spaniel.) Sarah was an attractive, African-American actress who had small roles on TV shows and in movies but made her living primarily by appearing in TV commercials. (We'd only spoken a few times previously by the pool.) When the moving men were finishing up, she asked, "So, are you ever gonna ask me out on a date? Or what?"

A few nights later, Sarah and I went for sushi. We confided to each other how burnt out we were from being single and dating. She invited me back to her place, and much to my surprise, insisted I fuck her on the couch. Maestro, who, with his eye patch, resembled Captain Hook the Pirate, watched us screw, while concurrently farting uncontrollably.

Sarah and I repeated our first date dozens of times. We'd go out to eat, then hit a liquor store and buy bottles of wine. Back at her place, we'd drink booze straight from the bottle until we were wasted, and then fuck and suck. An actress with an extensive wardrobe, Sarah would wear costumes and wigs for me in bed. She was the most powerful lover I ever had. Sex with Sarah was epic.

One night, she called me into her bathroom. She'd lit a dozen candles in the tub and was laying in a bubble bath. I joined her, and, together, we drank wine and kissed. At the point when my hard on poked his way up through the bubbles, we went to the bed for some doggie-style action. I was drunk off my ass and fumbling with a condom. "Do NOT put that thing on!" she barked. "I need to feel your hot, sweet cum deep inside me." Oblivious to reality, we had another round of Herculean sex for the ages. After four such sessions that night, I passed out. "What's up, baby? she asked. Me: "I'm out. I'm done." "Honey, you better wake up, cause this pussy's just getting started," she replied.

Thanksgiving came around, and my family convened at my new place. Sarah swung by with a pie, and joined us in the board game "Taboo." My family LOVED her. She was cute, funny, charming, and outgoing. After I walked her to her car, my mother said, "She's probably the nicest girlfriend you've ever had. Too bad she's a 'Shvartza' (Yiddish for a Black person)."

I was making breakfast the next morning, when my mother approached me: "I had a dream that Sarah was pregnant!" Taken aback for a quick second, I said, "No, mom…that's not possible. We always use protection." Mom: "I sure hope so. I don't think you want any more kids!"

New Year's Eve. Sarah invited me to a friend's party at a Hollywood nightclub. She was dressed in pink and reminded me of a Hostess "Snowball" dessert snack. The party was packed, and we had a bunch of drinks. After about an hour, I became quite depressed when I realized I had no real feelings for her. Although Sarah was a lot of fun, and the sex was great, I didn't see any kind of future for us together. I simply wanted to be in love.

I became silent. "What's wrong?" she kept asking. How was I supposed to tell her I'd lost interest? We left the party early and wound up back at her apartment, where we lay at opposite sides of her couch watching Dick Clark announce the start of the new year. After the Times Square ball dropped, Sarah said, "Can I interest you in a New Year's fuck?" Me: "Uhm, thanks, but, ahh, I'm just not in the mood. Sorry." A short time later, I drove home, alone.

Sarah and I went out again once or twice, but I simply wasn't into the relationship anymore. At the end of a movie, she pulled me aside in the theatre lobby. "I've lost you, huh?" she asked. "What's going on?" Me: "You're a really great girl, and I like you very much, but I don't think this relationship is going anywhere. I'd like to get re-married someday, and unfortunately, I just know in my heart that you and I will never be that couple. I'm really sorry." Sarah's beautiful, sunshine face became dim, as though the flashlight behind her smile suddenly had a dead battery.

We drove back to her place in silence and kissed goodbye. "Friends?" I asked. "I guess so," she answered. I honestly was not expecting to ever see her again.

One night, about a week later, I got a phone call that <u>ALMOST completely changed the course of my life.</u>

"I'm pregnant," Sarah announced. You know how in a movie, when someone learns that their child's been kidnapped, the camera rotates around them in slow motion, and their world comes to a frozen standstill? Speechless, I simply could not believe what I was hearing.

"Are you sure?" Sarah: "Yes, women tend to know these things." Me: "Is it MINE?" Sarah: "Who do you think I am, the world's biggest whore? Yes, of course it's yours. I haven't been with another man in two years." Instantaneously, a million thoughts flashed through my brain: I already have two kids! How was I going to pay for another? College? A kid out of wedlock? This would simply kill my father. What would Kim say? My friends? Mom? My children? I almost fainted.

"You'll have an abortion, right?" I asked. Sarah practically exploded: "Honey, this is MY BABY, and I'm gonna keep MY BABY. There's nothing YOU or ANYBODY ELSE is gonna do to take away MY BABY. The good Lord Jesus Christ is telling me to raise this child, and that's exactly what I'm gonna do."

Sarah hung up the phone. I walked into my living room, stared at the wall then remem-bered my mother's dream. "Oh my God, she knew!" I said out loud.

Every night for the next week or so, Sarah would call to discuss her pregnancy. I'd beg her to PLEASE consider an abortion, because I absolutely did not want a third child. I couldn't afford it and had NEVER planned on having another one after breaking up with Kim. Every night, I heard the same performance on the phone: "Sweet Jesus spoke to me and told me to keep this baby. This child is a gift from Lord Jesus Christ, Our Lord and Savior, and there's nothing you can do or say or do that's gonna change my mind." I implored her, "Sarah, please don't do this to me." She attacked: "You already have two kids! What if you were to lose them? I know where they live. **What if they both somehow died in a mysterious fire?**"

OK, so now I realized I was dealing with a psychopath. I was scared – chills ran up my spine. I realized there was likely no way out of this mess, and that Sarah, clearly a nut job, was going to have my third child without my involvement. Then, I decided I had one possible "out"—one chance to play to her vanity. A basic Hollywood truth: Actresses love attention!

"I'll be your publicist for two years at no charge if you have an abortion," I offered. She went silent, then whispered: "I want that in writing." Me: "Are you serious?" Sarah: "Yes, and we're both gonna sign it." Incredulous, I drew up possibly the world's first, and only, "Abortion Agreement" (something I believe I may have invented?) – a contract between Sarah and myself, that stated I would provide public relations services to her for two years, and that I would also take her to and from the abortion procedure.

A nurse led us into a small operating room at the doctor's office, told Sarah to put on a blue paper gown, and lay on the table. I sat in a chair in the corner of the room. While waiting for the doctor, Sarah asked me to hold her hand. I did. Out loud, she began praying: "Sweet Lord Jesus, please forgive Daniel for making me do this, my fourth abortion." FOURTH ABORTION? Holy Crap! This woman was an Abortion Junkie!

As I sat holding her hand, listening to her prayers, I felt about three inches tall. It was, without question, one of the worst moments of my life. I was wracked with guilt and shame and would have rather been anywhere else on the planet.

Just then a very beautiful female doctor, who resembled a young Heather Locklear, entered the operating room. She took one look at me, then at a sobbing Sarah, and shot me a look that said, "you are a piece of utter shit." She then hooked up a vacuum cleaner-type tube, inserted it into Sarah, and sucked out the bloody fetus. Truly a horrific hour of my life.

That night, I slept on Sarah's couch, getting up every few hours to check on her. The next morning, she walked into the kitchen and seemed to be in a cheerful mood. She made me a terrific breakfast, and we talked about everything <u>but</u> the nightmare from the day before. "Listen, I've got to go to work now," I said. "You're gonna see me tonight, right?" Sarah urged, almost panicked. "Sure, OK. I'll even take you out for a nice dinner if you're up to it."

After work, I took Sarah to a fun restaurant nearby. She was laughing and happy, having returned to the "Sarah Classic" character I'd dated the four months previous. During the meal, while smiling to her face, I decided I never wanted to see her again. Yes, I'd agreed to be her publicist, but I had no real intention of keeping that promise. (What was she gonna do, sue me?)

As I drove Sarah home through the winding, twisting turns of Laurel Canyon Blvd., she suddenly shouted, "Stop the car! Pull over right now!" I thought she needed to puke. "I need to suck your cock!" I careened the car into a pitch-black ditch off the side of the canyon, and parked. Sarah leaned across from the passenger seat, unzipped my fly, and gave me, without question, the most loving and passionate blow job of my life. It was breathtaking and mind-boggling – unbelievably hot and erotic. After I finished, she said: "OK, NOW you can take me home."

As we walked up to her apartment, I was consumed with conflict. This woman was funny, attractive, madly in love with me, and gave the best blow-jobs on the planet. She also had threatened the lives of my children, and for that I would never be able to forgive her. We reached her door. Sarah grabbed me, and with words that resonate in my ears to this day, said, "Honey, YOU AIN"T NEVER GONNA GET SEX LIKE ME AGAIN!" "Trust me…I know that already," I responded, slowly turning and slithering away.

Miraculously, Sarah never once requested my PR services, nor every contacted me again. Since that night, I've seen her on TV commercials a number of times selling toothpaste, mouthwash, and auto insurance.

Having somehow survived a near-tragic and very close call, I had a vasectomy about five weeks later.

CHAPTER TWENTY-TWO

Serial Dater

Business was booming. I had six employees, an office in New York, clients falling from trees, and money in my wallet. The other good news was that Kim had moved to Valencia, a city much closer to Los Angeles, making my weekend jaunts to pick up my children more convenient by many hours.

It was during this phase that women seemed to be drawn to me from all directions. I'd become a serial dater, and while I was in a position to really "sow some wild oats," didn't often do so with stellar results:

Claudia was an attractive, older blonde I'd also met at a Speed Dating event. A successful litigation attorney, she walked into a hotel restaurant for our first date wearing a sharp business suit and glasses, her hair pulled back in a stereotypical librarian's bun. She was smart, direct, and concise, and we had a good talk about life, dating, and current events.

After about three martinis apiece, I happened to mention that the next day was my birthday. Claudia removed her glasses, pulled her long hair out of its bun, leaned much closer in toward me, and said, "Well then, we need to celebrate, don't we Danny boy? Why don't you get us a room. I'll go to my car and get a few things."

Suddenly, I was Dustin Hoffman in "The Graduate." I scored the only room available, a suite which set me back $500. To pursue an opportunity this unique, I thought little about "investing" in my sex life.

I entered the beautiful room, opened the curtains, and saw a terrific view of Los Angeles. I kept the lights off. A knock on the door. Claudia quietly walked in, pushed me against a wall, and said "shush." She unbuttoned her shirt, unsnapped her bra, and pressed herself against me. "Are you going to fuck me hard, birthday boy?" she whispered. I was in heaven. Hand in hand, we walked into the bedroom, where she revealed red-and-black lacey lingerie. Our session began.

Claudia and I fucked four times in five hours – one of the more Herculean performances in the history of my sex life. This was especially impressive considering I was completely drunk, and not yet using Viagra. However, our sex was not the least bit romantic, tender, or gentle. This was porn star fucking. We did it in every position, upside down, inside out, backwards and forwards, on the bed, on the floor, in the bathroom. I felt like a jack hammer. "Harder, deeper, faster," Claudia kept demanding, and who was I to deny her?

About two-thirty, I was spent. "I'm done," I said. "Let's get some sleep?" Claudia stood, glasses back on, very methodically rolling her hair into a bun. Now re-dressed, she said, "Happy Birthday. Thanks for the fuck. You have a good cock. I've gotta go. Ciao."

As I lay in bed, naked and alone, longing to simply hold a woman and "cuddle," the robot named Claudia left me in the dark. She never returned future phone calls, and I never saw her again.

A friend of mine who ran a Jewish dating service hooked me up with Diane, a short, sexy woman, and a lot of fun. After dinner on our third date, while I was driving, Diane said from nowhere, "I think we need to talk. Can you pull over?" "What's up?" I asked. "I don't know how to say this…but, normally, after a third date with a guy I'm attracted to, I ask him to take me home to fuck. But, with you, I don't know…there's just SOMETHING ABOUT YOU…I can't describe it, but I just know that I'm NEVER GOING TO SLEEP WITH YOU."

I screeched the car off to the shoulder. This woman was a living, breathing testament to what my fortune teller had said in 1979. "I need you to tell me EXACTLY WHAT YOU MEAN, right now," I begged. "Can you describe why you feel this way?" I'd instantly given up on any future relationship with her, but thought, perhaps, she could shed some light on the "Carrots" phenomenon.

"I'm really not sure," Diane said. "You're nice, and you're funny, and I enjoy being with you. I also think you're cute. I honestly have no idea why, but I just get this feeling – this strange kind of vibe – that if I did have sex with you, something bad would happen. You just give off that aura....I know that makes no sense, right?" Me: "Do you like sex?" Diane: "You have no idea – I'm a fuck machine. Last year, I went on a singles cruise and never left my room. I fucked at least a dozen guys that week."

Diane and I went back to my house that night and played with my son's "Simpsons" chess board ("Homer" is the king, "Marge" is the queen). To rub salt into my gaping ego wound, Diane won the game.

My Jewish matchmaker set me up again, this time with Angela, a redhead with enormous boobs. About eight years younger, Angela was divorced, with a young son about my daughter's age. We were both single parents with a lot in common. When I met her, she'd just won a large lawsuit against her boss for sexual harassment and had recently purchased a brand-new condo.

"Wanna help me 'break in' my new place?" she asked at the end of our second date. Angela and I then proceeded to screw all over the house.

Once while fucking fast and furiously, Angela and I went "flying" off the bed. We were interlocked, cock in pussy, as we soared across the room, both orgasming together in mid-air. We hit the floor and laughed. That was hot.

Angela and I dated for months. We saw a bunch of movies, had a bunch of dinners, and had a lot of sex. One morning, we went out for breakfast to a local restaurant. At the end of the meal, I had to go to the bathroom, and simply said to her, "I'll be right back…can you please get the check?"

When I returned to the table, Angela was fuming – steam shot from her head. "What's wrong? Did you get the check?" Angela: "I can't believe you want ME to 'get the check'! I thought YOU were treating ME! Just because I have money doesn't mean I should pay for everything!" She was beyond angry. Me: "What are you talking about? I just said, 'get the check.' I didn't 'mean that you should PAY the check…I meant for you to LITERALLY JUST GET THE CHECK."

Angela: "I don't believe you," she said, storming off, a dozen paces ahead of me. I paid and caught up with her. We drove back to her place in silence. Hours later, the argument subsided, we kissed, and Angela invited me to spend the night for the first time. (Her son would be with his dad that evening.) During our sexcapades, I had to be extra careful not to squeeze her breasts too hard, as she'd just very recently had breast reduction surgery.

In the middle of the night, I was awakened by Angela's voice: "I'm a dirty, filthy whore, and I need to be punished." Me: "Wha, huh?" Angela: "I'm a dirty whore. I'm a very bad girl. I need to be fucked hard and deep in the ass." Having never before heard such a sentence in the history of my life, my eyes blasted open. Still mostly asleep, I kneeled behind her and fulfilled her request. Having never done this before, I was surprised how incredibly pleasurable it felt. After our "ass play" was over, I went back to dreamland.

The next morning, Angela, wrapped in a bathrobe, opened the shades in the bedroom, blinding me with the light. I was sound asleep. I saw her face and knew something was wrong. "You OK?"

I asked. "NO!" she replied. "I didn't get ANY SLEEP last night! You snore like a fucking symphony orchestra! So fucking loud! It's no wonder you're still single!" Angela stormed through the hallway, and down the stairs. "Well, that's NOT good," I said to myself. I got dressed and met her in the kitchen for some coffee. "Catch ya later?" I asked. "Don't call me, I'll call you," she said. And of course, she never did.

I'd joined a professional entertainment industry organization which held monthly mixers. I was doing my usual green apple martini thing, when I bumped into a woman standing next to me, spilling half my drink onto the open toes in her high heels. "Wow, I'm really sorry," I apologized. The woman laughed. "Don't worry about it… my toes needed a bath anyway," she said.

A bit older, Jeri was also divorced and lived near me. A freelance writer of Internet advice columns for single, working mothers, she and I became friends almost instantly. A model in her 20s, Jeri had appeared as an extra in Prince's movie *Purple Rain*. She remained striking, with a slender build, shaggy, dirty blonde hair, and a pretty face. Jeri and I dated for about five months, saw a lot of movies and ate a lot of Thai food. But whenever I'd make a romantic move, I'd get the "I'm not ready" line I'd heard, years earlier, from Lynda.

Jeri threw herself a birthday party. By the time I arrived, she was quite drunk and surrounded by a dozen guys. Clearly reveling in all that male attention, Jeri was beaming. I walked up to kiss her, but she kept me at arm's length, introducing me to her guests as, "My friend, Dan." Insulted, I decided to get drunk by myself in a corner. Just then, I noticed a beautiful blonde sitting at a table, alone. "Can I join you?" I asked. "Sure, I'm Jeri's friend, Shelly." Shelly and I spent at least two hours together, talking, drinking, and observing Jeri's peacock behavior during the party. Shelly worked for one of the major movie studios, and we exchanged business cards.

Hours passed, and Jeri, now sloppy drunk, was slurring her words and stumbling into people. "You should probably drive her home," Shelly said. "She's pretty wasted." I slung Jeri's arm around my neck, got her into my car, and then waltzed her up the stairs to her apartment.

"My presents!" she cried in a drunken stupor, "A birthday girl needs her presents!" I got Jeri situated in her living room, then made several trips back and forth to my car, schlepping her stupid fucking gifts up her stupid fucking staircase.

"Let's drink!" Jeri shouted, pouring two glasses of straight vodka. We sat on her living room floor for half an hour, unwrapping her gifts. I had no interest in her this way, sloppy drunk off her ass, and demanding the spotlight simply because it was her birthday.

After the last gift was opened, I said, "You need to get some sleep." I escorted her into the bedroom and plopped her onto her bed. I turned to leave. Almost unconscious, Jeri whispered, "Make love to me." I was really surprised at this turn of events. It was about 2 AM. I was drunk, very tired, and all I wanted to do at that point was go home and jerk off to mental images of Shelly's cleavage. Suddenly inspired, I headed straight for Jeri's pussy with my mouth. "Oh, my God, oh, God, that feels so fucking good!" she moaned, as I ate her out with wild abandon.

My cock now rock-hard, I quickly installed a rubber, and demanded, "Turn over, you little whore. I want you doggie style." Jeri got on her hands and knees, and I mounted her from behind. Her pussy was hot and tight, and I pounded away like a dog in heat. This had nothing to do with love making. This was AN ANGRY REVENGE FUCK. "Who was this bitch to ignore me all night, then make me haul her fucking presents up and down her fucking stairs? I'll show her," I thought to myself, shoving my cock deeper and deeper inside her, and slamming my balls against her ass cheeks.

"Oh, my God, I'm gonna cum. I'm gonna cum. I'm GONNA CUM!" Jeri screamed, her face shoved hard into a pillow. I continued plowing away, faster, deeper, harder, each thrust filled with more and more anger. I finally exploded.

Panting, I remained upright on my knees. Jeri turned onto her back, and began crying. Tears streamed down her face. "What's wrong?" I asked, not really caring. "That just felt so incredibly good," Jeri said, "I can't even put it into words. That was the most erotic thing I've done in years."

Back at my place that morning, the first thing I did ensured a screeching halt to any future relationship I might have developed with Jeri. Just hours after I'd fucked her best friend so hard I made her cry, blonde bombshell Shelly received an email from yours truly asking for a date! In my note, I told her how much I'd enjoyed meeting her, how attracted to her I was, and how much I was looking forward to seeing her again. I gave ZERO SECONDS of thought to the obvious—It NEVER ONCE occurred to me that Shelly would, of course, relay my email to Jeri, the woman whose pussy I'd just battered hours before.

My phone rang: "I can NOT BELIEVE you!" Jeri shrieked. "What is WRONG with you? I finally let you FUCK ME and then you ask my best friend out for a date the NEXT MORNING? You have GOT to be kidding me!"

And the truth is, I was focused solely on the "Carrot" – the beautiful "Shelly Carrot" – instead of trying to develop a normal relationship with Jeri, the woman I'd finally "conquered" after months of sexual frustration. Having finally fucked Jeri, I no longer had one ounce of interest in her. "Been there, done that," I figured. "Moving on."

"I thought I could trust you, Dan, after so many months together," Jeri continued. I finally gave myself to you with love, and then you immediately go and stab me in the back the very next morning? I can't see you again."

And let's face it, she was right. I never blamed her. The only reason this story remains upsetting to me is that because I'd finally had sex with Jeri, I never had a fighting chance at dating the much more alluring – and elusive – Carrot named Shelly.

Accepting my mistake with Jeri, I called a friend of mine, Sherry, who, along with her mother, ran a match-making service called "Meet A Mate," which specialized in hooking up Jewish singles. Sherry set me up on a date with Lauren, who I barely remember. I had just returned to LA from a business trip that afternoon and had extremely bad jet lag. We were to meet at a restaurant/bar, and, as usual, I'd arrived much too early, so I began to drink. And drink. By the time Lauren arrived, I'd had at least three green apple martinis which, combined with the jet lag, made me incredibly sick.

Lauren was a fairly attractive, short, brunette (I think.) She might have been a school teacher, I don't know – I'd rarely been more drunk in public. As we were following our hostess toward our table at the restaurant, I excused myself for a second, went outside into the patio area of the building, and explosively threw up behind some bushes. Very classy move. I returned to Lauren at the table, with the entire restaurant spinning round in my head. I have absolutely no idea how I managed to not only remain there having a conversation with her, but actually eating dinner!

Lauren had a few drinks, also, and was quite obviously attracted to me. I don't recall one word of dialogue, but I knew that we had some kind of chemistry.

As I walked Lauren outside to her car, we passed mine first. I pointed it out to her. "Wanna make out?" she asked. "Sure, why not," I said, still nauseous and shaky. We got into the back seat of my car, making out like teenagers for a while. My breath must have been horrific.

"Wanna see my tits?" she asked. "Sure," I said, and her shirt and bra came off. As I began fondling her big, majestic breasts, Lauren whipped out a condom and said, "I need you to fuck me." We were in a public parking lot, with other cars everywhere and people constantly coming into and out of the restaurant. "OK, I guess so," I replied.

The only time in my life I've ever had intercourse in a car was that night with Lauren. It was awkward and uncomfortable, and I thought for sure I was going to throw up all over her.

Miraculously, I didn't. Lauren took charge of the session, and essentially raped me. I didn't care. My eyes were closed most of the time.

When we were finished, Lauren kissed me goodbye, said, "Thanks, honey," and split. I never saw her again.

I was attending a multi-day television conference in Miami at which several of my clients were exhibiting. My (late) father and his Cunt of a Wife lived in Boca Raton at that time, about an hour north of Miami, and I was planning to visit them after this TV event had ended.

On the last night of the conference, two of my clients (producers of music for TV shows and films), took me out for drinks at a Miami hotspot. I stood at the bar with these clients and had my "signature" green apple martini. Then another. And another. And another. I was so engrossed in conversation with these guys that I kept drinking, not realizing that I'd simply forgotten to eat dinner.

The club was becoming more crowded, and the music was getting louder. Women were everywhere—at least four women to each man present. After my fourth drink, I spun around to see an older woman with long, dirty blonde hair, dancing alone. I "flashed back" to meeting "Kim 1," and knew instinctively that I needed to dance with her. "Thanks for the drinks, bro," I told one of my clients, "But that woman is calling out to me."

I took Martha by the hands and started dancing with her. She smiled. We danced song after song, while the club got more and more crowded. We were squished together inside a Miami sea of revelers, and I knew there'd be more than "just dancing" with this woman.

After about two hours, I said, "Come back to my hotel with me." Martha: "OK." Simple as that. I've discovered in life that women who want to give you sex, WANT to give you sex. There doesn't need to be any begging, pleading, crying or manipulating. While this hasn't happened all that often to me, when it did happen, it was obvious, and occurred with minimal effort.

Martha and I took a cab back to the Fountainebleau Hotel, where I was staying. I'd had at least six martinis that night, and, miraculously, not only didn't get sick or have the room spin, but managed to be in complete control of my penis.

I'm pretty sure Martha and I had sex five times that night and into the next morning. We didn't talk much. There was no "Where you from? What do you do for a living?" conversation. It wasn't necessary. Martha was clearly older than me, in her late 40s, and, when we finally fell asleep, I'd realized that during the course of my sexual "career," I'd now slept with women ages 16-46.

The next morning was incredibly awkward. I could tell Martha was surprised at her actions. ("Wow…I NEVER do things like this!" she said.) We got dressed, I checked out of the hotel, and we had breakfast in the lobby restaurant. Conversation was strained and unnatural, and neither of us was really interested in the facts of the other person's life. I did learn that Martha worked for a TV music company based in Manhattan, and that her elderly mother lived with her. She had grown children and had been divorced for a very long time.

That afternoon, I drove my rental car an hour north, to visit my dad and his wife. The minute I arrived at their house, I had a major diarrhea attack! I had the runs that entire afternoon, as a result of my "martinis-without-dinner" adventure the night before. My poor father and I had to make an emergency run to a local drug store to buy a large bottle of Kaopectate.

Sad Update: A year later, that same TV conference was going to be held in Los Angeles. I called Martha's company in New York, to ask her if she was going to be coming out to LA. I figured I'd have another shot at a night of "hot sex without feelings," something I'd learned to master.

A colleague of Martha's answered the phone. "Martha there?" I asked. "Oh, my goodness. I guess you haven't heard?" she said. Me: "Heard what?" Woman on phone: "Oh, Martha died about two months ago." Me: "Martha DIED?" Woman on phone:" Yes, she was walking her dog. It was a beautiful, sunny day, and she suddenly had a massive heart attack and died. She literally died on the sidewalk. Her poor dog…"

I hung up the phone, thinking, "If Martha had had an unknown heart condition, she could have DIED while she was in bed with me!"

To date – and as far as I know – Martha is the only "Dead Carrot" on my ridiculously stupid "Carrots" list.

CHAPTER TWENTY-THREE

Everybody Wants to "F" My Personal Trainer

I attended an advertising industry event in Bel Air, and, during the post-event wine and cheese reception, met two young, Jewish women who blew my socks off. They were Jennifer and Jenna, both in their early 20s, with long brown hair. However, Jennifer's body (like the name of a Megan Fox movie), was supernatural, and could, almost literally, stop traffic.

I met the two "J" girls toward the end of the affair, told them they were "hot," and that I wanted to get to know them better. They laughed and gave me their phone numbers. About a week later, the three of us had dinner at the "W" Hotel (the scene of my "crime" with Claudia, a few years previous).

During the meal, it was revealed that Jenna was single, but Jennifer had a long-time boyfriend named Peter, whom she'd been trying to dump for months. Unfortunately, poor Peter was unable to get over her, even telling her that he masturbated to her photograph every night before he went to sleep.

"I want to date you," I said directly to Jennifer's face. She laughed. "Yeah, right! Are you a millionaire?" "No, I said." Jennifer: "Then, you have no chance with me. Plus, you're way too old. But Jenna will probably date you, right?" We turned to see Jenna's face. "Sure, why not…you seem fun," Jenna said.

Jenna and I had one date—a sushi dinner. We ended up talking about Jennifer the entire time. "All the guys want Jennifer," Jenna said, "With that body, who can blame them?" Me: "I know…it's unbelievable—like a gift from God."

The next day, Jennifer called. "How'd it go with Jenna?" Me: "All we did was talk about you. I think she wants to fuck you as badly as I do." Jennifer howled with laughter.

At this time, Jennifer was working for a temporary personnel agency, placing people who had special skills in the digital and technology industries within ad agencies and marketing companies. "You like your job?" I asked her. "No, I hate it. But it embellishes the money I make on the side as a personal trainer." This was when I realized why Jennifer had such an amazing figure.

Over the next many, many months, Jennifer and I became extremely close friends, having countless lunches and dinners together. Although I liked Jenna, I was simply smitten with Jennifer and couldn't get enough of her "chutzpah," her boldness, and her unbelievably sexual charisma.

A few months into our friendship, Jennifer decided to drop her 9-5 job, and focus 100% on her personal training business. Almost instantly, she lined up clients left and right, including some young singers and actresses who would become quite famous a few years later.

To ensure that I could be with her as much as possible, I hired Jen to be my personal trainer as well, working out with her three times a week, religiously. I was making plenty of money and could afford her hourly fee (which she'd slightly reduced for me). We'd meet at a grassy area just in front of a spot in Santa Monica called "The Stairs," where hundreds of people exercise on a daily basis. Health nuts climb up and down those stairs, repeatedly, like lunatics, for hours at a time. During my best ever session, I was able to do six "round trips" on those mother-fucking stairs, before almost collapsing from what I was convinced had been a massive heart attack.

Beyond just the stairs, Jennifer made me run for blocks, jump rope, do endless sit-ups atop an enormous plastic ball, throw a heavy medicine ball back and forth to her, and stretch my calf and thigh muscles in excruciatingly painful exercises.

As our post work-out session "reward," Jen and I would almost always wind up having dinner at either our favorite Chinese restaurant ("Chin-Chin"), or at a nearby (celebrity favorite) sushi house. Again, because I was making a lot of dough at the time, and was consumed with the idea that "someday, I'm gonna get this girl into bed," I ALWAYS paid for these VERY EXPENSIVE meals. ALWAYS. (Jennifer, who never gained an ounce, could eat like the Green Bay Packers. She also had a special flair for driving waiters crazy with her "customized" Chinese chicken salad instructions, which would have baffled Nasa scientists with their specificity.)

Jennifer was a very sharp chick. She could see bullshit a mile away and had no tolerance for it, whatsoever. We would talk for hours and hours about everything, and I learned that I was one of four guys in LA who "fed her" on a regular basis. The others, including a successful dentist, a marketing executive, and the head of the home video division of a major movie studio, were each obsessed with the idea that they, too, would somehow, somewhere, someday wear down this diamond and sleep with her. She knew that she was playing each of us, equally, and simply had no qualms about it, whatsoever.

Jennifer was fascinated with my love life, or lack thereof, depending on which "Carrots" were in my purview at the time. She was also, I believe, the first woman (other than a therapist) that I ever talked about masturbation with, in extraordinary detail. I confessed to her about my "Whack Shack" days, the Korean massage parlors, phone sex fantasies, and Las Vegas call girls. She found these stories hilarious, often asking me, "How many times did you jerk off this week? How'd you do it? Who were you thinking about? Tell me everything!" (I'll admit that revealing these stories to Jennifer turned me on even more than actual sex with her probably would have done.)

Jen was far less forthcoming talking with me about her sex life, but, after so many months of insisting, she began to dole out little tidbits here and there. I'd hear stories about her boyfriends: "This guy's cock was too big; this one's penis was the size of a baby's pinky," etc. I hounded her to tell me about her masturbating habits, until, she finally said, "Well, I used to have a vibrator a long time ago, but it broke. I use my fingers, but not that often. I'm certainly not addicted to 'doing myself' like YOU ARE!" she mocked.

For her birthday during our first year of friendship, I bought Jennifer a "Rabbit" vibrating dildo, which had been featured in an episode of *Sex and the City*. She seemed shocked, yet turned on, when I gave it to her. "Now, I want to hear the details about how you use this," I said. "Yeah, sure, that'll happen," she replied.

For 18 straight months, Jennifer and I were inseparable—the closest of friends. We confided everything to each other, and she even started training my daughter (to whom she'd become something of a "big sister"), in kickboxing. Everywhere we went together, people assumed Jen was my girlfriend, and, on more than one occasion, strange men would approach me and say, "God, you are one lucky son-of-a-bitch!"

The longer Jen and I were together, the more two things in particular would happen:

1) My conviction that she would fall in love with me eventually, and
2) The phenomenon of guys blatantly hitting on her, right in front of me, as though I simply didn't exist and was invisible.

Jennifer and I would be eating sushi, when a good-looking guy sitting at the next table would shoot her a smile. "Terrific," she'd say to me, under her breath. "Here we go again." The guy would come over to our table, flirt with her without even acknowledging my presence, and then ask her for her phone number. "Give me your card," she'd say, "I'll call you."

"It must be something to have guys throwing themselves at you," I said one time. "Most of them are idiots," she'd say. "I'm not out for sex. Sex doesn't mean that much to me. That's too easy—there's no challenge for me in that. I can have sex anytime I want. What I'm looking for is the right guy who's Jewish, has tons of money, looks and connections. Without all of those things, I couldn't care less." Me: "Of course, I'm the exception, right?" Laughing, Jennifer: "Yeah, sure."

One time while we were working out together, Jennifer's mother came by to visit. Jen introduced me to her, and then returned to her exercise routine. The mom observed, as I blatantly watched Jen's perfect ass wiggle away. Jen's Mom: "She's too young for you!" she admonished. "Find someone your own age." Her words cut me to the core, yet I knew she was right.

"I know," I said, "But I can't get her out of my head."

"Try harder," the mom added.

After we were "together" for about two years, Jennifer met a very handsome, Jewish, multi-millionaire and basically was rarely seen or heard from again. No longer in "need" of my free sushi dinners, Jen was now being wined and dined around town, hanging out with celebrities, and attending all the "right" Hollywood parties, rock concerts and events. However, after Jen discovered that her boyfriend was cheating on her with a porn star, she broke up with him, briefly re-appearing in my life for a few more free meals.

Years later, during a blind date set up by her mother, Jennifer was having lunch in LA with a guy from Canada, when she got a phone call from her mom telling her that her father had had a heart attack. Her date drove her to the Palm Springs hospital, where the two of them spent the next 10 days in a row together, later attending her father's funeral. The son of a billionaire Toronto real-estate developer, this guy proposed to Jen after those 10 days, and they were married a few months later. Jen lived with him for a few years in Canada, until she realized she hadn't found true love, in spite of his fulfilling her "husband criteria."

After her divorce, Jennifer moved back to Los Angeles, and, while still pursuing wealthy, well-connected men, met a successful LA-based marketing consultant. She married him and together they have two children.

Along the way, Jen also wrote an exercise book, invented a line of running shoes, and became a mini-celebrity in the field of health, appearing on several high profile TV shows. Later still, she morphed that career into becoming a highly-sought-after Motivational Speaker, delivering lectures, as well as Ted Talks, all around the globe.

Although we've seen each other just a few times since she became a mom, our bond of friendship still exists. We had a blast during our most recent evening together (early 2022,) when she actually carved out some time from her busy life to hang out with me. I've always enjoyed talking with her a great deal, but getting her to commit to a reunion will forever remain a truly difficult assignment.

CHAPTER TWENTY-FOUR

The Comatose Three-Way and the "Spanish Orgasm"

About to enter an entertainment industry party in Beverly Hills, a young Hispanic girl (early 20s) approached me on the sidewalk. "Can you help me get inside?" she asked. "I'm not on the list, but I'm supposed to meet some friends." Unconventionally attractive, I was instantly intrigued.

Once inside the club, Ruthie and I sought her friends, who were not to be found. We talked and drank, and she took hold of my hand. A few hours later, and drunk off my ass, I leaned over: "Come home with me tonight. I want to have sex with you." Without pause, she answered, "Take me to a nice hotel and I'll fuck you all night long." We drove to the Four Seasons, and for the tidy sum of $650, I secured a beautiful suite for the night.

Upstairs, I gave Ruthie oral sex, and made her cum, repeatedly, in my face. "Oh my God, where have YOU been hiding?" she said. Ruthie then insisted on shaving my scrotum in the bathtub. I was so wasted, I let her. Afterwards, we had sex, although I gave her a truly poor performance, having only gotten semi-hard. "You don't have sex very often, do you?" she asked, and I had to admit that that was the case. "You're such a sweet guy, and you're so incredibly sexy, I can't believe you don't have like a million girlfriends," she said. In her unadorned simplicity, Ruthie made me feel content and at ease.

I dated Ruthie for several months. We'd go out for dinner and end up back at my house for sex. She was always upbeat and spunky, and her sexual appetite inspired me—my manhood became more powerful and solid with each session.

I wanted to take her someplace fun that New Year's Eve, so we hopped a ferry and sailed to Catalina Island (popping ecstasy along the way.) At our hotel, she put on a bikini. "Let's go play in the hot tub," she said. While there, Ruthie took off her bikini bottoms: "Finger fuck me, baby" she requested and I obliged, as other hotel guests clearly watched through their windows.

We spent that New Year's Eve dancing at a Hawaiian-themed nightclub. After a great deal of drinking, we were essentially humping each other with clothes on. About 3 AM, we left the club to head back to our hotel room. An enormous sign heralding the new year – "2001" – appeared in bright white lights on the side of a Catalina mountain. In our hotel lobby, we saw a young man passed out on the couch. Off to the right, we also saw a very attractive young woman sprawled on the floor, as though she'd been murdered. "Is she dead?" Ruthie asked. "No, just drunk, I think," I said. I kneeled next to the woman's face. "Honey, you OK?" She struggled to open one eye – clearly incoherent, she was unable to respond. "Let's get her upstairs." Ruthie and I lifted drunk lady off the floor, and with each of her arms over our shoulders, slowly escorted her up two flights of stairs (the hotel had no elevator) and into our bedroom.

We laid the woman on our bed and stood back, soaking in the sight. Comatose gal was about 30, terrific body, long, dirty blonde hair, and a very pretty face. I vaguely recalled having seen her and her boyfriend (the guy passed out in the lobby) earlier in the week, from a distance. Ruthie took the woman's shoes off. "She's completely wasted," she said, "But she is pretty hot. I'll bet you'd like to fuck her, wouldn't you?" "Yeah, of course…she's beautiful," I said. "I'd like to fuck her, too," Ruthie informed me. "You're bi?" I asked. "I'm everything sexual," she answered.

I went into the bathroom for a pee and looked at myself in the mirror. Even for me, I was extraordinarily drunk. It was very early in the morning, and I was in a tiny hotel room with two women, one of whom was passed out in my bed. "What the fuck are you supposed to do now?" I asked the man in the mirror. I was really stupefied – I had absolutely no idea how to negotiate the scene that awaited me on the other side of that bathroom door.

I returned to the bedroom to find Ruthie, completely naked under the covers, stroking our newfound friend's long blonde hair. I stood feet from the bed, frozen. "You gonna join us, or what?" Ruthie asked. I took off my clothes and joined her under the covers. Comatose woman (still dressed and atop the covers) groaned. "Hey, what's your name?" I asked. Unable to verbally respond, she did, however, look up at me with starry eyes. Much to my own surprise, I leaned over, and started kissing her. She responded, sticking her tongue deep into my mouth. I then started rubbing her crotch, and she wiggled, grinding her vagina against my hand in response.

It was the closest I've ever come in my life to necrophilia.

Kissing this strange woman was incredibly exciting. But then I noticed Ruthie was getting jealous. "You're ignoring ME for HER?" Realizing I was hurting her feelings, I turned to my left and began kissing Ruthie, next giving her oral sex. She moaned and came. Having alleviated that problem, I returned to dead lady, hoping to pick up where I'd left off. Perhaps repulsed by the fact that my lips had just been on another woman's hey-nonny-nonny, the comatose one nudged me away, no longer allowing me to molest her.

Ruthie: "Hey, drunk lady…wanna make love to my man?" Uttering a guttural noise, comatose girl slowly rolled onto her right side, literally giving Ruthie and I the cold shoulder.

"Fuck her – she's boring," Ruthie said, "Fuck me instead." Ruthie and I then had sex, our coupled bodies pounding up against dead lady's backside. After we both climaxed, Ruthie and I fell asleep, me with an arm around a blonde, female corpse.

About 6 in the morning, I was awakened by the comatose one, who'd suddenly leapt from bed, picked up her shoes, and was tip-toeing from the bedroom. "Hey, you alright?" I whispered. She looked at me with a semi-smile, said, "I'm OK now, thank you," and split. (I think her "thank you" really meant, "thank you for not raping me.")

Back in LA, Ruthie and I continued dating for a while, but I noticed that the dynamics between us had changed after our Catalina Island adventure. Our sex was more distant and mechanical, and I could see we weren't really that "into each other" anymore. At the end of a dinner date, Ruthie made a surprising confession: "Danny, I never told you this before, but you should probably know that I'm a prostitute." I was pretty shocked—she'd never charged <u>me</u> for sex. "I really do like you, a lot," Ruthie continued, "But, I've been building up my client base lately, and I decided that if you want to keep seeing me, I'll have to start charging you. Of course, I'll give you a good discount, because you've been so super sweet to me all this time."

Surprisingly hurt, I paid the check: "Take care, Ruthie, have a nice life." I split, never looking back. And, of course, I never saw her again.

For my 46th birthday, I decided to treat myself to a real vacation, and booked a ten-day trip to Cancun, Mexico. I had three goals in mind:

1) Drink to excess
2) Sleep to excess
3) Fuck to excess

I'd been working out with a personal trainer the two-years previous, and my body was in its best shape since college. I was feeling pretty good about myself, and I figured I'd go someplace where I'd be surrounded by women wearing minimal amounts of clothing.

I checked into Club Med's Cancun Village and hit the bar. The place was beautiful, but I noticed right away that everyone there was either much younger than me, or a couple. The girls seemed to be in their early 20s, and the couples were in their 40s or older. Instantly, I was a fish out of water. So, I did what all fish do.

I drank.

I'm pretty sure I consumed more alcohol during my time in Cancun than I'd had in my entire life, combined. Drunk from early morning till late at night, I did my best to relax and tried (in vain) to make some kind of connection with the other vacationers. I'd walk around smiling or winking at the young, hot, bikini girls walking past me, but they'd ignore me, giggle at my flirtations, or shoot me back a look that read: "Yeah, right! As if!" These hotties wanted absolutely nothing to do with this balding, old Jew.

At night, the DJ located at the bar would corral everyone together for mass dancing sessions, set to blaring "Euro-trash" techno music. There must have been at least 250 people there, but as far as I could tell, most of them were part of a couple. One night after the dancing ended, I was walking back toward my room, when I felt a pinch on my ass. I turned to see a short, plump woman, holding her husband's hand, walk past me, smiling. She licked her lips and winked. "What the fuck?" I thought. "Why would she do that? She's clearly married." Even though I didn't find her remotely attractive, I was oddly aroused by her actions.

After the ass pinching, I tried to sleep but couldn't. There was just no way. I'd promised myself I would not masturbate during my time in Cancun, but now that promise came back to haunt me. My cock was so angry: "What's wrong with you? You're surrounded by pussy here…I MUST HAVE pussy!!" I sat up in bed, found a phone book, and although it was in Spanish, began leafing through. I found a bi-lingual ad for "Female Entertainers." I called, and through broken English, ordered myself a companion.

About 2 AM, a knock on my door. There stood a Mexican beauty named Lorena, whose long, dark hair, gorgeous face, and perfect little body reminded me of Salma Hayek. Walking in, she hugged me, and I realized she spoke virtually no English. Lorena and I sat on my bed, and I tried through sign language to communicate. She laughed and smiled, but I had no idea what she was saying. She was perhaps 19 or 20 and could easily have been a model. After we both realized that "talking" wasn't getting us anywhere, she stood, took off all her clothes, and slipped under my covers.

"You think me is sexy?" she asked, in what I was sure were the only words of English she knew. "Yes, I think you is very sexy," I answered. I held her in my arms and we just kissed for a long time. It was fantastic. Here in the Mexican darkness, I was romancing a stunning young girl.

She moved herself down my body and started giving me oral sex. It was sweet and tender—not "vacuum cleaner"- esque, as I'd experienced with other prostitutes in the past. When I was ready to rock and roll, I put on a condom, and gently rolled her onto her back. This petite Mexican hooker and I made love, instead of my usual anger pounding, porn star athletics. This little charmer was sweet and romantic, and reminded me of the night I'd spent with Candy, a million years earlier.

In no hurry to cum, I was able to maintain a hard erection inside Lorena for quite a long time. After about 30 minutes of intercourse, her face began to glow, and her body started to tremble and shake. She orgasmed, crying out, "Si! Si! Si! Aydios Mío! Si! Si! Si!" Then, she began crying, triggering my orgasm, which, in turn brought her to climax a second time.

Finished, we lay back on the bed, exhausted. She held me close, her long, dark hair on my shoulder. "Te'Amo!" ("I love you") she whispered. We lay together for quite some time in silence, until my phone rang. It was Lorena's Madame, wanting to know if we were done. Through broken English, the Madame instructed me how to pay my little lover. I just fanned all of my local currency before Lorena, allowing her to pick and choose the various paper bills that were appropriate. (Whether or not she ripped me off blind, I'll never know.)

On my last full day at Club Med, I noticed a tall, very pretty, blonde teenage girl eating with her parents. Because I'm always the most attracted to women completely and totally out of my reach, I became obsessed with her. After dinner, I walked about 30 feet behind her and her parents, as they walked along the beach, picking up seashells.

At dusk, all the young people headed to the bungalow nightclub. Like a retarded child, I followed my new "mystery girl" into the club from a distance. The place became packed quickly, the music got loud, and everyone was drinking and dancing. I inhaled three drinks in a row and forced myself to meet my new "goddess."

Melissa was a total joy – she seemed to be instantly attracted to me. We danced and drank, drank and danced, for several hours. She pressed herself up against me and, I guess you could say, we began "dirty dancing," whatever that even is. She rubbed my bald head as we danced, and placed my hands on her ass, grinding her luscious body against me. My heart was filled with joy. Single-handedly, this young girl was making up for the painfully long nine days I'd experienced up until that point. About 1 o'clock, the nightclub filled with foam – if you've never experienced "foam dancing," you haven't lived. Maybe the most fun I ever had in my life. The foam, up to my neck, reminded me of the times my mother used "Mr. Bubble" in the bathtub, when I was a small child.

An hour later, the club was stifling. I asked Melissa if we could take a walk outside and she agreed. Hand in hand, my blonde bombshell teenager and I were strolling along a perfect Cancun beach. The waves were still, and the full moon was so bright, it lit the entire ocean and the white sandy beach. The stars were overwhelming. The further we walked from the club, the quieter it became.

Melissa and I sat side by side on some beach rocks, still holding hands. I stroked her long blonde hair and asked if she liked sex. "Love it," she said, "Especially when a guy eats my pussy…that's my favorite." "Finally!" I thought to myself, "I'm going to make love to a beautiful girl on a perfect beach before I die." I leaned over and we kissed. It was magical. It was mind-boggling.

And, like my experience at an 8th grade party, it only lasted about 20 seconds.

As though suddenly struck by a bolt of lightening, Melissa sprang from the rocks, brushed the sand from her long, beige dress, and said, "Oh my God! I'm only 17! I can't have sex with YOU! You could be my FATHER!" Within seconds, she vanished from sight. And I mean that literally—she VANISHED into thin air. Supernatural, the moment could easily have been a scene from *The X-Files*. I walked back to my hotel room in a complete daze.

Cancun Coda: The next morning, I awoke to find the pupils of my eyes "bright lobster red." Apparently, I was having a major allergic reaction to the nightclub foam. Back in LA many, many hours later (after my first plane caught fire,) I drove myself to St. Johns Hospital in Santa Monica. The ER was empty, and I was whisked into a patient area inside. Without a single second of advance conversation, a doctor walked up to me, looked directly into my bright red pupils, and said, "Mexico, right?"

I haven't taken another vacation since.

CHAPTER TWENTY-FIVE

Shiksa Blondes and the Missing "Zap"

I jumped back into the dating pool, attending every singles party I could find. It sucked living alone in a beautiful, huge, brand new Santa Monica apartment building. All I wanted to do was find a "compatible companion" to share my life. For some inexplicable reason, the next batch of women that breezed all just happened to be blondes.

** Zappy: I met Zappy at a party in a popular sushi restaurant. She had long, straight blonde hair, green eyes, a very good figure, and reminded me a bit of Meryl Streep. A divorced accountant with two kids in college, she told me over drinks that she was there simply to "meet a new guy and have a good time." I walked her to her car, and we kissed briefly. "Call me anytime," she said, handing me her card. "You're cute. I'm sure we could have some fun."

I had my first date with Zappy that weekend, feeling rather guilty because my children were staying with me. Although my kids were now old enough to stay by themselves, this was the first time since my divorce I was out on a date during a "kids weekend." After our dinner date, we wound up in my car, parked just outside my building.

About to tell her I had to check on my kids, Zappy threw herself on me, shoved her tongue down my throat, and began grinding her body up against mine. My daughter called my cell phone: "Daddy, when are you coming home? Jordan and I are really bored." As the Zapster tried to unzip my jeans, I replied, "Honey, I'm outside right now…I'm just saying goodbye to my friend. I'll be there in a few minutes, OK? I promise." My date's hands were down my pants – my "daddy guilt" was overwhelming.

"I can't do this right now, sorry," I said to my gal pal. She responded: "Fuck me in the backseat. Just stick your cock inside me and cum. We can do it in three minutes. You know you want to."

Strongly considering her proposal, I glanced around the street and realized at least half a dozen Orthodox Jewish parents were returning from Temple, pushing their kids in strollers. Adding this paranoia to the sound of my daughter's voice, I was compelled to stop everything. "Listen, I am SO attracted to you, you have no idea. But I HAVE to get back to my kids. I CAN'T have sex with you right now. I'd love to, but I can't. And especially not out here in public. Sorry…Rain check?"

She finally got the message and backed-off. "OK, next time," she said. "But you owe me some dick."

For the next several months, Zappy and I really, truly fucked. The routine was always the same: She'd come to my place, we'd go to a local restaurant for dinner and drinks, and return to my place, wasted. Having just discovered the joys of Viagra, I would surreptitiously pop a little blue pill into my mouth before each meal. Without question, this lady was one of the better looking women I'd ever dated. Our sexual chemistry was powerful, but, every time we were in bed, we had porn star sex. We kissed only briefly, and she really wasn't interested in oral copulation. Our relationship was based solely on a "cock-pounds-hard-the-pussy" scenario.

During our months together, we managed only one daytime date. Walking along the Santa Monica Promenade, we held hands, ate pizza slices, and bought each other cheap sunglasses. It was the one time I considered her a "girlfriend." That night, we fucked three times in a row. Sweating and exhausted, we finally fell asleep.

About 4 AM, I was awakened by a tug at my arm. Me: "Huh? What's wrong?" "Danny, you're a great guy, really. I'm attracted to you, and I like you a lot. But you and I don't have any 'Zap.' I'm so sorry." Dreaming at the time, I had no idea what was happening, or if this conversation was even real. "Oh, no problem," I replied, dead asleep.

Later that morning, I awoke to find Zappy inserting my "morning wood" into her vagina. "Fuck me goodbye," she commanded, and fuck we did, both cumming very quickly. Hopping off my bed, she showered, dressed, then said, "Walk me to my car?"

We kissed. "Thanks…I had a nice time," she said, and drove off. I went to work. About three hours later, the word "Zap" popped into my head. "Did she actually tell me we had no "Zap?" Confident it had been a dream, I called my lady friend at her office: "Did you tell me last night we had no 'Zap?' Or was that my imagination?" "No, it wasn't a dream," she said. "I think you're a really sweet, funny guy, and I like you every much, but we have no future. We just don't have any 'Zap' in bed. I'm sorry. I'm not trying to hurt your feelings. I just wanted to be honest."

More than slightly dumbfounded, I replied, "Didn't we fuck like four times in the past 12 hours? Isn't THAT 'ZAP?' What is 'ZAP?' exactly…I don't understand." Without hesitation, she said: "Zap—either you have it, or you don't. We have sex, we have fucking, we have orgasms. But, I'm sorry to say, we just don't have 'Zap.' Goodbye."

So now you know how this particular "Carrot" earned her nickname.

** Chubsy-Ubsy: During yet another torturous "Rapid Dating" event, I met Chubs, a hefty blonde woman who had, quite possibly, the most beautiful, angelic face, I'd ever seen. I'd noticed her when I first walked in the room—she stared at me from afar and never stopped. I approached her: "Clearly, you're attracted to me, huh?" "Yes, I am. Very much so," she replied. "How could you tell?"
On our third date, Chubs and I wound up on her living room couch, making out. But with two cats nearby, I could feel my allergies acting up, so I stood to leave. "Wait a minute," she said, "Let me put

them in the other room. I need to talk with you." Chuby-Ubsy then regaled me with her tale: She'd been married for 12 years, divorced for eight, and had two small kids. She hadn't had sex since her divorce, when her husband left her for his secretary.

"Eight years…really? God, you must be the queen of masturbation," I joked. "Would you like to see my vibrator collection?" she replied. Large Marge looked me in the eyes: "I'm ready to be with a man again. And, if you're interested, I'm inviting you to have sex with me tonight." This woman's face was as beautiful as her body was large. I must admit I was scared at the prospect of having to fuck such a heavy partner, but I knew this woman was truly attracted to me, and who was I to turn down her offer?

The physicality of fucking Chubs was a bit tough, as her thighs and legs were huge, and difficult for me to maneuver. We did it missionary style, one time, and she came rather quickly. Honestly, I wasn't turned on all that much, but the sight of her massive breasts bobbling around was visually interesting, and it did help me climax eventually. Shortly after she came, she said, "Thank you so much… that was wonderful. Can you please sleep with me tonight? I don't want to be alone." I reminded her about my cat allergies. "Don't worry about that," she said. "I'll keep them locked in another room for the night."

Moments later, the Chubster was out cold. And then she started snoring. And I mean SNORING. I have never, ever, in my life, heard a louder sound coming from another person's mouth that wasn't a scream. I lay next to her for hours, wide awake, cringing at the inhuman (and inhumane) sounds emanating from her enormous gullet. (I was reminded of how I must have tortured redhead Angela in a similar fashion, years before.)

Every time I was thisclose to sneaking out of bed, getting dressed, and heading back to my place for peace and quiet, pangs of guilt overwhelmed me: "This woman hasn't had sex, or trusted another man, in eight years, and YOU'RE going to run away in the middle of the night? She'll be devasted. You can't do that to her—she's too nice of a person. You just have to eat shit tonight and wait for daybreak."

Morning finally arrived. I was unbelievably irritable, having been subjected to her interminably long, God-awful, snort-and-gasp session. When she walked me to her front door, she smiled. "Sleep OK?" No longer able to hold my anger, I replied, "Yeah, terrific. I especially enjoyed listening to your unbelievably loud Snoring for 9 hours. Gee, I wonder why your husband left."

I apologized immediately.

Chubs and I had several more dates after the "snoring fiasco." But as she was also one of the world's most boring conversationalists, I made sure I always had something else lined up at the end of each night. I simply had zero interest in ever fucking her again. Trying to be especially nice, she took me to see a live band for my 50th birthday. I should have told her in advance I have a hearing condition called "hyperacusis" – to me, listening to loud music, live, is comparable to someone sticking a nail file deep into my ear drums. After just minutes, I insisted she drive me back home.

"I'm really sorry I fucked up your birthday." The look of disappointment on her face was sincere. I felt like the biggest asshole in town. "Not your fault," I said. "Besides, I hate my own birthdays with all my heart. They don't interest me." I got out of her car, watched her drive away, walked inside my apartment and KISSED MY LIVING ROOM FLOOR. I looked skyward, and said, out loud, "Thank you God."

My phone rang about five days later. Chubsy: "Hi, there, listen, I don't think it's gonna work out between us. So I just wanted to say I enjoyed meeting you, and I hope you find what you're looking for. So long." Me: "Oh, really? Oh, OK, I understand. Thanks for the call."

I'd rarely been more elated.

** Ten: While attending another singles event, I bumped into Ten, by far the most attractive "Carrot" I ever pursued. I'd spent the last two hours striking out, left and right, with every other woman at this nightclub, and was just about to walk out the door when our paths crossed. A stunning blonde along the lines of a young Christie Brinkley, Ten and I sat for a time and talked.

Hand in hand, Ten and I then briefly ran three blocks to her car in the pouring rain, laughing. Inside the car, we kissed for just seconds, before exchanging phone numbers.

I wined and dined the Ten for several months, taking her to very expensive sushi, steak, and seafood restaurants. I once bought her a bottle of pricey, perfume, "because I really dig you." "Obviously," she replied.

Ten and I spent a good deal of time together, with only brief smatterings of kissing involved. One night at a club with her best friends, we had a few drinks, and danced for a while. Like magnets, we kissed passionately for the first time, and, again, in the parking lot afterward.

Ten was my date for a client Christmas party that year. Every guy's head turned as we walked into the restaurant—she was the most attractive woman in the room. My male clients were "high fiving" me during the night, assuming that I was sleeping with this raging beauty. I wasn't.

During dinner at that party, I realized I needed to have a "Come to Jesus" talk with my stunning "Carrot." "So, listen, we've been dating for a while, now. Can I ask you why we aren't having sex?" Without missing a second, my Ten replied, "Are you gonna marry me and give me two babies? Because if you'll commit to me, right now, I'll give you all the sex you could ever want in your life."

I was dumbfounded – Ten was so extraordinarily attractive, I thought I would have said or done anything to sleep with her. However, since I already had two children and a vasectomy, I knew that her request was simply not something I could have fulfilled without lying.

"Uh, err, ahm," I stammered. My penis was livid: "Tell her you'll do it, schmuck! Tell her ANYTHING! Just get me inside those panties!" My good guy/angel voice quietly whispered: "I'm afraid you'll need to let this lovely woman go. You're not going to have more children with her or anyone else, ever. Continuing this will only frustrate both of you. You have no future here."

"I adore you and I'm incredibly attracted to you," I finally answered. "But I already have two kids, and I had a vasectomy years ago. I can't give you what you're asking. God knows, I really wish I could, because I could so very easily fall in love with you. I'm really, really sorry."

Ten made a sad face. I never saw her again after that evening.

** Frenchy: I'd heard that a great place to meet singles was at the monthly gathering of an organization called "EuroCircle." Primarily a group of professionals between the ages of 25-55, EuroCircle was comprised of transplanted foreigners to Los Angeles. When I approached the check-in desk for my first-ever EuroCircle party, I was asked, "What country are you from?" "New Jersey," I replied.

The party I attended was held at the Beverly Wilshire Hotel, in a beautiful ballroom. The place was packed, and, as usual, I hit the bar immediately, quickly downing a few martinis. I scouted the place, and noticed that while many of the women there were truly beautiful, most of the MEN were even better looking. Standing in the middle of "Male Model Central," I'd suddenly become "George Costanza."

Standing in line for hors d'ouevres, I began talking with a group of five women – four of them were Russian, while the fifth, from Paris, was a thin, muscular blonde with slightly masculine features.

Frenchy and I caught a quick "spark," and, although we never sat together or even drank together (she doesn't), I boldly said, "So, we should date some-time." Without missing a beat, she handed me her card. "Call me," she said.

On our first date, she and I had dinner at a Morrocan restaurant. We sat on pillows on the floor and watched a belly dancer. That was fun.

Date two: Frenchy asked me to see an indie film about a man and a woman who abuse young children, keeping them hostage in their barn. The movie infuriated me, and I stormed out of the theater half-way through.

I had no intention of ever seeing Frenchy again after that movie disaster. But about four days later, I got an email from her. It read, "So I guess you don't want to date me, and that's fine. I understand. But to be honest with you, I'm not looking for a boyfriend. I find you attractive…so if you're interested in a purely physical relationship with me, please let me know. Otherwise, I enjoyed meeting you."

I read her message several times. "Purely physical relationship? I guess that means she wants sex with me?" I really wasn't sure.

Frenchy and I became "Fuck Buddies" for the next several years. We developed a routine that rarely varied—we called it "S & S" - "Sushi and Sex." I'd pick up a ton of sushi and bring it to my apartment. Frenchy would swing by my place about one night every two months, an exotic, French, chocolate pastry in hand. I'd have a DVD movie at the ready, and we'd eat our sushi mostly in silence while watching about 2/3rds of the film. After the food was gone, I'd take her hand and place it against my hard crotch—no words were spoken.

In my bedroom, our sex sessions usually lasted exactly an hour. The first time I saw Frenchy topless, I was shocked. She was flat as a board, with nipples that resembled small, dark brown, thumbtacks. I'd never in my life seen a woman without breasts. As I'm painfully visual, I always preferred having sex with Frenchy doggie-style, so I could look at her sensuous back, long, straight blonde hair, perfect ass, and long muscular legs (she was a runner.) While so doing, I fantasized that I was screwing Gwyneth Paltrow.

We never once changed our routine. For years and years, it remained an exact replay of the session that had come before. During our last evening together, I was giving Frenchy oral sex, something she'd always enjoyed. She asked me to stop. "You know what? I'm not feeling it anymore," she stated rather matter-of-factly. We didn't have intercourse that night, just simply finished watching the movie. She left.

The next day, Frenchy emailed me: "Just a quick note to say thank you for the years of 'S&S'. I enjoyed knowing you very much, but I have to be honest and tell you that I'm no longer sexually attracted to you. I think it's time for both of us to find new sex buddies. Let's stay in touch, and I hope we can remain friends."

Once in a very blue room, I will email Frenchy to try to lure her back to my house for one final "S&S" session. She politely blows me off, every time.

** "Manny:" I'd joined an expensive dating service called "It's Just Lunch," which—oddly enough—only arranged dinner dates for its clients. I got fixed up with a real estate developer, 20 years younger. She had a nice figure and a pleasant face, but I found her extremely short, wavy, blonde hair distracting. Her haircut made her look like a man ("Manny"—get it?)

Manny was really a great lady, but I was truly conflicted about dating her. Of course, I knew how shallow I was being. She really liked me, but I was just unable to overcome my ambivalence.

Manny and I had numerous dinners and saw a bunch of movies, usually making out briefly at the end of those dates. Shortly after we'd first met, she called me about 2 AM one night from Las Vegas: "I'm in love with you. I thought you should know that." "You're just drunk," I groggily replied. "I know," she replied, "but that's still the way I feel."

My physical reticence toward Manny remained a problem during our many months together. We had sex several times, and while it wasn't bad, it wasn't quite "right," either. After a time, I began avoiding sex with her, and, once or twice, was unable to get hard in the bedroom. "What's wrong?" she asked. Realizing it was time for some honesty, I said, "I think it's your hair. I'm attracted to women with long straight hair, and, for whatever reason, I'm not getting turned on by yours. I feel terrible about this, but I realized I can't disguise these thoughts any longer."

A few days later, I was at an amusement park with my kids, when I got a cell phone call. Manny was at an expensive, Beverly Hills hair salon: "I'm about to get long, blonde hair extensions," she informed me, "And they're thirteen-hundred dollars. I need you to split the cost, OK?" I was on the spot. "Six-fifty?" I replied in disbelief. "Is this really necessary?" Manny: "I need you to be attracted to me. So this is how we're gonna do it. Are you IN?" Me: "Yeah, sure, I guess so."

A few days later, Manny arrived, unannounced, at my office in Beverly Hills, sporting her new, long blonde locks. I was stunned— they looked so incredibly phony, I was aghast. She had tried so hard to please me, yet I felt her extraordinary efforts were in vain. During lunch that afternoon, she asked, "So, what do you think?" Me: "Urgh, ah, uhm, it looks great...very sexy...really nice job," I lied, while writing her a check for six hundred and fifty smackers.

Because I'm the world's most shallow man, I didn't see, or call, Manny again. Like the little boy that used to ring neighbors' doorbells, I was, once again, simply running away.

A few months later, Manny contacted me, and we had a brief reunion. Her hair had returned to its normal state, and she honestly looked much better that way. She told me she was dating someone new, and, much to my surprise, I felt a bit jealous. As I walked her to her car after this get together, I leaned in, and we kissed for a quick moment. Then she pulled away.

"Oh, no, get lost," she said, half-kidding. "I gave myself to you a long time ago and you blew it, buster. I'm not going to be your 'I don't have any other woman in my life right now' fuck friend. If you're horny, just go masturbate. I know it's something you enjoy doing, and you do it well. So, what's the big deal?"

CHAPTER TWENTY-SIX

Bella & Lilly

I rejoined the Speed Dating organization, in my on-going attempts to discover "The One." As I walked into a hotel lobby for yet another torturous such gathering, a woman seated there said, "Hey... remember me?" I had NO idea who she was, so I sarcastically replied, "Don't tell me we already dated?" Woman: "Well, actually, YES we have."

This woman's (not real) name was Bella ("B" from here on.)

Because she was seated at the time, I did not remember her. We'd only had one date, years earlier, when we were both members of Great Expectations. But once she stood, I did remember her, because she was so tall, I'd joked to my friends that I'd just had dinner with Kareem Abdul-Jabaar.

When B sat at my table during the speed dating evening, I had zero interest in her. I'd asked her out for a second date years ago, and at the time she blew me off. Now sitting opposite me, she took my hands into hers: "I am so sorry I didn't go out with you for that second date, when you called. That was stupid. I'm so incredibly attracted to you right now, I can't even believe it." Staring into my eyes, if I didn't know better, I would have said she was in love with me. "Can you forgive me? If you pick me tonight, I promise I'll make it up to you."

("Picking" someone meant that both the man and the woman each circled "Yes" on the "Yes" or "No" speed dating sheet handed out to all participants as they sat down.) Flattered, I did pick B that night, along with several other women.

A few nights later, B called, and asked me out for our "first new date." Wanting to keep it simple, we met for dinner at a deli near her apartment. Afterward, she invited me back to her place. There, I met "Lilly," her incredibly furry, bright white cat, and immediately felt my flesh crawling up my spine. Of the many, many cats I've had to endure in relationships with women during the course of my life, Lilly made me feel, by far, the most allergic.

B lit some candles, poured some wine, and kindly "whooshed" Lilly into the other room. I don't believe we watched the film—we instantly began making out. I ripped open her shirt and started sucking her beautiful titties. She then unzipped my pants and took the tip of my penis into her mouth, teasing it with her tongue for just a few seconds.

Pulling away, she said, "I don't want to make you cum tonight," she explained. "It's too soon. You won't see me again if I give it up so quickly. I promised myself NO SEX tonight, but I can't help myself. I'm just VERY attracted to you." I was flattered. As I walked back to my car, a throbbing Johnson in my pants, I realized she was right. I couldn't wait to see her again—soon.

The next three dates were similar—dinner, her place or mine, and making out, but no orgasms or sex—yet.

After dinner at a Thai restaurant for date four, B and I were walking along the Santa Monica Promenade. "I have something important to tell you." ANYTIME a woman says that to me, I IMMEDIATELY respond with the joke, "Don't tell me you're really a MAN??" She said: "I've been dreading this since I met you. I have to tell you two things. One is that I am incredibly horny for you and I want to fuck you so badly, you have no idea. I think about it all the time. But, the second thing is that I have HERPES. And I wanted to be honest with you. I don't know how you feel about that…"

The truth is, I didn't know <u>how</u> to feel about that bombshell. I'd been with quite a few women by this point, but never had this conversation with any of them. On one hand, I was dating a woman who turned me on sexually (even though Bella was, by no means, a looker.) But on the other, I could possibly get a disease that would affect the rest of my life.

"I really would like to have sex with you," I replied. "But I'm not sure how I feel about this. I need to give this some thought. I guess we're gonna have to hold off on our activities for a while…"

"I can still suck you off," she suggested. "I only have vaginal herpes, and it only shows up once every few months, just for a few days. I'm not contagious the rest of the time." My cock twitched. "Are you feeling 'oral' tonight?" I joked. "Honey, I'm always feeling oral," she answered.

B and I drove about 15 minutes north, to an empty parking lot in Malibu, adjacent to a noted seafood restaurant. It was pouring, pouring rain, and the lot was secluded. We both hopped into the backseat, where she practically tore my pants and underwear off. While crouching on the floor of the car, B started inhaling my penis and testicles.

After just a short while, however, and from NOWHERE, my stomach began to make an ear-numbing "gurgling" noise, and I realized that if I didn't take a massive poop within the next three minutes, B would be covered head to toe in undigested Thai food. "Oh my God," I whispered. "I have GOT to go the bathroom, RIGHT NOW!"

I pulled my pants up in seconds, leapt from the car, and ran through a hurricane-like downpour without an umbrella. I "flashed" through the parking lot and the restaurant, tore through the bar area, and zoomed into a men's room stall, convinced I'd just broken Usain Bolt's Olympic record as the world's fastest man. Miraculously, shit did NOT cover my pants, shoes, or legs, but actually went into the toilet bowl.

Re-entering my car, I felt like a complete dumb-fuck. "Sorry about that," I sheepishly said. B: "It's OK…not a big turn on, but I understand." We drove home through the pouring rain with minimum conversation.

For the next two weeks, I discussed "Bella's Herpes Condition" with everyone I knew—my friends, my doctor, my brothers and their wives. ALL of them, without exception, said "DO NOT HAVE SEX WITH THIS WOMAN! You need herpes like you need cancer." They were adamant. My sister-in-law yelled at me for even considering the option.

Having not seen her for two weeks, I called B: "Let's have a nice dinner and talk about this." I took her to my favorite, upscale Italian place, and we were seated in a very charming, corner booth, next to a young, very much in love couple, who couldn't keep their hands off each other.

"I'm really conflicted," I told her, having absolutely no idea what I was going to say next. "I'm attracted to you, I enjoy being with you and talking with you. Sex is unbelievably important to me. I masturbate daily and I think about cumming every few hours of my life." B: "Me too. I'm a sexaholic. Sex is my favorite thing on the planet. I got herpes back in high school from some asshole guy I only dated a few times. I don't reveal this to every guy I sleep with, but I knew that I had to be honest and tell you."

We sat and looked into each others' eyes, and then glanced again at the madly-in- love couple at the next table. "They seem happy," B said. Me: "So, you really, really LOVE sex? You love it as much as I do?" B: "Probably more. I'll give you all the sex you could possibly ever want or need. That's a promise."

I was completely torn. My brain shouted: "Asshole, why even take the smallest chance of getting herpes? You'll have that for the rest of your life!" While my dick countered with: "This woman will make you cum six ways to Sunday. Look at her amazing tits! What the fuck are you waiting for?"

A few more minutes of silence. And then I made my big decision. "OK, let's do it. Let's have a sexual relationship with two conditions: You have to swear that you will always tell me when you're having a flare up. And you have to always be 100% sure that I'm wearing a condom, because sometimes when I'm drunk, I forget. Deal?" B: "Absolutely. Deal." We shook hands.

B and I went to her place that night, and fucked and sucked for hours and hours, in spite of the fact that, honestly, I was never really physically attracted to her. After our sex-athon, B and I lay in her bed, exhausted. "Spend the night?" she gently requested. "Sure," I said. But after about 90 minutes, I got a severe asthma attack, something I'd not had in a million years, since childhood. I could hardly breathe. "Bella, I'd love to stay here with you, but I can't. I'm SO allergic to Lilly it's incredible. I have to go home." I split out of that apartment like Richard Pryor in 1980, after he caught fire freebasing cocaine.

For the next dozen dates or so, B came to my place, and we had massive amounts of fun, lusty, sex, likely working off some weight in the process.

NY Eve was fast approaching. "Come away for a weekend with me," I said. "I'd like to take you to my favorite, romantic getaway."

I took B up to the El Encanto Hotel in Santa Barbara (the same site where I'd had both my honeymoon with Kim, and my incredibly romantic getaway with Sharon, five years earlier). The MINUTE we got into our little bungalow room and finished putting our things away, B said, "Well, I've got a surprise for you. I JUST this SECOND got my period. Great timing, huh?"

In spite of her bloody mess, Bella and I participated in a variety of sex acts that weekend, that did not involve her troubled vagina.

During our New Year's Eve dinner, B and I had perhaps three or four drinks apiece and were laughing like idiots in the hotel restaurant. We were wearing the requisite funny pointed hats, and, at midnight, blew the requisite funny horns. On a WHIM, and DRUNK OFF MY FUCKING ASS, I leaned over the table: "Bella – I have an idea. I want you to live with me. Your lease is almost up. My lease is almost up. Let's get a brand new apartment together and make a life for ourselves. We have nothing to lose."

B started to cry. "Are you sure? Is this just drunk talk? Or do you mean it?" Me: "I want you to live with me. I want to do this. We're gonna do this, OK?" B: "Yes. OK. I'll live with you." Back in LA, we took turns during our spare time to investigate potential new apartments, investigating buildings throughout the city of Los Angeles.

"You have GOT to see this incredible place in Beverly Hills I'm standing in right now," B called me at work. "I think you'll like it." Situated in a classic building from the 1920s, this enormous, three-bedroom place had a fireplace, hardwood floors, and arched hallways. "I love it. This is it. This is our new home," I said immediately.

An "Early Warning of Impending Doom" occurred while B and I were packing up the stuff in her existing place. (She'd been living there for more than 12 years.) We broke a big fucking mirror—glass shattered everywhere. "Oh, fuck, that's not good," B said. Me: "I never told you this, but when I break glass, it always means 'Major Change.' In my world, breaking glass is a good thing." (This actually is true…usually.)

Because our existing leases were set to expire two weeks apart, B moved into the new, Beverly Hills apartment first. The moving men set her up, and I spent my evenings there afterward, helping put things in order. Then, it suddenly hit me like a brick pile. HOW THE FUCK WAS I GOING TO LIVE WITH LILLY THE CAT? "Hey, B," I called out, rooms away. "We need to talk about something." I told her that I was really nervous about Lilly, and about the possibility of having future asthma attacks. "What are we going to do if I simply can't live with Lilly?" I asked. "I'll tell you what," she said. "The new place has hardwood floors, and I'll sweep up her furballs everyday. And, if you still feel sick and you can't deal with it, I'll have my mother take her, OK?" Me: "Do you PROMISE?" B: "Yes, absolutely, I PROMISE."

If ever there was a "Promise" that I should have gotten in writing, it would have been that one. I moved into the Beverly Hills place on the first of April. This date is more commonly known as "April Fool's Day." Can you guess who the "April Fool" was that year?

(During our first weeks together in the new apartments, B and I experienced a poltergeist, who we named "Joe the Ghost." Inanimate objects moved, strange voices were heard, doors slammed, and knocking sounds banged the walls. After a Ouija board session, we determined that the "ghost" was my late Grandpa Joe, who, according to the board, told us "I am a stranger here." After we asked him to please (and politely) move along—the other-worldly activities in our house ceased instantly.)

Once I rid the apartment of my dead grandfather (by asking him nicely to leave, via Ouija,) I next began to devise a plan for doing the same to Lilly. Now living with B and her cat for two months, my allergies were in hyper-drive. My flesh crawled when I came home, my eyes were constantly red and tearing, and my nose was dripping 24/7. I'd been getting allergy shots once a week for over 25 years, and I even asked my allergist to add some "cat dander" into my allergy serum mix, so that I would, perhaps, become immune to the presence of cat.

The new shots were killing me. I never felt sicker in my life. B and I entered a new era in our relationship. All we did now was fight, bitterly, over her promise to give Lilly away. "Sorry, I changed my mind," B said during these arguments. "I'll give away my cat when YOU give away your DAUGHTER." To say these fights were becoming more and more heated would be a significant understatement.

I began to daydream, almost constantly, about ways in which I could "off" Lilly:

** I could stuff her behind our washer and dryer units, then pretend she somehow had gotten stuck back there;
** I could hire a friend of mine, a security guard who'd served in the Israeli Military, to pretend to break into my apartment, ransack the place, and kill Lilly in the process;

** I could pour clear, odor-free poison into Lilly's water dish, and then feign my sympathies when she "passed".

Of course, <u>this</u> big pussy did none of those things to Lilly, that big, white, fluffy, actual pussy.

B and I took a weekend retreat to San Diego, where we had massive amounts of sex. But when we weren't screwing, all we did was nag each other to death about the status of Lilly. Back home a few nights later, I returned from work to find B on the living room couch, sobbing. "What's wrong?" I asked. Through a barrage of tears, B whispered: "I love you so much. I thought you and I were going to get married, buy a house, and make a baby." Me: "Make a baby? You know I had a vasectomy!" B: "My father said he'd pay for you to have that reversed."

According to my surgeon, a reversal of my vasectomy would have cost over $10,000.

Me: "You know I can't live with Lilly much longer. I can't live with a cat. This experiment was a mistake. It was my mistake, and I'm really sorry." B continued to cry for hours. I went to bed.

We would sleep in separate bedrooms for the rest of our time together – a reminder of the time I did the same with my fiancé, Kim, after she discovered Jesus, exactly 20 years earlier.

My birthday was fast approaching, and my mother came to stay with us for a few days. She had a private talk with B. "Bella, dear," she said. "You and my son could really have a nice life together. I know you love him. You both have good jobs and you're making a lot of money." (B was an accountant for a top Hollywood

TV production company.) "All you have to do is get rid of your cat, and the two of you can move forward with your lives." B: "I can't do that. I love my cat more than anything else in the world. I'd sooner cut off my hand than give away my cat." My mother: "Well, then, I'm afraid the two of you are doomed to fail as a couple."

My family and friends threw me a small birthday gathering at a steak joint in Beverly Hills. As my kids, my mother, and I were getting dressed for the event, I saw that B was sitting in bed, reading. "You gonna get ready?" I asked. Calmly, B said, "No, I'm not going. I've decided not to celebrate your birthday with you. In fact, I've found a new apartment for myself and Lilly. We'll be moving out next weekend. And, by the way, I got a gift for your birthday. But I've decided I'm going to return it tomorrow."

I stood a bit stunned, frozen in my own (former) bedroom. I wasn't surprised at this news, but I was taken aback by the calm, almost psychotic manner, in which she delivered it.

Dinner sucked. B and I were breaking up, and it was announced to me on my fucking birthday. My mother took me aside. "Let's be honest," she said. "You don't really love this girl. You only THINK you love her, because she's SO IN LOVE WITH YOU!" The old bag's insight was dead-on. She was absolutely right.

When my kids, my mother, and I returned to my apartment, I entered our bedroom.

"Quick, close the door," B said. "Why? What's wrong?" I panicked. "I want you to fuck my brains out RIGHT NOW!" B pulled aside the covers, showed me her naked body, and spread her legs wide apart. "Fuck this pussy as hard as you can, birthday boy," she demanded. Ever the horny bastard, I fulfilled her request, albeit reluctantly.

It was by far the best fuck we ever had.

I watched with mixed feelings as moving men removed Bella's possessions. I would now be fully responsible for the lease agreement on this very expensive place. I also had to fork over to Bella 50% of her share of the security deposit, the washer and dryer, the draperies, and the custom closets we'd jointly purchased.

This, my "second divorce," cost me many thousands of dollars.

I walked Bella to her car. She placed Lilly inside, hugged me, and whispered, "I'm sorry this didn't work out." "A noble effort," I replied. Moments after she drove off, I found a broom, and swept every fucking square inch of that enormous apartment. It took me over two hours, and I was sweating like a pig. When I was done, I scooped up a Volkswagen-sized ball of errant cat fur and tossed it into the trash can behind the garage.

I came back inside, opened every window in the place, took in a long, deep inhale, and then slowly and gently exhaled.

At that moment, I never felt happier, healthier, or freer, in my entire life.

CHAPTER TWENTY-SEVEN

Marti and Tales of Auschwitz

I'd been invited to a "Summer Singles" party at the Bel Air Bar and Grill, where I quickly downed several martinis. An hour in, a woman entered the room, as though moving in slow motion – a soft spotlight seemed to shine on her long, light brown hair and angelic face. I knew instantly I had to meet this person, and intro'd myself quickly. "You caught my eye," I said to her, "And I need to know who you are." "I'm Marti," she replied. "And if you wanna buy me a Cosmo, I wouldn't say 'no.'"

We sat on a bench at the side of the restaurant, drinking and talking, for some time. We covered a lot of ground. Just a few months younger than me, Marti worked as the office manager for a chiropractor, was a long-divorced mother of four adult children and was even a grandma. "Are you serious?" I asked. "My grandmother didn't look like you." We laughed.

We also covered favorite TV shows, and realized we had *The X-Files* in common. When she had to leave, I walked Marti to the valet parking attendant, who quickly pulled up her car. We exchanged phone numbers, and did a quick huggie/kissie thing, before she drove away. Standing next to the valet, I said, "I think I just met my second wife."

On our first date, Marti and I had Italian food for dinner, then attended a movie, but didn't see much of it. Marti had placed her legs in my lap, and we were making out like idiots during much of the film (shades of my *Schindler's List* experience.) A few dates later, while walking along Santa Monica beach on a wonderfully sunny afternoon, I decided to have my famous "Do you happen to enjoy sex?" talk, but she beat me to it. "You should probably know I'm a nymphomaniac," Marti revealed. "So anytime you might wanna have sex with me, all you gotta do is ask."

We ran to my car, flew back into my apartment, and leaped into bed. We had sex for hours. It was exhilarating to be with someone new who loved sex for sex's sake and had no interest in getting married or having any more children.

I learned early on that Marti's parents and two brothers were Orthodox Jews, and that she had also been Orthodox during the marriage to her husband (the father of her four kids.) A few months into our new dating relationship, Marti told me that her parents had invited me to their house for Rosh Hashanah, the Jewish New Year. Having not attended a dinner for a major Jewish holiday in decades, I was flattered. While driving together to her parents' house, Marti happened to tell me, "Oh, by the way, my parents are both Auschwitz survivors. My father will probably bore you to tears with some of his stories…"

My dinner with Marti and her parents that night was mesmerizing. Her mom, busy serving food and cleaning up, clearly did not enjoy talking—or reminiscing—about her years as a Nazi concentration camp "guest" at Auschwitz. However, Marti's father had no such qualms, and began regaling me with his tales of wonder. As he did, I saw tears in the mother's eyes, and noticed a faded ID number still tattooed on her right forearm.

Long story short: Marti's parents were third cousins to each other, and grew up together in Micalovce, Czechoslovakia. As teenagers, they'd just begun to date, until one day, a Nazi soldier came to the home where the mom and her family lived. The six of them were quickly swept away to the camp. Martin, Marti's dad, was working as a clerk in a watch repair store, when another Nazi soldier entered and asked him for his I.D. Martin said, "It's in the back room. Please give me a minute to bring it to you. I'll be right back." Brilliantly, he calmly walked through the rear door of the store, devoid of any possessions, and fled for his life.

Martin and a small band of fellow Jews from his hometown lived in the nearby woods—they LIVED IN THE FUCKING WOODS—for the next several years. They slept in the mud, froze their balls off, and killed small animals with their bare hands to eat. They would ambush the occasional one or two Nazi soldiers who would be riding horses through the woods looking for a place to piss or shit. Martin and his cohorts would jump on these bastards from behind, slitting their throats, removing their uniforms, and killing their horses for food.

At one point, Martin learned that a nearby schoolhouse filled with Jewish children was going to be inspected by Nazis. Their assignment was to lead those kids to a train car for a trip to the camps. Martin put on the uniform of one of the Nazi soldiers he'd killed, and, nonchalantly, marched into the town and straight to the school. He managed to corral the Jewish children into a single line, and whispered to them that, if they followed him closely, he'd lead them from danger. The kids did as they were told, and Martin led them through the center of town, as several other Nazi soldiers who were smoking cigarettes nearby, watched. Laughing, they waved Martin on, as if to say, "Good job! Get those little Jew fucks onto the trains!" Once past the town square, Martin led the children to safety in the woods, where they were joined by other refugees.

Somehow, Martin had learned the exact location of the concentration camp housing structure where Marti's mother and her family were confined. He'd bring a loaf of bread with him, and, while standing on the other side of a barbed wire fence, would throw hunks of the bread over the top and into their eager hands.

I listened to Martin's stories for at least an hour, in complete silence, tears streaming down my face. Marti seemed restless—she'd obviously heard these stories countless times throughout the course of her life. Her mom kept her head down at the table, teary-eyed. She remained silent during the entire dinner.

I realized that it's one thing to read about—or watch a documentary film about—the Holocaust, but it's something entirely different to hear these stories, in person, from an actual survivor. At the end of Martin's tales of horror, I wiped off my tears, looked at both he and his wife, and said, "Both of you are heroes. Thank you for surviving. And thank you for making Marti."

During the months Marti and I were together, we met many of each other's friends and family members, celebrated numerous holidays together, watched every single episode of *The X-Files* on DVD, and had massive amounts of sex.

However, the longer I was with Marti, the more I realized a number of things were bothering me:

** Marti was slightly deaf. During sex, I'd whisper dirty talk like, "Oh, baby, that feels so good when you suck me," to which she'd reply, "Eh, what? What'd you say? Huh? Didn't hear you?" A terrific mood killer;

** Marti was incredibly soft spoken, and mumbled. Since I, myself, also have a slight hearing problem (certain frequencies have been lost to me,) this made for a "double whammy" in the miscommunication department;

** Marti's life revolved around the activities of her children and grandchildren. Almost every weekend involved a religious service, a holiday meal, a baby-sitting assignment, a wedding, a briss, etc. I hadn't felt this "Jewish" since my Bar Mitzvah, and, quite frankly, wasn't all that interested in re-visiting that era of my life;

** This one is painfully shallow, but I have to include it here: Marti's left breast was about ½ the size of her right one. While I don't consider myself anywhere near handsome, I can't help but be visually "disturbed" by a woman's flaws, likely a result of my years of worshipping Playboy centerfold girls. Every time Marti and I had sex, I'd do my best not to look at her left tit, focusing my line of sight, instead, on the right, normal sized one;

> ** Marti took FOREVER to cum. By this point, I'd become pretty accomplished in bed, and usually didn't have a problem bringing a woman to climax. Marti, however, simply could not cum from intercourse or even from oral sex. She could only orgasm from a man's hand rubbing her clit in a swirling, circular motion. Most of the time, this rubbing activity took anywhere from 20-40 minutes. I'd be laying on my back, falling asleep, while my right hand would become numb from over-stimulation. She'd say things like, "Faster, slower, little circles, big circles, clockwise, counter clock-wise," etc. My poor wrist felt like it was in the Marine Corps.

Marti and I took a trip back East that fall, to visit both my mother and her daughter, then attending college in Manhattan. We met a bunch of relatives and friends and had a terrific time. My childhood buddy, Steve, now owned a very popular nightclub in NYC called "The Cutting Room," where Marti and I spent a few hours drinking. About to get sick from one too many of Steve's freebies, Marti called a cab, and ushered me back to our hotel.

"You know I love you, right?" I drunk-declared, the hotel elevator spinning like a top. Marti, "Yeah, yeah, you love me. I love you, too. But you're pretty wasted right now, so this doesn't really count."

Just a hair before Christmas, Marti came down with a terrible case of the flu. We were supposed to attend a holiday party in Hollywood being thrown by one of my clients, but when I arrived to pick her up, she was green, puking and had a fever. "Go without me…I'll be fine," she said. "No way," I replied. "You're sick as a fuck. I'll stay here with you."

Ill for weeks, Marti recovered just in time for New Year's Eve. I made arrangements for us to attend a party at a hotel in Santa Monica and booked us a room that overlooked the Pacific Ocean. That night, we ate a wonderful dinner, drank a ton of liquor, danced to a live band, and had what was probably the hottest sex of our "career."

Two weeks later, for Marti's birthday, we had dinner at a dark little Mexican restaurant in West Hollywood. Back at her place, we made love on the living room floor. For the first time, the idea of possibly proposing marriage momentarily flashed through my mind.

The next day, Marti called: "I need to talk with you." I knew, instinctively, something was wrong. She continued, "I love you, and you love me. But I've decided I don't ever want to get remarried, and I don't even want a boyfriend right now. I think I need to be alone for a while, and re-discover who I am, and what I want. You're a great guy, but I think we should probably both walk away at this point."

While I certainly was taken aback by this phone call, I was also quite relieved. I'd been rehearsing a "Marti, I love you, BUT..." speech in my head for weeks. Now here was Marti, once again beating me to the punch. "Can we have a goodbye dinner, at least?" I requested. "Sure."

We went to an Italian joint in Beverly Hills and had a number of cocktails along with our pasta. Afterward, we stood on the sidewalk, waiting for a valet to bring our cars. Drunk, Marti slurred: "You wanna know why I REALLY broke up with you?" "Yes, of course," I replied. "Your penis is too big for me! Every time we had sex, I got a yeast infection, and it hurt." She started to laugh. I said, "Marti, that's called a 'back-handed compliment.' Most guys would kill to hear a woman tell them that their Johnson was too big. But I'm really glad you told me – it explains a lot of things. I'm sorry for any time I hurt your poor little pussy."

We kissed briefly, until the valet arrived.

When my mother asked why Marti and I had broken up, I was honest with her: "Ma, my cock was too big for her pussy." Without missing a beat, the old crow, God bless her, actually said, "Hasn't she ever heard of LUBE?"

Marti and I became extremely close, both as lovers and friends. But throughout the course of our relationship, I always knew in the back of my mind, that our time together would be finite. If ever I'd had a girlfriend who could have been described as "close, very close, but no cigar," Marti would have been that one.

CHAPTER TWENTY-EIGHT

Hollywood Hotties

As my business continued to prosper, I was now attending film festivals, movie premieres, luncheons and parties on a regular basis. I was also asked several times to speak about the entertainment public relations business at various industry events and colleges, including UCLA. As a result of my new-found Hollywood "exposure," I was also now meeting more and more women in "the business" who worked either in front of, or behind, the camera lens.

** The Sitcom Blonde: I was running the PR for the Hollywood Film Festival, and had to ensure that the guest of honor, Kirk Douglas, was escorted onstage to receive his Lifetime Achievement Award. During this organized chaos, I was stuck at one point amongst the crowd in the hotel's ballroom and found myself standing next to a very attractive woman. I recognized her immediately from her role as the "hot blonde daughter" from a classic '80's TV series.

Sitcom Blonde and I had instant chemistry, and her smile made me completely forget what I was doing there. We spoke for just a few minutes. I said, "Listen, I would do anything to just stay here and flirt with you tonight, but I'm running the PR for this event, and I've gotta go get Kirk Douglas. Sorry!" "No worries," she said, taking a business card from her purse, and stuffing it into my jacket pocket. "We can always continue this conversation another time. Call me." Big smile.

I felt like I'd just been handed a winning lottery ticket.

Cut to my "Carrots" reality: I called her several times in the coming weeks, and she spoke so softly on the phone I could barely hear. She was completely depressed, her sorrow unmistakable. "I'm going through a terrible divorce right now...a really, really, awful divorce," she whispered. "I probably shouldn't have given you my number. You seem like a cool guy, but I'm just not ready to date."

I added her card to my collage of useless phone numbers.

** The Competitor: I appeared on a panel for the Publicist's Guild, and afterwards, a knock-out brunette approached me. The owner of a very successful entertainment PR agency, she was one of my competitors. "Let's have dinner sometime," she suggested.

We met at my favorite Beverly Hills restaurant (the "late" Kate Mantilini's,) and the first half hour of the date was very pleasant. Then, I ordered my third martini, and shortly thereafter devolved into "Buddy Love," the arrogant character played by Jerry Lewis from *The Nutty Professor*.

During the course of the next 90 minutes, I managed to insult my date repeatedly by:

** Telling her that her middle name sucked;
** Insinuating that her most recent boyfriend, who dumped her without a good reason, "was probably gay and was afraid to tell you";
** Joking that my favorite hobby was "masturbation;" and
** Commenting, "God, you must look so hot in a bikini!"

I was so intimidated both by her looks and the fact she was a competitor that I became an extraordinarily obnoxious idiot.

When I wasn't busy insulting her, I tossed out other great lines, such as:

** You are so <u>fucking beautiful!</u>
** Where have you been all my life?

And of course, my personal favorite – telling the valet parking lot attendant, "Guys, say hello to my second wife!"

When I emailed her again a few days later for a second date, she responded with the longest "go fuck yourself" note imaginable, one detailing my every faux pas. She began with, "You seemed like a great guy at first, and you're very cute BUT," and then detailed for me, line by line, the countless screw-ups I'd made that night.

Had I been a normal person, I think this woman and I would have made an excellent match. But after all those drinks, my lack of self-confidence returned, and I felt I didn't deserve to be with such a "winner."

I suppose I blew this one on purpose.

** The Bikini Model: I met this 21-year-old blonde beauty at the launch party for a new Hollywood magazine. She was so pretty, I could have sworn a spotlight followed her around the room. A dead ringer for a younger, thinner, Jessica Simpson, she was a professional bikini model. Her manager handed me her card: "She could use a good publicist," he told me.

Bikini Model and I had dinner at a very stylish Japanese restaurant overlooking the city of Los Angeles. She was so striking, heads turned when we walked into the place. As we ate, I realized that not only was she a quiet talker, but she also had "mush mouth"—basically she was unable to complete full sentences, pronounce words clearly, or even articulate a cohesive thought, in anything resembling the English language. This young girl either had a serious speech impediment, ADD, or, most likely, was simply a bimbo. Perhaps some combination of all three of those afflictions?

Because her face and figure were so extraordinarily heavenly, however, I just didn't care. I faked my way through the meal, not understanding two words she said. As we waited for the valet to bring my car around, we kissed, briefly. It was sweet and lovely and very romantic.

For date two, we went out for sushi. Again, I couldn't understand her words, and just nodded my head a lot. In front of her apartment upon our return, she refused to kiss me goodnight. Intuitively, I think she was on her period.

Our third and final date: Dinner at a fun Chinese place. I was beginning to understand how to "interpret" her unique form of the English language, and we almost had a real conversation. After dinner, we wound up playing videogames at an arcade.

I drove her home, she invited me upstairs. Inside her small apartment, we stood a foot apart, staring at each other. After a few awkward seconds, she said, "I just got a new mattress." Sitting on the bed, she began to demonstrate its "bounce" factor, by pushing down on it several times. She then smiled up at me. Was this her way of "inviting" me to have sex with me? Or, in her child-like simplicity, was she just proudly showing off her new bed?

Jiminy Cricket's voice popped into my head: "Dude, she is SO young! How can you even THINK about fucking her? You could be her grandfather." Call it guilt, call it conscience, call it fear. For whatever reason, I remained standing, then made an executive decision: If she was this responsive to me on our NEXT DATE, I'd make a move for sure.

"I should go," I said. She walked me down to my car, and we hugged goodbye. "I had a really fun time," I THINK she mumbled. A week later, I called for another date. No answer. I emailed her. No answer. This continued for about a month, until she responded. She'd been travelling across the country at various bikini competitions and had been too busy to get back to me. I asked: "When can we have dinner again?" to which she replied, "Soon. I'll let you know."

I never saw her again. When I look at her photos now, I can't believe I didn't "go for the gold" that one night, when she might have been offering me sex on her new bed, via her inimitable and unintelligible, way.

** Stallone's Friend: I met this brunette, a friend of Sylvester Stallone's, at the Beverly Hills Hotel's world-famous Polo Lounge. A "match" from Match.com, we had an impromptu dinner date – our chemistry was great. I was so nervous, though, I, once again, went into buffoon mode, quickly downing three martinis in a row. Before coffee and desert, the Polo Lounge began to spin like a Ferris Wheel – I excused myself from the table, went outside onto the patio, and surreptitiously threw up into some bushes.

This woman suggested I take her home. The world's biggest moron, I DROVE my car from the hotel, taking both of our lives into my drunken hands. (The valet attendants there had no business handing me back my keys.) We marched into my apartment, and she headed straight to the bedroom. She lay on my bed, pulled off her shoes, pants, and panties, and spread her legs. "Feel like eating pussy?" she asked.

I felt like I was dying. I was so drunk that my brain was hurtling down an enormous abyss without bottom. My world was spinning out of control. In spite of my death throes, however, I managed to shove my face into her snatch, and began showing off my honed oral sex techniques.

Under normal circumstances, I would have fucked this woman silly just then. But I was so beyond drunk, I had to stop "eating" after just a few minutes. I rushed into the bathroom for another vomit session.

"I'm not feeling well...I better get you home now," I somehow announced. "Really? Oh, that's too bad. You are a very good pussy eater," she nonchalantly said, pulling her clothes back on. "I was just getting into it."

The world's biggest putz, I once again drove my car (she lived not far from me.) After dropping her off curbside. I raced back to my bathroom, where I remained praying to the porcelain God for the rest of the night.

** The Crime Scene Queen: I was introduced to this actress through mutual friends. A Russian native, where she'd been a renowned ballerina, this woman had next worked as a stripper in Las Vegas before moving to Hollywood to pursue acting. Recently, she'd become established as a regular, recurring character on a hit cable TV crime drama series.

I picked her up, and we had a great sushi dinner, talking and laughing for hours. A soft blonde with sky blue eyes, I was extremely attracted to her, and honestly felt we had a connection. Early in the meal, she told me she was divorced and that her ex-husband was her best friend. She also said her life would become fulfilled if she could just meet a "great new guy to become involved with and make some amazing sex."

The SECOND I got the check at the end of this two-hour meal (somewhere in the neighborhood of $140,) this stunner said: "You know what? I've changed my mind. I've decided that it's OK for me to be alone. I'm not interested in DATING or MEN, anymore. I think I wanna just stay single."

This 180-degree change of direction happened before my very eyes! Somehow, I'd managed to alter this woman's life goals during the course of just one meal!

The "Carrots Curse" strikes, yet again.

** The Soap Star: One of my longtime clients created special effects makeup, characters, and creatures for major TV shows and movies like *Star Trek*. For many years, he also threw the most amazing Halloween parties in Hollywood, since most attendees worked in the special effects industry, and tried to out-do each other with their extraordinary costumes.

During one such Halloween party, I was dressed as an escaped convict from Alcatraz. I saw, from across the room, a killer, beautiful blonde, wearing a policewoman costume, complete with black mini-skirt and fishnet stockings. Boldly, I approached her and said, "You should arrest me," to which she replied, "You're right. I think I will." She handcuffed me, and we danced for hours.

A former (and quite well-known) daytime actress, Soap Star was now going through a painful divorce, having just found out that her husband had been cheating on her for many years. "Forget him, you've met me now. I'll take care of you," I drunkenly said. "Great!" she replied, "That makes you my new best friend."

The next week, we had a very romantic dinner at my favorite Japanese place. We were there for hours, and I felt we'd truly bonded. "I'm so glad I met you," she said softly, gazing deeply into my eyes. "It's so great to finally meet one man in Hollywood that I can trust." I walked her to her car, and we hugged goodbye. "Next week, dinner and movie, OK?" I asked. "Absolutely," she answered. "100 percent yes."

I called a few days later for the follow-up date. Soap Star on phone: "Listen, Dan, ahh, err, uhmm, I'm not sure how to tell you this. But I just hired a divorce lawyer, and he's so fuckin' hot, it's scary. So I decided I'll be dating him now, instead of you. Sorry! But let's stay in touch, OK?"

Only in Hollywood, folks.

CHAPTER TWENTY-NINE

UFOs, Bethany and the Field of "Orbs"

Wandering through a bookstore, I came across the "Paranormal" aisle, and noticed a sea of books about UFOs, extra-terrestrial beings from other galaxies, and alien abductees. The sight of those titles made me "flash back" to an incident that I'd completely forgotten about, which took place when I was just 13.

My father had just picked me up from Hebrew school one sunny afternoon. We'd turned onto our street, when I peered through the windshield, and saw something enormous in the sky. "Dad, stop the car!" I demanded. I hopped out quickly, and stared in disbelief at the ENORMOUS, FLYING "V" UFO that was slowly and silently gliding across the sky, directly above our heads. When we got home, I ran to the phone in our kitchen, and called the editorial department of our area newspaper. A woman answered: "Yes, young man. How can I help you?" Breathless, I relayed the story of my sighting. She responded: "We're getting dozens of calls about this right now. I've gotta go but thank you for letting us know." I checked our newspaper every day for the rest of that week, but nothing ever ran about my tri-tipped spacecraft sighting.

Suddenly re-discovering a long-lost topic of personal interest, I left that bookstore with an armful of books, and began reading about the study of "UFOlogy." I was fascinated by legendary UFO sightings that took place in Washington State, Mexico City, Florida, Texas, Phoenix, Washington, D.C., the Bermuda Triangle, the UK, and above New York State; UFO saucer crashes covered up by the government, including those in Roswell; Aurora, Texas; Kecksburg, PA; and elsewhere; the abductions of Betty and Barney Hill; Hitler's flying saucer research and "flying disc" program and the various theories behind the international, governmental cover-up of visitors from Outer Space.

After extensive study, I came to realize that extra-terrestrial biological entities have been visiting Earth for tens of thousands of years. I joined MUFON (the Mutual UFO Network) in Los Angeles and began attending that organization's monthly meetings. I also heard lectures across Southern California on this topic, one that had become unexpectedly important to me.

Concurrent with my newfound UFO fascination, I got a call from a woman I'd paid $1500 to for matchmaking services a year earlier. I'd forgotten that she even existed. "I've found the perfect woman for you," she said. "An Emmy Award-winning writer for television. She's smart, funny, Jewish and has a great sense of humor." Me: "Is she attractive?" Lisa: "Well, I think so."

Bethany became my next "Carrot."

Our first date was very pleasant. She and I went to an Indian food restaurant near her apartment in Studio City. We talked and joked and laughed for a long while. I learned that her father was also a brilliant scientist who'd invented technology for the government (we had that in common,) and her mother was a retired schoolteacher. She also had a sister who was a schoolteacher in Massachusetts, but one who'd never married. "She's the oddball in the family," Bethany revealed of her sibling.

For our second date, we had Chinese food, and I drank two martinis. We saw a movie, and afterward, (as she'd say later) I "kidnapped her" into having an ice cream sundae for dessert. I walked her to her apartment door and tried to kiss her goodnight. As Bethany later told it, my mouth was open as "wide as a lion's. I thought you were going to eat my face off! You scared me away."

That Christmas Day, I spent time with my children, when I got a call from my matchmaker. "What did you do to poor Bethany?" she asked. "She wants nothing to do with you." I was taken aback. First of all, I barely remembered even trying to kiss her, and secondly, I thought she kissed me back. "I tried to kiss her goodnight, that's all. I didn't jump on her, rape her, or grab her boobs. What is she telling you?" The woman explained that I'd been "much too aggressive" with Bethany, and that, "unless you do some serious apologizing, you'll never see her again."

The rest of that holiday weekend, I was so annoyed, I cleaned my enormous apartment from top to bottom. I scrubbed every hardwood floor in the place, on my hands and knees, with a bucket, Playtex gloves and a scrub brush. I could not believe that I'd scared this new woman away so quickly.

Finally, I got up the nerve to call Bethany. "Listen, I hear that I mauled you last week. I'm sorry. I didn't mean to do that. I would never hurt you, ever, in any way. I'd like to see you again, but if you don't want to, I understand. I just wanted you to know that I am truly sorry." She admitted that she was attracted to me, and that I was a "great guy," but she was NOT seeking a highly physical or sexual relationship "just yet." "If we have chemistry together," she explained, "then I'm certainly open to sleeping with you. But that's not what I'm looking for right away."

Bethany gave me a shot at a third date. A total gentleman, I never once touched her. Dates 4, 5, and 6 were similar, and, by date seven, she agreed to come to my apartment for dinner by my fireplace. I cooked the one and only dish I knew (lemon chicken). We ate, drank wine and watched TV. After we cleaned up, we curled up next to each other on my couch, the fireplace roaring, and we kissed.

The first second I kissed Bethany, I had the utterly odd feeling that she and I were RELATED. Kissing her felt like I was kissing my Aunt Edie (my mother's sister) back in Brooklyn. The feeling wasn't sexy or intriguing or romantic. It felt like I was literally kissing my SISTER, if, in fact, I actually had a sister.

After just a short time we both stopped kissing each other. "Well, that was interesting," she said. "Interesting…yes, I think that is the right word for it," I added.

For the next ten months, B and I became inseparable. She met all of my friends, my children, my parents, my brothers, and even my ex-wife. Everyone told me that "Bethany was 'The One.'"

Bethany made dinners for me at her apartment at least once or twice a week, and we'd take turns renting old, classic movies, that one, or the other of us, had never seen before. After the movies, we'd kiss for a while, hop into bed and have unbelievably awkward sex.

The first few times we screwed, Bethany said, "You fuck like you're starring in a porn film!" (Little did she know.) "You fling me across the bed, turn me upside down and inside out, and expect me to talk dirty to you and fulfill your perverted fantasies! I just want to make love with you…can't we just simply make love to each other?"

I had a huge problem: I was NOT at all sexually attracted to Bethany. She reminded me of a blood relative. Plus, her appearance just didn't "do it" for me. She wasn't exactly "thin," and her clothing, hairstyle, and choice of eyewear all made her resemble an old Jewish "Bubbie" from 1940's Brooklyn.

I did my best to "make love" to Bethany for the months we slept together, while she also tried—a few times—to "porn-up" her approach to the process. One afternoon, we spent an hour in the "Trashy Lingerie" store in Beverly Hills, as she tried on a variety of sexy outfits. Not to be cruel, but her "zaftig" figure simply did NOT work well in the red and black bustier costume she wound up purchasing. It made me cringe.

After the first few times I had sex with Bethany, I realized my penis was disinterested. He wasn't getting as hard as he should, so, halfway through each date with her, I'd sneak off to the bathroom to pop a quick Viagra pill. Once or twice, when she wanted spontaneous sex, she'd rip off my clothes and try to mount me. But without the advance kick of my little "blue friend," those efforts were in vain.

The therapist I was seeing at the time suggested that I hire a hypno-therapist she knew to HYPNOTIZE ME so that I would be attracted to her! This hypnotist happened to be an incredibly hot, older blonde woman, whose blouse was half unbuttoned during our entire session, distracting me no end. She managed to plant the suggestion in my subconscious that the next time I slept with Barbara, I would "think about the hottest sex I ever had with a different woman, and fantasize about her, instead." (I wound up thinking about Sarah...)

This post-hypnotic suggestion actually worked one time, although while I was screwing Bethany, I felt like I was cheating. Once I realized that having to be hypnotized to be attracted to my girlfriend simply was NOT the kind of relationship I wanted, I told her we needed to talk. "Bethany, I love you. You're the nicest, smartest, best woman I've ever known. But our physical connection just doesn't work—I think you know that already." Bethany: "Yes, of course I do. I'm not stupid." Me: "The only way I can explain it, is that it feels to me like we're related somehow. When I'm with you in bed or kissing you, I feel like I'm having sex with one of my aunts from back East. It's the strangest thing—I've never had this experience before with any other woman. I'm really, really sorry, but I just can't be sexual with you any longer."

Bethany nodded. "I absolutely agree. I really wish we had that physical chemistry thing, because I love you very much also. I think we're probably doomed to just being friends, I guess." "Best friends," I added.

Both of our mothers thought we were nuts. "So what's holding you up in marrying my Bethany?" her mother once asked me, point blank, during a deli lunch also attended by Bethany and her father. Me: "Well, urh, ah, uhmmm, I love her, I really do love her, but I don't think we're 'IN LOVE' with each other." B's Mom: "Well GET IN LOVE!" Her father was awash in embarrassment.

After my mother met Bethany, she said: "So what's wrong with THIS ONE? This girl is PERFECT for you. You should marry her tomorrow." Me: "Ah, mom, our sex life is terrible. It doesn't work. Screwing her is like screwing Aunt Edie." My mother: "That's ridiculous. You could find a pimple on Jesus' ass. You're obviously a moron."

For the next eight months, Bethany and I did, in fact become BEST FRIENDS. Together, we went everywhere, did everything, helped each other with every problem, on a virtual 24/7 basis. She helped my daughter write a major essay for college, helped me identify the fact that my son had Asperger's Syndrome, and took my daughter to her first, ever ballet.

I gave Bethany feedback on the book she was writing, advice on how to get payments from her freelance writing clients who were in arrears, and even attended her parents' 50th wedding anniversary dinner as her "boyfriend."

I was also able to interest Bethany in my UFO studies. She and I would attend MUFON meetings together, fascinated by the speakers and their home movies. We'd laugh hysterically by the questions asked by some of the whack-o attendees. ("Do you think that Mr. Spock and Darth Vadar were related?" asked an enormous man, of a world renowned UFO investigator. Bethany and I nicknamed the huge guy, "Tiny.")

One such MUFON seminar featured a cleric named James Gilliland, who owned a ranch in upstate Washington. His property was a world famous UFO hot spot, as the skies above it offered spectacular UFO shows almost nightly. The site had been researched by hundreds of authors, scientists, and professors, as well as by the U.S. Air Force, NASA, and the FBI. Gilliland held an annual 4th of July gathering at his ranch every year, attracting UFO buffs from around the world. I asked Bethany if she'd go with me. "Are we gonna sleep in the same bed?" Me: "Yes, of course." Bethany: "Let me think about it."

After a couple of weeks of my hounding her, Bethany finally relented. "OK, I'll go to the UFO ranch with you, but you have to promise me that you'll bring your CPAP machine. You snore like a wild boar." (I'd invested in a machine that alleviated my snoring the year before. It was heavy and clumsy and had to be filled with water, but my gal-pal insisted I schlep it to upstate Washington.)

We flew first to Portland and stayed one night (in twin beds) at an old hotel. We had dinner and drinks, then returned to our room. Later, as she drifted off to sleep, I surprised even myself with: "Hey Bethany, I'm horny…wanna screw?" (I really have no idea why I said this.) She was completely upset. "I knew you'd do this to me. You don't care anything about my needs or feelings. No, I don't want screw. Go jerk off in the bathroom…leave me alone."

I apologized profusely, and the next morning we drove a zillion miles through the magnificent mountains and forests of upstate Washington, until we finally arrived at a cozy little bed and breakfast place. That week, Bethany and I attended several seminars about UFO sightings, heard theories about ancient aliens (those who helped construct the pyramids in Egypt and Central and South America,) and watched an interesting documentary film about "Orbs," something I'd never heard of before. Orbs are bright, usually round-shaped lights that appear only in digital photos or on film. They often appear floating about a person or group of people. Theories about orbs vary. Some believe they are physical manifestations of the dead, either human or animal. Some people think they're visitors from other dimensions.

That first night, dozens of people set up lawn chairs on Gilliland's ranch property, and shot hundreds of digital photographs of themselves, dancing and singing. Bethany and I joined in the activities, and each of us taking turns with the camera. Very prominent orbs appeared surrounding us, within those photos.

While sitting in the field of "Orbs" every night that week, we'd see bright lights, moving in all directions across the sky, every few hours. However, I was skeptical—these lights could have been meteors, or comets, or shooting stars, or satellites. It wasn't until our third night in the field, that we all saw an enormous, bright light – a greenish color you'd never find in nature – slowly skimming across the sky. The light STOPPED directly above us, BLINKED ON AND OFF A FEW TIMES, and then SIMPLY VANISHED. Clearly NOT a meteor, comet, shooting star or satellite, everyone in the field applauded. My heart beat fast. This was, without question, a bona fide, 100% UFO sighting!

For the next five months, Bethany and I continued our "best buddies" routine without interruption. We'd become family to each other and did everything possible together under the sun EXCEPT have sex. Then, one day just before the holidays in December, she called me. "I need to talk with you about something. It's important. Can I come over now?" I knew this wasn't gonna be pretty.

I was cleaning out my car, which was parked in my garage, when Bethany pulled her car up in the alley where I was standing. I could tell immediately she'd been crying. "We need to talk," she said. We sat on the ground between our two cars. "I love you very, very much, and I know that you love me, too. And I just have to tell you that it's killing me that we're never gonna marry each other. I decided I can't just be friends with you any longer, Danny. I love you too much."

She began sobbing. I felt like a total piece of crap. "I am so, so sorry," I offered. "I really wish things were different between us. I don't understand why 'karma' or 'fate' or 'destiny' would play this cruel trick on us." I held her in my arms as she cried.

"Listen, I'm starving," I said, trying to alleviate the sad moment. "Can we at least have a goodbye deli sandwich?" She laughed, "Sure, I guess so." After a quick lunch, I managed to talk her into helping me shop for a hat to cover my bald head.

Back at my house, I drove her to her car. "We can still be friends, right?" I asked. "No, I'm sorry. You don't understand. I CAN'T SEE YOU ANYMORE AT ALL. It's too painful," she said. At that moment it really hit me. I was about to lose my very best friend. A few tears filled my eyes, and I realized she wasn't joking around.

"Fuck!" I said. "I don't think I can live without you. What am I supposed to do now?" Sobbing again, Bethany waved goodbye, and drove away. While we've emailed each other a few times afterwards, I haven't seen her since the day she helped me select the "rakish" hat I wear to this day.

It took me many months to "de-Bethany-ize" my head, my heart, and my life.

CHAPTER THIRTY

"These Are a Few Of My Favorite Whores"

I was sick to death of trying to pursue, develop, manage, and maintain a relationship. Having tried and tried, and failed and failed, I realized I had no idea how to make one work. I thought about the lyrics from a song Neil Diamond wrote for The Monkees:

"I thought love was only true in fairy tales.
Meant for someone else but not for me.
Love was out to get me.
That's the way it seemed.
Disappointment haunted all my dreams."
The only problem was, I was incapable of becoming "A Believer."

My sexual hunger was out of control. Having just come off a series of fairly regular sexual encounters, Mr. "Angry" in my undershorts had become accustomed to frequently exploring the cavernous regions of vagina. "More, more, more," he'd scream at night – his voice so pervasive it was impossible to ignore. I was making more money than I could spend, and decided, after much inner-debate, that returning to the world of "pay-per-play" offered me the best option by which to feed my insatiable little friend.

I'd remained in touch with Ava Cadell, the actress/model who I'd befriended during my years at The Playboy Channel. Having not seen each other in many years, we wound up having lunch. During the interim time apart, she'd become a noted therapist, author and lecturer on all things sex-related. I confided in her my dating dilemma and my ceaseless sexual urges. Without missing a beat, she said, "Dan, every normal man needs to get laid several times a week. If you're not in a serious relationship, why don't you just hire a Call Girl? I know lots of beautiful women around town who you'd love to be with. Their rates are reasonable, and they're full-service. They'll come to your home and will give you as much pleasure as you pay for."

I told Ava that a number of times in the past, I'd enjoyed having sex with hookers, prostitutes and street-walkers. My heart racing, my palms sweaty, the entire interaction, from the first meet to the money negotiation to the stripping of clothes to the act itself, provided me with sexual stimulation at a greatly heightened level. The adrenaline rush, coupled with the thrill of the unknown, provided me with far more excitement than I was able to achieve by "making love" with a girlfriend or a "normal" date. Knowing that something could go wrong at any moment – I could be robbed, ripped off, arrested – also added to the "high" of the entire experience. It turned me on beyond words.

Plus, to paraphrase Charlie Sheen: "I don't pay hookers for sex. I pay hookers to leave."

My bosomy friend gave me a phone number. "Call J," she suggested. "She's an attractive blonde with a terrific body. She's a friend of mine. Tell her I sent you."

The first time J knocked on my door, I was instantly attracted to her. She was a killer in tight jeans. A mid-30s blonde, J looked like sex to me, and had a wacky personality that I found uplifting. "What do ya have to drink around her?" she asked the moment she waltzed in. We wound up killing a bottle of Chardonnay after her first 15 minutes inside.

My house had a large hot tub in the back, which I never used. J saw it and said, "Hey, let's screw out there." We went outside with our wine glasses, stripped, and had sex in the tub.

This, for me, was a form of heaven on earth. I didn't care if any of my neighbors saw or heard us. I was in a "pleasure zone," unaware of any other outside stimulus.

J gave incredible blowjobs, and also liked getting fucked doggie style. In between fucking and sucking, I'd regale her with tales of my "bad dates" with "real women," and she'd howl with laughter. I also once showed her a very expensive toupee I'd just bought. She laughed so hard, she fell to the floor, crying. "Oh my God," she said, "That's the worst thing I've ever seen in my life! Please tell me you're not going to wear that dead raccoon in public?" (After she left, I tossed the $1,500 rug into the trash.)

J became my "go-to" fuck pay-pal for months. Shortly after we met, she set up a new apartment near me as her own private whore house. She'd admonish me to "be very quiet when you come here… I don't want my neighbors to bust me." I'd tip toe into her apartment, where she'd greet me, topless, with a glass of wine and a hug. "Hey sexy," she'd say, "Hold on a minute." Standing in her little kitchen, she'd be counting massive piles of $20 and $50 bills, which had been neatly stacked along her countertops.

J would lead me into her bedroom, where a porn film would be playing on the TV. While I only paid Janey for an hour, she so enjoyed hearing my "bad date" stories after we had intercourse, that she'd often grace me an extra half hour or more, laying naked in bed, just so I could entertain her.

One night when I went to get a "J Fix," her girlfriend Gina, a short, stacked, brunette Italian, was visiting. As I walked in, Gina shot me a big smile, turned to J, and said, "This one's pretty sexy. I can see why you like fucking him so much!" Popping an instant boner, I asked J if we could "invite Gina into bed too?" For an additional fee, my request was granted.

I'm not sure why J became mentally removed, but when I fucked her that night, I felt like I was humping a blowup doll. She wasn't the sexy, zany whore I knew and loved. I stopped "doing" her, and, instead, turned my attention to Gina, clearly hungry for sex. J left the room. Gina and I fucked for at least an hour. I made her cum several times. Her pussy was very tight, and she gave me such wonderful pleasure, I completely forgot I was screwing her in J's bed.

While I continued to see J every so often, the original chemistry we'd enjoyed drifted after the Gina affair. She began gaining weight – all she ever did was stay in her apartment, eat, fuck johns, and play with her cash. She once confided in me that she was a multi-millionaire. When I asked why she didn't just move to Hawaii and retire, she said, "What would I do there? The ONLY thing in the world that makes me happy is having complete control over men and making them cum. My life is perfect the way it is, right now."

The last time I saw J, she'd gained so much weight, I was no longer attracted to her. Coupled with her now complete lack of enthusiasm for sex, I realized our glory days were over. After one last lackluster performance, I hugged her goodbye, knowing full well I'd never see her again.

I called J and asked her if she knew any "hot redheads." "I have the perfect girl for you," she replied. "I met her at The Playboy Mansion. She's a 'plus-sized' model who needs some cash. I just started recommending her to some of my clients."

I met Sher in a small apartment she was sharing with a girlfriend in West Hollywood. A complete and total knock-out, Sher WAS BIG, but in perfect proportion to her height and weight. I could tell she was nervous when I first met her. "Just so you know, I've only been doing this a few weeks, because I really need the money," she explained. "I don't want you to think I'm a pro at being a big ole whore." She gave me a nervous giggle. I was smitten.

Sher and I had loving, passionate, lusty sex, many times. I often invited her to my place just minutes after I'd arrived back home from dates with "real life" women I had minimal interest in. Originally from Texas, Sher was dating a quasi-famous musician known for his work in television. She was frustrated by this guy, because she was in love with him, but he simply would not ask her to marry him. "I just don't get it. I know he loves me. He's introduced me to his family and friends. But he just won't commit. He's breaking my heart. If he doesn't make a move, soon, he's gonna lose me forever," she confided.

Many months later, Sher sent me an email saying she'd relocated to New York City, because she was getting so many modeling assignments there. I began to see her on TV commercials, and in print advertisements in magazines. She broke up with her LA boyfriend and was being chased by multi-millionaires in the "Big Apple."

A few years later, well after she'd moved to Manhattan, I saw Sher twice more. Once, when I was in NYC for a trade show, we met in a hotel room. We hadn't seen each other in a time, but our sexual chemistry was still as powerful as it had ever been, if not more so. The final time I saw her, she called from a hotel near LAX. She was in town for a photo shoot and had been thinking about me. I brought a bottle of champagne and a variety of sex toys. At one point, she asked me to "take her anal virginity." Having already orgasmed twice, and drunk off my ass, I couldn't get hard enough, and was unable to oblige her.

Another call to Ava led me to the truly beautiful Marsella, 19, who'd just arrived in California from Italy. A young, perfect, Gina Lollobrigida-type, Marsella spoke almost no English. When she knocked on my door, she was clearly apprehensive.

During sex, the look on Marsella's face was beyond description—she glowed. The joy and rapture she expressed as we came together was truly memorable. Afterward, she went silent, and just held me, her whole body trembling. "Thank you, my lover," she said in broken English. "I never before 'did orgasm.'"

I could have continued on with Marsella indefinitely. But each time I called her thereafter, she'd commit to a date, but then, within an hour of our designated meet time, would flake out. A friend would pop into town, she didn't feel well, or she was on her period – I heard every excuse in the book. I realized my little Italian movie star was gone, and it was time to continue my quest for the perfect call girl experience.

A friend of mine turned me on to a website that showcased local girls, and featured photos of them in scanty lingerie. Dozens and dozens of choices were just a mouse click away. Now a true call girl aficionado, this online "shopping" for sex partners became almost as thrilling as the sex act itself. One Friday night, a photo on this site stopped me in my tracks. A tall, blonde goddess, in white lingerie and white go-go boots named Kamila was available. I HAD to have her. I called the number posted, and spoke with an older woman, Kamila's madame, Christina. Her Russian accent was almost unintelligible. After a good deal of effort, I was able to learn that Christina had an endless supply of young, perfect blonde girls, "fresh off the boat from Russia," available to her clients.

Ding-dong. Dressed exactly as she'd appeared on the sex website, Kamila was, without question, the most gorgeous woman to ever enter my house. This Russian beauty, perhaps 21, took my breath away. She entered my living room in slow motion, and, honest-to-God, I felt like I was watching a *Victoria's Secret Lingerie* TV special in 3D.

Kamila's English was nearly as bad as Christina's. But she wasn't there for the conversation. A gifted sensualist, Kamila's love making was equal to her physical attributes. She was tender, romantic, and giving, without inhibition or reservation. She told me she'd just come to the U.S. from Minsk (birthplace of my mother's father,) had a boyfriend there who "bored her," and had come to Hollywood "to meet sexy, rock and roll, guitar boys."

Kamila and I had sex three times that night. The most beautiful woman I ever had sex with in my life, she became one of my "regulars." Every Friday night, Christina would call to ask if I wanted to see Kamila again, or if she could interest me in another of her many girls. Sex with Kamila was amazing every time, and I never got tired of it. But one night she had the flu, so Christina sent Elena to my house.

Elena spoke NO English. But she certainly DID speak the language of sex. Her body was so perfect, and her face so delicious, I came in under 10 minutes. While I like to pride myself on my ability to control my orgasms during sex, I was a goner with this girl. As I was climaxing, she laughed: "Good, yes?" "You could say that," I beamed.

Unfortunately, after just a few months, Christina informed me that both Kamila and Elena had moved back to Mother Russia. I'll miss them both, forever.

Trolling once again online, I found Jackie, a tall, well-built redhead, who loved to drink beer, smoke pot, and fuck. She lived with her boyfriend and his struggling rock band – the boyfriend actually encouraged her to "fuck guys for money" so they had food on the table. Jackie had a crazy ex-husband back East someplace, and a four-year-old son, whom she'd lost custody of years earlier. (Her ex's parents were raising the kid.)

A total slut and legitimate white trash, Jackie was the polar opposite of the "real women" I was pursuing at the time. In spite of her low-level stature, I enjoyed being with her countless times, because there was no pretense. She was there simply to suck some cock, get fucked, and drive back home with enough cash in her hot little hands to eat food. I had no qualms about helping her out.

Our sessions were particularly hot and nasty. Afterwards, Jackie and I would occasionally talk for hours. I tried to encourage her to save up enough money so she could attempt getting back custody of her son from her ex-in-laws. "Well, they really hate my fuckin' guts, ever since I got busted for prostitution and went to jail," she revealed. "They think I'm the biggest whore on the planet. I don't know if I'll ever get the little guy back."

The last time I fucked Jackie, she looked extremely thin and pale. Her health seemed questionable, and I realized that continuing to see her in the future would be playing Russian roulette with my much beloved penis.

Jackie often raved to me about her best friend, V (her actual nickname,) who was also in the "sex business." I hired V to come to my place, and I'm quite sure she would agree we were an instant chemistry match. A tall, thin woman with modest titties and very long, straight, dark black hair, V reminded me immediately of Cher from her "Gypsies, Tramps and Thieves" era. The second V walked into my living room, we started making out hungrily, and flung each other onto the couch. Without words, she pulled down her panties, I licked her clit, and she came in my face, her whole body trembling. "Oh my fuckin' God!" she said. "Now I know why Jackie kept seeing you! You're a champion pussy-eater!"

V and I had sex together innumerable times, either at my place, or at her rented apartment in West Los Angeles, where we put to good use her astounding collection of impressive lingerie, wigs, and adult toys. V also liked anal sex and would specifically request that action from time to time. I was always glad to deliver.

When we weren't on top of each other, V and I would, like Jackie, also spend hours of time talking after sex. She told me about the thriving call girl business she used to run in Florida when she was a madame. "I made a lot of girls A LOT of money, Danny," she'd say. "And so few of them ever even thanked me. Some of them ripped off clothes I loaned them, stole cars of mine, or even started competing businesses against me." V also opened up to me about her father, a former Vietnam Vet/now homeless schizophrenic. She'd placed him into various mental hospitals for many years, but he kept escaping. "I just can't be in charge of the guy anymore, Danny," she'd lament. "I've done all I can for him."

Of all the many call girls I spent time with during this era, I always felt particularly close to V. In spite of her external self-confident aura, she was really just a vulnerable little girl, burdened with a troubled soul and a mess of a father.

V gave me Lisa's number. A cute blonde in her 20s, Lisa came to my place once on Halloween. Dressed as a "Sexy Kitty," her costume was complete with cat ears, a long tail, and facial whiskers. While I was completely nude, I insisted that Lisa keep the costume on while we fucked. She simply pulled her kitty panties off to the side, and I humped her brains out on my couch. I couldn't tell if she was experiencing pleasure or pain—she kept whispering "My God, you're SO big!"

In some weird, way, since I've hated cats my entire life, I felt like I'd gotten "revenge" against them all, by fucking sexy, blonde "Kitty Lisa" that Halloween eve.

In search of someone new, I called Ava again: "You should meet Tanya. She used to be a Playboy model back in the '80s. She doesn't kiss because she's married, but she's very sensual. I'm sure you'd like her."

Not a thin woman, Tanya, in her late 40s, had shoulder length, curly blonde hair, blue eyes, big, botox-laden lips, and enormous, REAL, tits. While coming off as something of a scatter brain, Tany was actually quite bright. Each time she'd walk into my place, she'd initially present an aloof vibe, until at least half a bottle of Chardonnay or champagne was consumed. Then, without prompting, her blouse and bra would disappear, and her large, very lovely tits would find their way into my mouth.

Tanya was never a wild, dirty, sex partner. She did like sucking cock, but the ONLY way she was able to orgasm was to masturbate herself (while I watched,) with a tiny, zebra-colored vibrator, which she'd rub against her clit for at least 20 minutes. When she finally came, she'd call out "Oh my GOD!" so loud, I was always afraid the neighbors would complain.

A model, Tanya never quite made the "big time" with *Playboy* by appearing in the magazine. Instead, she did photo assignments for some of their print advertisements and was often hired to "pretty up" various company events at the Playboy Mansion – when Hugh Hefner threw parties for his elderly cronies.

As soon as our sex sessions were finished, Tanya would polish off any remaining alcohol left in my house. She'd then sit on my couch, naked, and talk to a series of friends on her cell phone. I didn't mind in the least. I loved sitting in my living room, drunk, staring at a beautiful, naked woman.

After a particularly fun Tanya "session," her cell phone rang, just as she was preparing to leave. "Hey, Whitney," she said. "I'm here in Beverly Hills with my friend Danny. God, he makes me cum so good." Tanya then said, "Here, she wants to talk with you." I took the cell phone. Whitney's Voice: "I hear good things about you, Danny," she said. "Any guy that can make Tanya cum must be special. So when do I get to meet you, too?"

I held the phone off to the side. "Does she know about our financial arrangement?" I asked. Toni: "Yes, of course, she's my best friend. We've been talking about having a three way with the right guy. Do you want to be that guy?"

I saved up my pennies, and a week later, I called Tanya. "I'm ready for that three-way," I said. "Great, let me set something up for Saturday night," she replied. I was incredibly attracted to Whitney instantly. She had long, straight, red hair, nice, natural boobs, a slim figure, and a very pretty face. The first time Tonya and Whitney entered my house together, I was ecstatic. Whitney loved to drink even more than Tanya—fortunately, I knew this in advance, and had plenty of liquor at the ready.

That night, Tanya, Whitney and I spent three straight hours in bed. I took turns giving oral sex to one, while the other watched and masturbated, and then, reversed the process. Although they were very close friends, not only had they never before had a three-way, they'd never even seen the other naked. Once their initial hesitations were calmed, they relaxed, and our first evening together was monumental.

I had at least a dozen three-ways with those two ladies over the next few years.

I called Tanya once again to arrange another get-together. She told me she was out of town. I then asked if it would be OK with her if I wanted to see Whitney alone? As Whitney and I had powerful chemistry, this certainly was not an issue for me. Tanya said sure, so Whitney came to my place, and, after the requisite drinks, we began a (surprisingly) romantic session on my couch. However, just as Whitney and I were about to screw, Tanya called to say that she and her friend, Samantha, had returned back to LA <u>many hours earlier than planned</u>! Since she knew Whitney was over, would it be OK if they "dropped by" also?

Drunk off my ass, my cock hard as a rock, I said, "Are you kidding me? Two MORE women in MY HOUSE? Three women?? Yes, of course, come over. And tell your friend I can't wait to meet her." Whitney was perturbed. "I thought I had you to myself tonight," she pouted. Me: "I'm sorry! But, isn't Tanya YOUR friend? Did you want me to tell her NOT to come?" Whitney: "No, that's OK. But I don't know this Samantha chick. What if she's not cool?" Me: "I'll call Tonya back right now to cancel." Whitney: "No, forget it. It's OK. I would imagine having sex with three women at the same time would be pretty exciting for a guy." Duh!

The second Tonya and Samantha walked into my house, Samantha, clearly very drunk, made a beeline for me. "Oh my God! You are so fucking sexy!" She pushed me against a wall, shoved her tongue down my throat, and began dry humping me. Tonya, Whitney and I were shocked. A short, adorable brunette, with a nice figure, Samantha took me by the hand. "Show me your bedroom," she insisted. (Note: Samantha was related to a very famous, now-deceased, comedian.)

While my two other lady guests went into my kitchen to pour themselves cocktails, I stood in my bedroom, Samantha on her knees. "My husband doesn't fuck me anymore. I NEED cock. Make me your gag whore, Danny." Sam began sucking me like a machine. Minutes later, Tonya and Whitney, now wearing just lingerie and high heels, and carrying mixed drinks, walked into my room. Tonya: "Oh my God, Samantha." she said. "I had no idea you were such a big slut!" They left.

Samantha tore off her clothes and hopped onto my bed. "Daddy, will you be my master and fuck me, please? I need cock, Daddy. I'm a very bad girl. Please make me fuck, Daddy." This woman was such an unexpected sexual "gift," that I must admit, even with all the sex I'd had with call girls previously, Samantha raised the bar by many notches. While fucking her with all I had, the two other gals returned once again to my room and sat on the bed. They watched in awe. "God damn, that's hot," Whitney said.

I was pounding away at Samantha, when Whitney kneeled beside me. "What about me?" She began kissing me. Tonya, meanwhile, laid beside me and said, "God, you're all getting me so horny. I really need to cum." She took out her black and white vibrator, closed her eyes, and began masturbating herself with gusto.

For many hours, I was in bed with a beautiful redhead, a former *Playboy* model blonde, and an adorable brunette. This was a dream I never even knew I had come true. I allowed each of them to take turns sucking me while I kissed another. I'd be fucking one, while the other two would masturbate with abandon. At one point, I glanced into the mirror and caught myself with the biggest smile I ever had. Throughout the action, I promised myself that, in spite of my drunken stupor, I would "Remember this night forever and ever." I literally "recorded a mental videotape" of every single moment – one I've replayed countless times since.

With very few exceptions – truly special moments laughing with my two kids when they were very young, or playing drums in high school bands during the '70s – that night was perhaps the most exhilarating experience in the history of my life.

CHAPTER THIRTY-ONE

Help! I'm in Love With A Supermodel!

In early 2009, just a few months after Bethany and I split, I stood in my living room, channel surfing on my large, hi-definition TV, when I came upon a program featuring an incredibly beautiful blonde woman sitting on the floor, vomiting into a trash can. Fascinated, I stood watching the rest of the show, *Celebrity Rehab Presents Sober House*, which aired on VH-1.

I'd never heard of the series, which presented eight "celebrities" (most of whom a far stretch from that word) going through withdrawal from their addictions to drugs and alcohol, on national television. There was a marathon of *Celebrity Rehab* episodes that day, so I sat watching half a dozen in a row.

Quite simply, I was mesmerized by this blonde woman, who was coming off a 20-year addiction to painkillers. As I watched her puking, sobbing, and wiping tears from her Goddess-like face, I HEARD A VOICE that whispered into my right ear: "You need to reach out to this woman. She needs your help." I swear to God, I really did!

Her name was Amber Smith. Go ahead, Google her photos. I'll wait.

I'd never heard of Amber before, so I looked her up on the Internet, and found her website. There, I saw photographs of perhaps the most stunning blonde sex-bomb model ever. I discovered she'd appeared on the cover of more than 300 magazines around the world, including a 1985 issue of *Playboy* that had been published when I was working there. Amber was a tall, extremely attractive blonde from Florida who, in the *Playboy* layout, had posed with large yellow feather-fans, and very dark red lipstick.

At the bottom of Amber's website was a phone number as a contact. I called and left the following message: "Hello, Amber, my name is Dan. I'm a publicist in Beverly Hills. I've been watching your show, and I simply have to say that it's breaking my heart. Your story has touched me, deeply. If you need some help re-starting your career, I'd be glad to try to help you. I know this sounds kind of crazy, but I simply felt compelled to call and reach out to you. If you'd like to have lunch with me sometime to meet, please let me know. My phone number is XYZ. Either way, I wish you the best of luck with your sobriety and I hope you're able to stay away from drugs in the future. Clearly, they're NOT your friends. Take care."

A few days later, I got a call. "Dan? This is Carol Smith. I'm Amber's mother. We were very touched by your message, and we'd like to meet with you."

I was taken aback. I'd actually gotten a response!

Over the course of the next few days, I researched everything I could find on the Internet about Amber Smith. I also developed a list of possible publicity, promotional, and marketing ideas for her, such as potential product endorsements, public appearances, speaker's bureaus, talent agents to meet with, etc. I wanted to be prepared for this meeting with my "Damsel in Distress."

I'd chosen my favorite Hollywood restaurant, Musso & Frank, for our lunch meeting. Arriving in an old, loud, junk-heap of a car, Amber and Carol got out. We sat at a plush red leather booth (Amber in the middle) and for the next two hours, I told them about myself, my career, and my ideas for Amber to pursue, now that she was sober. She revealed a good deal to me about her struggles with drugs—an addiction she shared WITH HER MOTHER—for over 20 years! Carol, also, had become clean but now the two women faced an even more prominent problem: poverty.

"I'm broke," Amber told me. "I had everything—a house, cars, clothes, money in the bank. It's all gone. My problem got really bad about five years ago, and my mother and I were almost homeless. We were living in a tiny Hollywood hotel room, and I didn't know where my next rent check was gonna come from. Then, I heard about the *Celebrity Rehab* TV show, and I called the producers, begging them to help me. I didn't do that show for the fame, or the money, or the publicity. I did it because without it, I knew I was gonna die."

Amber's ability to articulate her struggles with drug addiction and the devastation it left behind in her personal life, were extremely powerful. I sat on the edge of my seat. I'd never, in my life, met a hardcore drug addict before.

I told Amber that "a voice" told me to help her, and that I'd like to be both her personal publicist and her manager, for free. "I'm not here for money," I told the women. "I'm here because I'm supposed to help you." I picked up the check for lunch and walked the two back to their shitty car.

Later that week, I invited Amber to have dinner with me. I wanted to discuss our new relationship and have her sign a management contract. I picked her up and drove her to a Mexican place. She looked stunning. As we entered the restaurant, I noticed that the head of EVERY SINGLE PERSON (both men AND women) turned, to watch her simply walk across the room. When we sat at the booth, I said, "Wow. Everyone stared at you walking in here. What's that like?"

She replied, "It's been happening to me since I was 15. I don't even notice it anymore."

Amber and I had a fun meal. Our "relationship" was fresh and brand new. We talked about our childhoods, our careers, and our lives, in broad strokes. The fact that she had been a true supermodel in the 1990s (*Maxim Magazine* once voted her "One of the Sexiest Women Alive"), never entered into the conversation. We were just "a guy and a girl" having dinner and bonding as friends.

During dinner, Amber told me she'd been invited to participate in another VH-1 TV show, this one called *Sex Rehab with Dr. Drew* (2009).

"Are you a sex addict?" I asked.

"Oh God, no, not at all," Amber told me. "I'm not even a big fan of sex, at all. Actually, I'm a LOVE ADDICT. It's something entirely different."

She went on to explain that during the course of her life, she'd had "a lot of sex with a lot of men," but other than the "15 seconds of cumming and then, so what?" she never enjoyed it. She confessed she'd never had a "real" boyfriend, had never been married, and had never experienced "true love." The concept seemed alien to her.

Her affliction in this area was a mental, romantic "disconnect." She'd meet an extremely good-looking man at a party or a nightclub, speak with him briefly, and then become completely and totally smitten with him, beyond anything resembling normalcy. She would start stalking these men, finding out where they'd be and when, and show up, unannounced, just to stare at them from a distance. Amber told me the "high" she felt from doing this was even more powerful than the high she got from drugs.

"Wow," I said. "I did that with a girl I couldn't talk to in college. I called her 'Long Red.' I never knew there was a name for that condition."

Amber replied, "Most people don't know anything about love addiction. It's not been discussed within popular culture. I'm hoping that my appearance on the new show will help spread the word about this disease to others."

For the *Sex Rehab* TV program, Amber, along with seven actual sex addicts comprised of rock stars, porn stars, models, and filmmakers, would be confined to the Pasadena Recovery Center for three weeks. She would have limited access to a telephone, and none to the Internet. During those weeks, I began reaching out to a variety of potential business partners for us, including talent agents, modeling agents, nightclub promoters, marketers of new products, ad agencies representing iconic brands, etc.

However, I quickly came to learn that because of her recent national "celebrity" on the TV shows that had aired the year previous (*Celebrity Rehab* and *Sober House*), Amber had earned a reputation for herself as, perhaps, the country's most beautiful drug addict. One noted talent agent actually told me, "She's probably the most stunning woman I've ever seen in my life. Unfortunately, she has the 'stink' of drug addict on her. I don't think that's something she'll ever be able to shake off, certainly not in Hollywood."

During her second week at the rehab center, Amber called and invited me to come for a "family and friends" BBQ visit, asking if I wouldn't mind picking up her mother along the way. During that car ride, Carol told me how sad it was that Amber just couldn't find the "right guy," had never been in love, and had never even had a real boyfriend. When we arrived at the clinic, Amber (and a TV crew) approached us. She looked especially sad.

"What's wrong?" I asked.

Amber replied, "The therapy here has been really tough. This is so much harder than even drug withdrawal." She explained that since she was now drug-free for the first time in 20 years, she was beginning to "feel again," and was delving into long-hidden feelings about her father's abandonment and guilt over his death. (Amber's dad, who left when she was five, drank himself to death. His body, along with hundreds of empty alcohol bottles, was found aboard a boat he owned. Amber, who was on the set of a low-budget movie at the time, blamed herself for "not being there" for him the day he passed away.)

After Amber was done with the three-week stint filming the new TV series, she and I, for the next four months, took meetings all over town with agents. Amber once turned down an offer for her own reality TV show (much to my dismay) because the powers that be wouldn't name her an executive producer! We also met for lunches at least a few times a week, visited each other at our respective apartments and spoke by phone at least four times a day.

I threw a birthday party for myself that June; my closest friends attended. About an hour late, Amber walked in, bringing all conversation to a screeching halt.

My friend, Jamie, pulled me aside. "Danny, I'm so NOT a lesbian, but for HER I'd make an exception!"

Jamie's husband, Andy, added, "God, she's so good-looking, it's off-putting."

Amber instantly eclipsed the attention of my gang, but it meant a lot to me that she showed up at all. When she left, she handed me an oversized birthday card. It read: "I know the going hasn't been easy so far, but I really appreciate all you have done to help me, and all of your selfless sacrifices. I honor our friendship and have had a lot of fun! You have quickly become a great friend and confidant to me. Here's to a wonderful, prosperous future. Happy birthday, and may this year be unforgettable for us both. Love, Amber."

Amber was invited to sign autographs at a booth at "Comic Con" (the biggest science fiction and comic book show in the world) that summer in San Diego. I suggested that she and I drive down together and stay at a (cheap) area motel. I'd help her set up her station at the booth. "Sounds like fun," she said.

From that Friday morning until that Sunday evening, Amber and I were inseparable, although I'd injured my right ankle dancing at my niece's wedding the weekend prior and was forced to walk with a cane the whole time! We drove down to San Diego together, picking up a wacky, model girlfriend of hers along the way, checked into our little motel rooms (side-by-side), and set up shop at the booth of her sponsor, a top comic book company. Amber was among at least eight other "Booth Babes" sitting there, including several former *Playboy* bunnies, rock stars' wives, indie film "scream queens," and one red-haired, WWF wrestler to whom I said, "You re-invent the word 'Hot.'"

While the attendance for the show was record-breaking, guys who wanted to shell out good money for photos of pretty girls weren't amongst the crowd. (These geeky guys wanted autographs from "Mr. Spock" from *Star Trek*, and "Captain Adama" from *Battlestar Gallactica*, not from half-naked babes.) Amber and I lost money that weekend when we factored in gas, motel rooms, food, and "bike taxis." After parking the car incredibly far from the convention hall, we had to ride, sitting closely together in little bike taxis, pedaled by incredibly muscular men and women. Laughing and talking incessantly, we had tremendous fun during those trips, with fees of $25.00 in each direction. Those costs mounted quickly.

One night after a Comic-Con appearance, Amber and I shared some fast food in her hotel room. I chomped down fries, as I watched her remove her makeup, kick off her high heels, and change into her casual clothing (averting my eyes on purpose).

"I wish I didn't have to do these appearances anymore," she lamented. "I've been doing them forever. Girls my age don't make much money from autograph shows these days."

I said, "I only wish I was still making the income I made up until last year. We could start a business together."

Amber: "What happened?"

Me: "Wonderful George W. Bush fucked the world and killed the economy. I'm only making about 12-grand a month now, down from 30-grand a month, which I made for years."

Amber stopped eating, rolled her eyes, said, "$30K a month?" and pretended to faint, actually dropping to the floor. We laughed. "God, I wish I was making that kind of money."

Me: "Didn't you make millions in your heyday?"

Amber: "A lot of people made a lot of money from me for a very long time, but during my very best year ever, I only made about $250,000. I was making good money for a while, but never 'Gisele Bündchen' money, even though I was her body double a few times."

Back in Hollywood, I helped Amber schlep her unbelievably heavy suitcases up to her apartment door. We hugged and then, as I turned to walk away, she said out loud, but perhaps more to herself, "I love you, Dan."

I froze in time. Did I just hear correctly? I turned around. Amber stood about 15 feet from me, staring. The moment was suspended.

Me: "Amber, I love you, too. You know that, right? You KNOW I love you, RIGHT?"

She smiled. "Yeah, yeah, I know. Thanks for everything. Good night."

We stared at each other for a few seconds more. Then I split. I didn't know what else to do. (I suppose, had she not been one of the most beautiful women on Earth, literally, I might have had the courage to kiss her then.)

For months that summer, I arranged public appearances for Amber around the U.S. at nightclubs, parties, autograph shows, and even at a college campus, where she spoke about overcoming drug and love addiction. While I was helping her generate a few thousand dollars a month (and constantly driving her to and from airports for those appearances), she hit a snag financially.

"Dan, I can't pay my rent. What am I gonna do?" she asked.

Deeply touched and completely smitten with her, I handed her $2,000.00. "You'll pay me back someday when you're making the big bucks again," I said.

Hugging me, she said, "You're the only man on the planet I can count on and completely trust. What would I do without you? You are truly my hero."

I arranged a meeting for Amber and myself with Neil Strauss, a multi-bestselling author who I was able to contact, as he was friends with my cousin Franz, the magician. This author (whose book *The Game*-about picking up women-was an international bestseller) was instantly smitten with Amber and agreed to help us pursue a book deal with a major, New York-based publishing company for rights to her autobiography. Then things took a strange turn. Neil hired a "nobody," young, "potential hot new author" he discovered from Toronto to write up a few sample chapters of Amber's life after having spent just a few days with her, one-on-one. When this famous author presented us with those sample chapters, Amber and I were shocked and disgusted. "These chapters are not remotely in "Amber's voice," we told Neil and rejected them.

Once that happened the whole thing fell apart, plus the publishing house this author was associated with decided that, while Amber's life story would "certainly make for compelling reading," they just didn't feel there would be "enough of an audience to actually buy such a product." Amber and I, who'd literally performed a dance for joy in the street after our first meeting with Neil Strauss, were crushed when the deal, which seemed like a sure thing, eventually fell through.

We decided to drown our sorrows over our lost book fortune at a killer Indian food restaurant in Beverly Hills. As I slathered up a big piece of naan with raita, and was about to inhale it, she said something like, "Yada, yada, yada, blah, blah, blah, AND IF WE EVER END UP HAVING SEX TOGETHER, etc., etc., etc., yada, yada."

I almost choked on my naan. I wished at that moment that the previous two sentences had been videotaped, so I could have played them back. I wasn't paying close attention to her preceding thoughts, so I wasn't 100% sure if her "having sex together" phrase was in reference to <u>me</u> or to one of the "love addiction" guys she was obsessed with from afar. (I didn't ask, so I'll never know.)

Amber and I went to see the incredibly scary horror film *Paranormal Activity* together. We were so frightened during the course of that film, we took turns grabbing each other's legs, and turning to each other with fear. (She was so scared she had her eyes covered at the very end of the movie, the most unsettling moment of all.) After the film ended, we were so rattled, we remained in our seats for quite a while, until the feeling subsided.

Leaving the theater, we went to a nearby nightclub, where we watched one of her best friends perform stand-up comedy. I hadn't felt this close to any woman in years. A Martian observing the two of us together would have said that Amber and I were on a date. (In heels, Amber was very tall. I used to insert "lifts" into my shoes to add some inches when together.)

Amber was invited to tape an appearance on *The Oprah Winfrey Show*, along with Dr. Drew Pinsky, and two other fellow "sex addicts" from VH-1. I worked with Oprah's team to make Amber's arrangements (the show taped in Chicago.) Weeks later, when that episode of Oprah's show aired, my daughter happened to be home from college. Amber came to my apartment to watch. There I was, sitting on the couch with my beautiful daughter on one side and my beautiful best friend, the supermodel, on the other, as the three of us watched Amber chatting with Oprah about the differences between sex and love addiction. It was truly a surreal moment in my life. (Oprah really seemed to "spark" to Amber's plight, even confessing a case of "love addiction" that Oprah, herself, had experienced decades earlier.)

"I got a great booking in Vegas," Amber called. "Fifteen hundred bucks to show up at a club and sign some autographs."

"Sounds like fun," I replied. I then realized I had both a brand-new Mercedes Benz, and absolutely nothing to do with myself that weekend. "Let's go together. I'll drive," I said.

"Great," she replied, "Should we stay there overnight? The gig will end around 2 AM."

Thinking quickly, I offered, "To save money, why don't I get us a room with two beds?"

Amber: "Perfect, thanks. Sounds like a plan."

I went online and arranged for a fairly inexpensive room with two beds, within walking distance of the nightclub in which she was to appear.

For the next four days, I was a nervous wreck. I was going to be sleeping in the same room with my best friend, a super model. I wrote down a little speech I planned to deliver during that weekend.

"Amber, I think I'm starting to have feelings for you, and I just felt the time has come for me to let you know."

I picked Amber up from her tiny dive apartment in Hollywood at 2:00 PM that Saturday afternoon and for the next six hours straight, we drove through a good deal of traffic to Las Vegas. We never once played the radio or the "positive thinking" CD she brought along for the road. We talked about everything under the sun, neither repeating a stream of conversation nor ever running out of stories to recount.

We arrived at the front desk of the Vegas hotel. I gave the female clerk my info and credit card, and she pulled me up on her computer. "Here you are," she said.

"The room's got two beds, right?" I said.

The woman slowly looked at me, then the blonde goddess standing beside me, then looked back at me. She said, "Yeah, sure, right." (Only in retrospect did I realize she was being sarcastic.)

Amber and I got upstairs and, you guessed it, there was only ONE BED in the room. We both stood, frozen. "Amber, there's only one bed in here."

Amber: "Yeah, I see that."

Me: "You KNOW I ordered two beds, right? I just want you to be sure that you KNOW I did that, okay?"

Amber: "Yes, I know. Don't worry, I believe you. What should we do? Should we go back down and switch rooms?"

Realizing she only had about two hours to eat dinner, get dressed, and walk over to the nightclub, I said, "You know what? I'll sleep on the floor. Don't worry about it, it's not a big deal. I really don't care."

Amber: "Thanks, Dan. I appreciate that."

For the next 90 minutes, Amber and I sat side-by-side on the bed, ate a really shitty room service meal (ice cold French fries and greasy burgers), and watched an old comedy movie.

"God, I have NO INTEREST in doing this appearance tonight," she said.

Me: "I know. I would do ANYTHING if you and I could just stay here on this bed all night and watch movies."

Amber: "Me too! That sounds like heaven! I WISH we could do that and nothing else!"

The time came for Amber to prepare for her appearance. Watching her stand in the bathroom in just bra and panties, putting on her makeup, installing her hair extensions, and slinking into her skin-tight sexy costume, I was greatly surprised to find myself <u>not</u> turned on! In all honesty, I actually felt like Amber was my wife and we were simply a married couple getting ready for a night out on the town.

We arrived at the club and Amber was asked to pose for some photographs with the owner in front of the entryway signage. The promoter handed me Amber's check for $1,500.00, which I pocketed, then led us inside. The place was packed, and the DJ's music was deafening. (I have custom-made ear plugs for such occasions.) The club owner then brought us to the VIP table, sat down with Amber and me, and had two very sexy waitresses bring us round after round of Petron tequila. Amber, a recovering alcoholic, said, "I SO shouldn't be drinking tonight."

"I know," I answered, "but I don't think there's much of anything else to do here right now."

Amber: "You're right. A little tequila won't kill me."

The club owner split, and Amber and I sat on our big fat asses for the next four hours, drinking. Occasionally, a club patron or two would approach her for an autograph or a photo but, by and large, we were on an incredibly loud "date," for which she was being paid solely for her wondrously luminous presence.

A club photographer came by at one point and snapped a Polaroid picture of Amber and me hugging. The SECOND I saw that photo I said to myself, "Oh My God! I'm IN LOVE with AMBER SMITH! What the fuck am I gonna do now?"

Every rap music song the DJ played that night sounded something like this:

"Gonna fuck you in the ass, in the ass, in the ass,
Gonna fuck you in the big black ass, fuckin' bitch.
Back it up, back it up, and let me fuck that big black ass.
Gonna fuck that ass that ass that ass."

Amber and I, now both drunk, were laughing hysterically, taking turns reciting the unbelievably nonsensical words to these horrific rap songs. "John Lennon must be spinning in his grave right now," I screamed into Amber's ears. She fell against me, laughing, her lovely breasts pressed against my shoulder and her long blonde hair flowing everywhere. Finally, 2:00 AM arrived, and the promoter "sprung" us from this hellhole. He walked us back to our room, shook my hand, hugged Amber goodbye, then split. We entered the room, drunk, and were both instantly reminded that there was just one bed.

Not wanting to let the tension last too long, I simply said, "Amber, I need to ask you a HUGE FAVOR right now."

Amber: "What's that?"

Me: "I really don't want to sleep on the floor tonight. Can I share the bed with you?"

"Yeah, sure, of course, that's fine," she said.

I popped on my PJs and slid under the covers, while Amber entered the bathroom to "de-supermodel" herself. She returned in sweat pants and a loose-fitting T-shirt with no bra.

Amber got under the covers and turned off the lights. I was now lying in bed with one of the most beautiful women on Earth, at 3:00 in the morning, drunk. Just inches apart, I realized if I didn't do SOMETHING just then, I'd regret it for the rest of my life.

I next did something so spontaneously stupid, I truly surprised even myself. I got onto my hands and knees, straddled Amber, and positioned myself directly over her face. "Amber, I need to kiss you right now," I declared. I stared into her eyes with love.

Her eyes were those of a deer caught in the headlights. She was horrified!

I slowly leaned my mouth down to press my lips against hers. She quickly turned her face. I got "the cheek." Truly surprised, I lifted my head back up, looked again into her shocked face, then went back down for a second try, this time kissing the other cheek. I lifted my head, looked directly into her face for a few seconds, then said, in hasty retreat, "Well, goodnight then." I got off my hands and knees, crawled under the covers, and instantly passed out, snoring just seconds later.

My friends have since asked me, "Why didn't you just ask her for sex?" The truth is, I knew instinctively that Amber simply had ZERO physical attraction toward me before I even went in for that first kiss. No amount of friendship-style love was ever going to change that, and it was just a fact of reality I was going to have to accept.

The next morning, my gal pal and I awoke about the same time. "Hey Amber, I just realized I can tell all of my friends I SLEPT WITH A SUPERMODEL!"

"Yeah, I guess that's true," she chuckled, and I knew she was not in the least offended by my reprehensible actions the night before.

We drove back to L.A., and again chatted non-stop for six consecutive hours. Amber brought up the "I've never had a real boyfriend, never been in love" theme she mentioned the day before, and I replied, "You know what? I actually find that hard to believe. Take me through the history of your love life, and let's be honest."

Hours later, Amber realized that there were a number of men she'd known in her past that truly DID love her. While most of them dumped her for becoming too clingy and needy, she did admit that she even dumped a few of them herself, when THEY became too clingy to HER.

"Wow," she said, "I never realized that before. I <u>have</u> <u>loved</u> some men, and some men have loved me."

"Of course," I said, "who could possibly date you and NOT fall in love with you?"

Then, the killer part came up. She said, "These days, it's so hard for me to find someone to date, because I'll only go out with extremely good-looking men, over six feet tall, who remind me of my father. My dad resembled Superman. I can't possibly be attracted to anyone else, for some reason." I believe this was Amber's cryptic way of telling ME that <u>I</u> simply would never make the "cut" within her stringent dating criteria.

I'd written my little "Amber, I think I'm starting to have feelings for you" speech on a yellow sticky post-it note, which was pasted to the left side of my steering wheel. I promised myself that at some point during our time in Vegas I was going to spill my guts, and let her know how I really felt. After the "I only date extremely good-looking, tall men who look like Superman" speech, we stopped off for gas. I surreptitiously tore off the yellow sticker from the dashboard and tossed it in the trash. "It's just NEVER GONNA HAPPEN," I said out loud to myself, as I filled the tank, preparing for our long drive back home to L.A.

A few weeks later, Amber met a multi-multi-millionaire at one of the Texas nightclub appearances I booked for her. This recently-divorced guy made his fortune by inventing some kind of unique dental implants. He bought a mansion in the Hollywood Hills solely to allow Amber to live there so she would be available to him at his beck and call. At this point, my relationship with her faded into history. My family and friends said to me, "God, she used you SO BAD," to which I, unfortunately, have no defense.

I became extremely disappointed that the minute Amber got involved with a mega-wealthy man, she was unable to find the time to maintain our friendship, dropping me like a hot potato. I honestly and sincerely believed that we'd become REAL honest-to-God friends, having shared so many intimate moments during our 10 months together.

With regard to our short relationship, I feel Amber's biggest flaw was simply her extraordinary inability to appreciate and nurture the love of a true friend. Her TV mentor, Dr. Drew Pinsky, once said of her, "Amber Smith is an empty person and she's struggling. She has a lot of emptiness and she doesn't even know sometimes what she's feeling." For me, those sentiments sum it up best.

I reflect back on Amber as my penultimate "Carrot on a Stick"—a woman with brains, beauty, honesty, sexuality and mystery—whom I truly loved, or thought I loved, but could never quite "attain."

Today, she will no longer return my phone calls, emails, or texts. So close and yet so far!

CHAPTER THIRTY-TWO

Meet My Dominatrix

50 smacked me in the face. Hard. By this point, I'd had sex with close to one hundred women. I'd also been married, was the father of two children, and had had romances with blondes, brunettes and redheads. I truly believed I'd done it all with members of the opposite sex.

And then one night, I took a wrong turn in Van Nuys.

"Live Lingerie Models" read a small sign in the window of "Eros Station." Assuming it was another whack shack, I entered what appeared to be an adult video and dildo store. I asked the long-haired guy at the register, "Models?" "Back there," he pointed, completely disengaged from reality.

I noticed a waiting room in the back, and approached two tall, stunning brunette models in lingerie and high heels, sitting at a desk. "First time?" said one. Me: "Ugh, yeah, yes it is." "What kind of action you looking for tonight, honey?" said the other. Me: "What do you girls offer here?" They pointed up to a small sign that hung above the cash register. It read:

Basic Show/Single Girl: $50
Two Girl Show: $125
Fetish Room: $175
Bondage/Dungeon: $200

"Wow, a sex menu," I said, chuckling. These chicks weren't amused – they'd heard it all, a million times before. "What's a basic show?" I asked. Said the better looking gal, "One of us goes into a private room with you, and we put on some soft music. You make yourself 'comfortable' and we dance for you." "Glass window?" I asked. The girls laughed. "No, that's for losers!" said the second woman, as she leaned closer toward me. "This is real-life, hot horny chicks shoving their tits right into face while you jack your cock!"

I decided to go with the flow, asked the prettier girl for a basic show, and gave her fifty bucks. "Charley, basic!" she called out to the cash register guy. She stood (on heels, many inches taller than me,) took my hand, and entered a secret code into the heavy metal backdoor that split the front of the store from the private sex rooms at the rear.

"Can I get a tour, first?" I asked. My lady showed me the fetish room for cross-dressers, the "doctor's office," the "businessman/executive" room, and the dungeon. "Guys actually use that stuff?" I asked, referring to the gag balls, leather whips, and spiked metal riding crops hanging on the walls. "Honey, you have no idea," she said.

My gal pal next led me into a small room, with a black leather couch, a small nightstand with a boom-box stereo and lamp on it, and a chair. "So how much do you wanna tip me?" she asked. "Tip?" I said, thinking, "Great, here we go … it's Vegas again." "Yeah," said the girl, "That fifty was for the house. If you want a hot, nasty show from me, you need to tip me separately." "What's the normal tip fee around here?" I asked, clueless. She shook her head. "The more you give me, the better the show. But, since this is your first time, I'd say the normal tip would be twice the fifty."

I hadn't planned to spend $150 that night, but I had it in my wallet, this woman was incredibly sexy, and I was dying of curiosity. I placed a hundred bucks under the boom-box and sat back on the couch. "Now what?" I asked. "Make yourself comfortable, baby," she said, "I'll be right back." Alone in the room, thoughts were swirling: Was this woman gonna fuck me? Suck me? Hit me with a riding crop? Whack me in the head? Steal my wallet? I had no idea what was gonna go down. I pulled my pants down to my ankles, and sat there, like a Schlemiel, in my underwear.

The hot chick came back in and laughed. "Is that really comfortable for you?" she asked. "Don't you wanna take off ALL your clothes and show me what a big, strong, beautiful COCK you have??" Doing as instructed, I got completely naked and sat on a black towel she lay out for me on the couch. This chick then turned on some music from a boom-box, pulled her chair about three feet in front of me, and began dancing and stripping, looking deep into my eyes the entire time. Her body was near-perfect. She stripped off her panties, and shook her ass, her pussy, and her breasts inches from my face. "Can you smell my sweet pussy, little boy?" she asked. "Jerk off for me, baby. Jerk off for your sexy mommy."

The experience was overwhelming. Although there was very little physical contact with this woman stripping just inches from my face (she would occasionally rub her legs against mine,) her words were remarkably powerful, and no fantasy was taboo. As long as her client remained seated on the couch, he could masturbate himself to his heart's content.

I came in ecstasy and as I did, my private dancer clapped. "What a good boy!" she said, "You shot a nice big cum load for mommy! Mommy's SO PROUD of you!!" she laughed. That evening, I experienced one of the most exceptionally powerful sexual experiences of my life. Something about having a perfect, naked woman inches from your face, combined with the fact that you couldn't touch her, made it seem like my old *Playboy Magazine* pictures had been brought to life—so close, you can smell and almost taste them, yet so far that they still remained fantasy figures.

This was truly a "Next-Gen" masturbatory experience.

I visited Eros Station several times a week, having been entertained there by dozens of different women. The strippers came in every size, shape and nationality—some had glasses, and one even had braces. But each and every one of these ladies represented to me "fantasy come to life." For $150 a pop, I could have a sexually stimulating experience that made me feel warm and fuzzy and connected.

My favorite fantasy girl at Eros Station became Roxy, a Cuban bombshell. A former professional bikini and lingerie model (and self-confessed sex addict,) Roxy LOVED to help horny pathetic losers jerk themselves off. She quickly became my new addiction. "It's the hottest thing on the planet," she'd say. Roxy was also the only woman at the place who would, herself, also masturbate during the dances, timing her orgasms to those of her perverted clients.

Roxy was gorgeous, filthy dirty, and a true sexual deviant. She told me she was my "Slut Girlfriend," and I felt, at times, that I was in love with her. I became completely addicted to sessions with Roxy, until, one night, I walked into Eros Station and was told by hippie guy, "She's gone. Your little whore Roxy quit two days ago. But she left you this note."

"Dear Danny Slut-boy," it read. "I'm evolving my business outside of this shit hole. I've decided to become a dominatrix. I meet my clients at the Miyako Hotel in the Valley. My sessions are $1,000 for three hours of pleasure. I'd love to play with you again. Call me… Love, Roxy."

Other than a few times in Vegas, I'd rarely come close to spending that kind of coin for sex. But Roxy was my absolute, # 1 "Cum Slut," and I fantasized about her daily. I called and asked her if she'd like to have a date with me. I'd never seen her before outside of Eros Station, and when she hopped into my car, I got a whiff of her perfume. Both my mouth and my penis "smiled."

I took her to my favorite—and expensive—Italian restaurant (renowned for having been one of Frank Sinatra's regular hangouts for decades.) We got a private booth and ordered martinis. She told me that during the past few years, her adult-filmmaker boyfriend had been urging her to become a dominatrix. She realized that she had a natural flair for it, and some of her former (and wealthy) clients from Eros Station were now flocking to experience her newfound profession.

"Guys will only pay so much to watch them jerk off," she explained. "But for me to humiliate them, tell them how pathetic they are, make them kiss my feet, and call them losers, they'll pay me a fortune."

Dying of curiosity, I told Roxy that I definitely wanted this experience. During the course of dinner, I devised a way in which I could become a client of hers, but for free, since her fees were sky-high. I told her that I could provide her with publicity in adult magazines and on adult websites to help her promote her business, IF, IN TURN, she would allow me to utilize her services at no charge. She also informed me that she wanted to evolve her new dominatrix persona, which she called "Z," as the icon behind a product line of adult toys, comic books, and a fictitious autobiography. I told her that I could—and would—help her pursue all of those endeavors, in exchange for my becoming one of her clients. A barter deal was struck.

After dinner, we went to a liquor store, bought some Merlot, then rented a motel room. For the next few hours, I experienced the universe of "Z the Dominatrix," which, for me, elevated my sexual career to an unprecedented new level. I will only say here that numerous props, costumes, wigs, items of lingerie, pieces of furniture and sex toys I'd never seen before, were incorporated into our session, along with a digital video-camera. This made for an evening I'll never forget for the rest of my life.

Surprisingly, instead of just letting Z dominate me that evening, I would also turn the tables on HER, and give her commands—things I wanted HER to do. She smiled: "You've got some big balls, mister…You want me to be a 'Switch,' eh?" I'd never heard the term before, but quickly learned that a "Switch" is a person who vacillates between being both a "Domina-Tor" and one whom becomes "Domina-Ted."

After our sex play was finished, Z and I took the hotel elevator down, making out the entire time. I'd never before kissed her, and

I realized this was the very first time my "Fantasy Girl" and I had made physical contact. (At Eros Station, she'd always remained at least four inches in front of me.)

I saw Z as often as her schedule would allow. A few times, in moments of completely drunken debauchery, she gave me oral sex and even allowed me to screw her! One night, a power failure occurred just as I'd arrived at her motel room. We had a full session by candle light, the ambiance adding to the mystery of our naughtiness. As we expanded our role playing and fantasy scenes, I felt that each session was more exciting and intense than the one previous. Every time I left, she'd say, "You are my favorite Slut Boy, little Danny," while kissing me goodbye.

I did manage to secure for Z a profile article in a national girlie magazine, but my success in promoting her career ended there. While I did also get her an offer from a MAJOR men's publication (best known for showing "pink,") she turned it down. She called me from her car while driving to meet this magazine's editor. "I can't do this one," she said. "Sure, I'm a big, fat slut and I'll do anything in private, but I don't think I can spread my pussy lips and asshole wide open in this magazine. My mother and brother are still alive, and they could wind up seeing it someday. I have to draw the line someplace, I suppose."

I also tried getting Z a few product endorsement deals, and some public appearances at sexy celebrity autograph shows, but nothing came through that, she felt, was the monetary equivalent of the services she was providing to me. Our "barter deal" was over. "You're a great guy, and I like being with you," she'd say, "But, if you wanna keep playing nasty with me, you're gonna have to start paying me 'tribute.'"

My relationship with Z would end up costing me many thousands of dollars.

However, as unlikely as this may sound, I can also say that the real woman behind the Z "character" became a very good friend of mine. We had numerous sushi or Thai food dinner dates together, sometimes just as friends, and often chatted on the phone about our lives and loves. During one of our dinners, she revealed to me what a "fucking slut" her mother had been, decades earlier. She'd cheated with several men in her neighborhood when Z was a child, driving her father out of the house in shame. Z would come home from school, or a date, to find her mother, on her knees in the living room, sucking cocks of strange men across all nationalities. It haunted her, still, these many decades later.

Of the numerous women with whom I've had sex, I believe that Roxy holds a unique place among them – a pay-for-play female who enabled me to explore my deepest, darkest, sexual fantasies. Roxy gave me countless hours of pleasure – she was the sole "Mommy the Whore" partner I'd apparently been seeking my entire life.

Yet, in the real world, Roxy remains merely a "Carrot" fantasy girl, albeit one of the highest order. Last I'd heard, she moved to the Bahamas. I've not seen nor heard from her in many years.

CHAPTER THIRTY-THREE

Sex Addiction Therapy and SAA

I happened to mention to my brother, Bobby, that during the course of the week prior, I'd spent well over $3,000 on my little "hobby." Disgusted, his wife emailed me the phone number of a Behavioral Health Center in Los Angeles. She insisted I find a new therapist immediately, and made me promise to do so.

"Why are you here?" the founder of this clinic asked me. I told her about my recent expenditures with Z and other call girls, my sexless marriage, my list of short term girlfriends, my phone sex habits and whack shack days, my nightly masturbation rituals, etc. "You've found the right place," she said. "We have many, many men AND WOMEN, who come here to talk about similar issues. You are NOT alone, by any means. Obviously, you need to talk about these troubling behaviors. I'm really glad you found us."

The woman assigned me one of her best therapists, Meredith. After less than ten minutes into our first session, Meredith stated, simply, "So, you're a raging sex addict." "I am?" I replied, incredulous. "You didn't know that?" she asked. I confessed that, while I'd heard the term, and knew women who were, I honestly had no idea what it really meant.

"Wow..you are a classic sex addict, Dan." Meredith explained to me that sex addicts got "high" not just from the sex act itself, but from planning their actions around HOW they would be getting that sex. She said that the whole ritual behind my hiring call girls was as enthralling to me as the high alcoholics or drug addicts got from their vices. "Your objectification of woman has eroded your capacity for intimacy, sabotaging any chance of developing a meaningful, loving relationship," she said, "You aren't seeking love, you're only trying to screw as much meaningless pussy as you can possibly find."

She continued: "You are more infatuated with call girls, strippers, and whores than 'real women,' because these women are just fantasy figures. They aren't real – they are simply transactional. Your immaturity with women has you stuck living in fantasy. You don't have the ability to share your emotions or feelings with 'real women.' They scare you, especially once they develop feelings for you. You're incapable of returning their feelings because you're more comfortable living in the land of make believe. You have no problem spending a fortune of money on meaningless whores, but you can't seem to invest real time and real emotions on women who aren't 'drop dead gorgeous.' You're unable to share your life with a normal woman who maybe has a few extra pounds. You're a 'cum-junkie.' The only thing you're in love with is your own penis."

Of the many, many therapists I'd had before, Meredith was the first to simply "nail" me, 100% accurately, practically scolding me in the process. She seemed to care, passionately, about my well-being, and wasn't just sitting there watching the clock, laughing at my tales, and collecting a check at the end of each 50-minute session.

Meredith "reached" me. I "heard" her. She opened my eyes to my behaviors and made me see what I was doing, really for the first time. She strongly urged me to join Sex Addicts Anonymous (SAA,) which, she felt, would allow me to "connect with other men like yourself." She wanted me to know that I was not the only person in the world with a similar fascination with all things "penis-and-orgasm" related.

The first time I went to an SAA meeting, I was shaking. I was terrified. How the FUCK was I going to talk about my 40-year history of jerking off, fucking call girls, going to whack shacks, and paying for phone sex, in front of a group of dozens of STRANGE MEN? The idea was beyond frightening—it was supernatural. "I'll just sit here, way in the back, and observe," I told myself. "There's no way on Planet Earth that I'm going to be able to 'share' ANY of my stuff with these creepy guys!"

The meeting was held in a small side room of a church, with the men sitting in semi-circles around a fireplace. The composition of the attendees covered the full gamut of society—Whites, Blacks, Asians, Hispanics, Hindu Indians, and even an occasional woman. It seemed to me that a large portion of the guys there were Jewish, something that truly shocked and surprised me.

I learned that SAA meetings were based essentially on Alcoholics Anonymous meetings. A group leader—different each time—read the preamble for the gathering, which explained who they were, why they were there, and what was going to take place during the next 90 minutes. The leader then spoke for 15 minutes about his own struggles with his sex addition, followed by a series of talks from attendees, each taking four minutes to share. The group's secretary then made announcements about future meetings, community events, etc., before passing the toy truck, which was used to collect the "seventh tradition" – usually a buck apiece.

The things I heard during that very first meeting reminded me of a line from "Amazing Grace:" "I was blind, but now I see." This meeting triggered the opening of my "secret life mental strongbox," and insisted that I examine what was inside. Men in this group spoke about how their addictions to Internet porn lost them their jobs, their wives, and their families. Others spoke about picking up homeless hookers in the middle of the night from skid row and fucking them in their cars, without condoms. Still more spoke of jerking off for 8-12 hours, straight, some while watching kiddie porn. One guy even talked about getting arrested while sitting in a tree, peeping at his sexy, next-door-neighbor through her window, masturbating in the process.

That first session was mind-boggling. I'd been pursuing a private "cum-centric" hobby for 40 years, only ONCE EVER sharing just a few minutes with a MAN—the psychiatrist who prescribed Prozac. Here I was now, in a room of men from every possible walk of life, confessing their deepest, darkest, and most shameful behaviors in front of an entire community. I was deeply moved by their bravery and painful honesty—more than a few men cried during their "shares" – something I couldn't even imagine doing.

Toward the end of that first meeting, the group leader asked if there were "any newcomers here tonight?" Reluctantly, I raised my hand, and announced my first name. "Would you like to share with us tonight, Dan?" he asked. Caught off guard, but not wanting to feel like a total pussy, I said, "Sure, OK, I guess."

I have no idea where the words came from, but, in just four minutes, I revealed a significant amount about my sexual history: My parents not telling me the facts of life; listening to them screw in the bedroom next door during my adolescence; fantasizing about my mother's friends; stealing *Playboy Magazines*; Dustin molesting me; my sex-less marriage; Sharon, Bella, Sarah, endless girlfriends with cats; whack shacks; phone sex with Shannon in Canada; the massive amounts of money I'd spent in the past few years on call girls, Z my dominatrix, etc.

I felt like a shark that had been caught, raised into the air on a pulley, and publicly gutted. Things came out of me that, in a MILLION YEARS, I would never, ever have imagined I could have revealed to MEN, and especially not within a large group setting. At the end of my share, the room was silent. I had 50 men smiling at me, and applauding. When the evening was over, at least six guys came up to me, hugged me, and said, "That was one of the most amazing 'shares' I've ever heard. We are SO GLAD you're here with us! Thank you SO MUCH for coming!"

For the first time in my entire life, I found a group of peers I could not only relate to and sympathize with, but one which embraced me, encouraged me, and allowed me to quite literally spill my guts about my sexual secrets.

The feeling I had driving home that night was one of pure elation. I felt higher than I usually felt even after a particularly good fuck session with one of my gorgeous whores. I realized that my whole life, I'd never discussed my sexuality with my father and my brothers, or with my best friends, co-workers, or cousins. I'd had ZERO "male bonding" in the area of my sexuality, for over 40 years.

That "aha" moment was extremely powerful for me. I had a few tears trickle down my cheeks as I drove home. I felt like I was no longer alone in the dark void of my weird sexuality. I had found my "missing tribe" of long-lost brothers. I'd found my "peeps."

Working with Meredith, I developed my "circles" chart. The chart chronicled my "Inner Circle"—my most destructive behaviors (including sessions with Z, call girls, phone sex, whack shacks, strippers and massage parlors); my "Middle Circle"—behaviors that I should try to steer clear from (such as watching porno DVDs, seeking online sex shows or perusing girlie magazines; and my "Outer Circle"—behaviors to pursue that were non-sexual in nature, such as exercising, reading, and spending more time with my children and friends.

After attending perhaps six SAA meetings, I decided to try an experiment. I wondered if I could become celibate. I stopped masturbating for three full months, not knowing if that would even be possible for me. During that time, I experienced a new form of gentle contemplation. I completely sublimated any sexual thoughts and desires – if I saw a pretty girl in a short skirt or tight jeans on the street, I looked away. If a gigantic billboard presented me with a shot of a goddess model in bikini lingerie, I turned my head. Instead of my on-going pursuit of fantasy sex sluts, I decided to jump back into the dating pool, and attended a new series of singles parties and events, talking with regular women.

With Meredith's help, this new approach to my sex life began to take hold, and I believed I could re-wire my brain. I was attending SAA meetings three times a week and was committed to the re-design and re-structuring of my behaviors with women and my relationship with my penis. I was ready to pursue the new world of SAA and wished to live a revised life of non-addictive sexual behaviors.

All was going well, UNTIL one SAA meeting blew me away. David shared with the group that, earlier that week, he'd gone to a small motel room with a bottle of whiskey and a bottle of pills. He had decided to end his life, because he could no longer live as a divorced man without the love of his wife. He drank half the bottle of whiskey and was JUST ABOUT TO DOWN THE ENTIRE BOTTLE OF PILLS, when his cell phone rang. Hesitating, he decided to answer, and heard his college-age daughter's voice. "Daddy, how are you? I miss you and I love you," she told him. He hung up the phone, flushed the pills down the toilet, and spent the night sitting on the bed in his shitty little hotel room, sobbing.

At the end of David's story, not only could you hear a pin drop, but there wasn't a dry eye in the house. Every single man in that room had tears flowing down his face, including yours truly. I felt overwhelmed by his share. I was moved to tears, but also terrified. The reality of his near-death experience shook me to my core. Unfortunately, it also turned me off of—and away from—SAA, for quite a while.

I relayed the "David story" to Meredith, and she understood my alarm. Slowly and gently coaxing me, I returned to SAA meetings, now attending them just once or twice a month. I came to terms with myself that there was no way I could remain celibate, so I determined that masturbation within reason (once or twice a week, max) wasn't the end of the world.

Meredith opened my eyes and made me realize that I'd lived for more than 40 years as a sex addict, completely unaware of this disease. It was an enormous revelation to admit this to myself and to embrace the consequences. While I understand the "highs" that I experience from my pursuit of "Carrot Fantasy Girls," I began trying to find some balance in my life.

There's more to life than sex.

Meredith also taught me to find a sense of harmony through my relationships with women who are "just friends." "You don't have to try to fuck every woman you meet," she said. "Learn how to talk to women. Enjoy them. Appreciate them. Respect them. Eventually, if you're lucky, you'll find one that fits into your lifestyle. Learn to enjoy every aspect of her company. Sex is terrific, but only one component of the overall female package."

CHAPTER THIRTY-FOUR

Psychic Readings, Past Life Regression and My Two Shamans

A few years after Bethany and I broke up, I began thinking that, perhaps, since she seemed so very "familiar" to me, that I'd known her from a previous lifetime. I sought out a "Psychic to the Stars," and arranged a meeting. Tom, an elderly, deaf medium, lived on a farm about 20 minutes north of LA, with his wife, Janet, another psychic. Tom was renowned for sending himself into a trance during a reading, and then, while talking to the ceiling, would reveal very specific details about each client's past, present, and future.

I was fairly apprehensive as I entered Tom's little office shack in his backyard. I sat in silence before the great man. He studied my face, then asked me to toss some coins onto his desk. I did. Tom then began chanting, softly, to himself, before entering a trance. When his eyes returned to normal, he again looked at me. In rapid succession, he said:

"Your ex-wife has a new boyfriend—a much older man."

"Your son's name is Isaac" and then…

"A woman writer—capital letter 'B'—has become very close to you…a dear friend…a colleague…but not a lover. A distant relative on your mother's side."

I digested all of the above: My ex-wife, Kim, had just recently met Hank, a much older man whom she was now dating. My son's middle name is Isak. And the capital letter "B" thing I had to assume referred to Bethany.

Tom's eyes rolled back into his head. He continued: "Yours is an old soul. You were a star in the Hungarian theatre in 1792. In the

1930s, you were a comedy writer for the 'Fred Allen Radio Show,' but you died of a heart attack. Your name then was Larry Marks."

He went quiet for a long time. Assuming he was finished, I stood. Then, his eyes shot open: "You were a sin-eater, a begger, in Scotland…1820s. Families hired you to absolve the sins of the dying by consuming food and drink. You sat beside their deathbeds, so the souls of the dying could rest in peace. Religious magic."

What the fuck??

Driving home from Tom's place, I was now more convinced than ever that past lives did, indeed, truly exist. And that my CURRENT life had been deeply affected by my past ones.

"You should see my friend Brianne," my friend Heather (a former employee of my agency) advised. "She's an 'Aura Healer.' Perhaps she can help cleanse you."

I met Brianne at her office in Beverly Hills. "Nice to meet you," she said, "Let's get started." She led me into a small room, closed the lights, and said, "I need you to completely relax and clear your thoughts. Do I have your permission to touch you?" Me: "Yes, sure." As I got comfortable in my chair and closed my eyes, Brianne gently ran her hands over my head, neck, shoulders, back and arms. She inhaled and exhaled deeply, and I felt a sense of sinking into my seat. After about 20 minutes, Brianne turned on the lights. "Wow," she said, "I have a lot to tell you." Me: "Great. Go for it."

Brianne said that there was an extremely dark presence that surrounded me and had been following me during the course of many past lives. "If that's true," I said, "Why?" She continued to say she "saw" that I'd been a murderer of two young women in the 1880s. "You raped and strangled two teenage girls in a forest," she said, "And then you went home and stabbed your mother to death. You were a psychopath – you terrorized your community. A hunter tracked you down and shot you to death in a field. Those terrible deeds from that life created powerful dark energy. It remains with you…it's something you continue to carry forward today."

"Can I fix this?" I asked. Brianne said she would try to remove this energy, and once again ran her hands over me in the dark. She did. I paid her and left. While I don't believe a single thing changed as a result of this visit, I did find her story rather compelling.

I attended a seminar at the "Whole Life" Expo led by a nationally renowned hypnotist (and former dentist) whom I will call Dr. Bruce. This guy had been profiled on dozens of television shows and in magazine articles during the course of the past 25 years. He was considered an "authority" on past life regression hypnosis. During the seminar, he presented videotaped sessions with several of his patients, each of whom described the facts of their lives during previous incarnations, while they were under an hypnotic spell.

Most impressive about these hypnotic sessions was the research that followed. Dr. Bruce investigated tidbits revealed by many of his patients during these trances, unearthing factual evidence of names and circumstances from past lives. One guy apparently had been a Civil War soldier, another a pilot from the 1920s. A woman turned out to be a Spanish Queen, while another had been a slave in the Deep South.

Whether or not these researched facts proved that these past lives existed remains open to personal belief. However, I was completely convinced that all of this stuff was 100% for real.

I contacted Dr. Bruce shortly thereafter and had a private session in his office. In a darkened room, I sat in a recliner, as he set up his audio recording equipment. He instructed me to relax, taking deep breaths. Counting backwards out loud, the guy managed to lure me into an extraordinarily deep state of tranquility.

After about 10 minutes in this bliss, he began to instruct me. "I want you to open your mind to what came before," Dr. Bruce said. "Remember who you were and where you lived—what you saw and how you felt." I saw a kind of swirling blackness during this hypnosis, flashes of colors and images sparking through my brain like a Tesla experiment. Then, a scene popped into view that was crystal clear:

"I'm in Egypt," I said, "I'm performing a burial service for a queen. I'm a priest in white robes. Her coffin is on a raised platform inside a large hole in the ground. I'm also in the hole, and I can see one of the great pyramids above us. I am walking in a rectangular shape around her coffin, chanting prayers. Slaves are standing above us, looking down into the hole. I'm some kind of holy man."

The scene was as vivid as watching a TV show. Dr. Bruce then decided to move me "forward in time," and after some more breathing instructions, and counting backwards, I came up with this next one:

"I'm a farmer. I'm plowing a field along with my teenage son. It's a sunny day. I see people riding past us on a dirt road in carriages pulled by horses. It's the 1890s. I'm Amish. I can see my house. I'm walking inside. There's something wrong. I go into the bedroom. My wife is sick—very sick. She's in the bed, sweating and crying. She's pregnant. She's in labor. A woman nurse stands beside her, holding her hand. There's a great deal of blood on the bed. I stand before the bed, tears in my eyes. My wife looks at me—she's in tremendous pain. She dies."

I went silent. Dr. Bruce asked, "What's happening now?" Me: "I'm back outside. The townspeople are walking down the dirt road, en masse. They're heading for a celebration of some kind. I walk up to them…a beautiful woman with long, red hair turns her head to look at me. She smiles and takes my hand. We walk off together."

When this vision ended, Dr. Bruce led me again into a more recent past life, through a combination of my deep breathing and his counting. "I'm a cop in New York," I said, "It's the 1920s. I'm walking my beat along the sidewalk, watching out for street thugs. I hear someone call my name—I look up into an open window of a brownstone building. A woman with a kerchief on her head waves to me. 'He's gone,' she calls, 'Come on up.' I walk up the stairs and knock on her apartment door. She opens it and leads me into the kitchen. We start kissing passionately. I'm her lover."

The scene continued: "Suddenly, her husband walks into the room and confronts us. I take out my gun and kill him. The woman screams. I run out the backdoor of the apartment, down a flight of stairs, and into a back alley. A dozen policemen chase me and force me up against a fence. Their guns are drawn, and they want me to surrender. I take my gun, point it at my temple, and shoot myself in the head."

Time ran out on my session with Dr. Bruce. As he walked me to the door, he said, quietly, "If you believe in such a thing, I would say you're someone with a 'carry over curse' from a past life encounter… maybe even from several. I've rarely heard this many stories concerning violence and death. You're an interesting subject – please let me know if you'd like to do this again."

The guy cost me a small fortune, but I did believe what he said to be true. Each of these past life encounters seemed so real to me, I could still recall the colors, the sights, even the smells, during my drive back home.

While discussing the possibility that, perhaps my "Carrots" situation was stemmed in part by the reality of past lives, Meredith suggested that I see a Shaman to learn more. I managed to find two female Shamans living in Los Angeles.

Amanda was an older woman who reminded me of Anne Bancroft in her later years. Living in a compound in a Malibu forest, she spoke with me for two hours about why I'd traveled to see her. I told her about my peculiar history with women, my mother's breakdown upon my birth, and my unending problems with the opposite sex.

The woman had me lie down and covered my eyes with a cloth. She began to chant, shook Indian rattles, banged on a drum, and blew across my neck and chest. While completely awake, I felt as though my eyes were in REM sleep, as they fluttered rapidly beneath my lids. I saw a series of amazing images, most notably my dead grandfather Joe, my kids when they were small, and a wild deer with dark black eyes, who came out from a forest to stare at me.

At the end of the session, the woman told me that the deer was my "animal guide." She also said that she'd had a powerful vision of the ancient Egyptian Goddess, "Nut," who'd descended from heaven to visit me, enveloping me in her arms, and vowing to protect me for the rest of my life. "Nut is one of the most powerful spirits imaginable," she informed me. "I've very rarely seen her at work before. She came to continue your 'female energy download.' Apparently, it got interrupted when you were born into this lifetime."

I left the woman's home that day elated and joyous. These emotions remained with me for a few weeks.

My second Shaman was a very attractive blonde woman named Erin, in Beverly Hills. Following a very similar modus operandi to that performed by Amanda, Erin had me lie down, and chanted, while banging musical instruments, and blowing over me while I relaxed on her table.

This time, I experienced a series of beautiful, flowing colors – oceans of blue, red, orange and yellow vividly filled my senses. The experience was peaceful and calming. Also, during this trance, I could feel Erin clasping her hands above my chest, as though she were extracting something from me.

Afterward, Erin told me that she, too, had had a vision. Hers was the following: Dressed in a flowing white gown, Erin was walking through a forest, when she saw another version of ME as a dark-skinned, mysterious, and evil man wielding a raised knife. "Are you here to hurt me?" she asks the man, who replies, "Yes." "Why? the Erin 'as vision' asks. The man answers, "Because my soul is dead inside."

Without giving her any "hints" about my belief in a past life curse, Erin experienced what she told me was an "evil presence that has long impeded my life." She explained that during this vision, she did her best to remove the bad spiritual energy from me—the "extracting" actions she'd performed with her hands above my chest, earlier.

While my visits to both Shamans were extraordinarily interesting, I'm not sure any concrete changes were made as a result.

I was walking down Hollywood Blvd, killing time one day, when I saw a sign on a small building that read, "Psychic Readings." In a virtually exact repeat of my story from 1979, I walked in at random, and met a short, young woman named Sarah. "Would you like a reading?" she asked. I paid her thirty bucks, and she led me into a small booth. "Hold out both hands," she said, "and let me see them."

In quick succession, Sarah told me that: I had my own business; I'd had financial problems the year before, but things were starting to turn around now; I had two children, both in their 20s; and that I was going to participate in a large family reunion, two months hence.

Every single one of these pronouncements was 100% true.

Then Sarah asked, "Would you like to know about your love life?" Me: "Yes, actually…that's really why I'm here." She stared into my hands for a minute, then said, **"You have the luck to find love… over and over again…but you don't have the luck TO KEEP IT."**

Three decades after my first-ever reading, another psychic, 3,000 miles away, delivered to me a corollary to that very first revelation:

"Many women are attracted to you, but something goes wrong with each one you meet."

Sarah continued, "Do you believe in past lives?" Me: "I do." She stared again. I saw her body actually shudder: "You have a lot of very strong negative energy from a past life. I see a great many deaths and tragedies. In an ancient time, you were murdered. In another, a woman you loved very dearly accidentally drowned. Before that, I believe in the early 1800's, you were in love with an older woman named Jessica Burrows. She was a dark-haired beauty, but she left you for another man. **You were so despondent, you hung yourself. Your suicide unleashed a black spirit—a very powerful, evil presence that haunts you, lifetime after lifetime. It prevents you from securing the true love that you seek today.**"

I asked Sarah if there was a way to get rid of the "black spirit." She told me that, for a fee of $1,000, she could order a rare "pink stone" for me. She and I would then sit in front of the pink stone for an hour and focus my negative energy into it. When it turned black, the evil, negative energies from my past lives would be gone, forever.

Of course, I knew the "pink stone" bit was a scam. I'm not a total schmuck.

CHAPTER THIRTY-FIVE

TEN YEARS AFTER: 2012–2022

My daughter, Anjuli, moved back to Los Angeles after having graduated from San Francisco State University in May 2012. As my ex, Kim, was then living with her old boyfriend, Hank in Phoenix, I had my wonderful daughter move in with me and instantly "uplift" my life. (My son, Jordan had moved in 2008 to Anchorage, Alaska, where he remains to this day.)

On weekends, Anjuli and I would rent bikes and ride them in Santa Monica and Venice along the scenic bike paths. These rides were among the happiest moments of my life, and I was ecstatic to be spending quality time with my daughter, who, I then realized, was not only my favorite person on the planet, but also the ONLY WOMAN I've ever known who never broke my heart.

My daughter often encouraged me to join Match.com, so I finally did. From that service, I met a very attractive redhead named Willow, who worked as a hairdresser in the San Fernando Valley. From 2012 – 2015, I would retrieve Willow from her small apartment deep in the valley, go out for nice dinners with LOTS of alcohol involved, then return to her place and have literally mind-blowing sex. I was so incredibly attracted to her, it was unreal. Sometime along the way, she turned me on to doing cocaine before sex – I only did it three times, because the following mornings I would invariably end up with the worst headaches of my life.

Willow turned me on a great deal, and even, on a few occasions, invited some of her attractive girlfriends – and female neighbors – to come over and join us in our sexual acrobatics!

But over the course of years, I realized that her behavior was becoming erratic, and she had developed a severe case of ADD. She could NOT STOP TALKING, ever, even during sex, and would dance around the apartment, trying on different outfits, changing channels on the TV, calling her sister, playing with her cat and dog and fidgeting with her hair and makeup, all while vacuuming her floors and rearranging her furniture.

I finally realized that, due to her cocaine addiction, Willow simply was not someone I had the patience to be around. We broke up on a New Year's Eve, after I'd watched her prance around her apartment for four straight hours, never once stopping to ask me how I was doing, or luring me into initiating sex.

In 2016 (the year of my 60th birthday,) I attended a singles party and met a remarkably beautiful brunette from Poland who was an actress on TV shows, films and even starred in a popular videogame. "A" was quite simply stunning, and we dated for many, many months, but, for some reason, without having sex. I asked her a number of times why we weren't having sex, and she told me that she had never been a fan of it, that she'd made her (now ex) husband sleep in another room from hers, and that, as she was raised a hardcore Catholic, she felt it was dirty, wrong and sinful.

Finally, at the very tale end of that year, she came to my place and had dinner. She then asked me if I had any pot? My daughter had left some in the house, so we got high, then drank champagne. We began to kiss for the first time and she said, "Do you think I'm a bad girl?" I replied, "A, of course not! I am SO INTO YOU, I have been waiting for this moment for SUCH a long time. Do you think we can finally have sex tonight?" She replied: "No blowjobs, and no intercourse. But otherwise, yes, we can fool around."

I led her onto my bed and we "fooled around" for about an hour before falling asleep. (I must saw that she had the most beautiful naked breasts I've ever seen in my life.) Then, perhaps at 3 or 4 in the morning, we awoke, and she said, "I need to go home now." I walked her to her car and hugged her goodnight.

The look on her face just before she drove off clearly indicated to me that she'd been traumatized by our sexcapades. While I have seen her a number of times since that night, we never had sex again. My gut is that something terrible happened to her in childhood and there was no amount of future "begging" from me that was ever going to change her inherent feelings about sexual intimacy with me – or any man – at any point in the near future.

In 2017, I reconnected with a long-lost friend – a woman I'll call KK, who I first met when she was dating one of my clients about 12 years earlier. She'd been living in Las Vegas for a while and upon her return to LA, looked me up. We would have many, many meals together, drinking, talking and laughing. She was a very tall, strikingly beautiful blonde, and when we went out together I felt like a Munchkin from *The Wizard of Oz*.

One New Year's Eve, KK and I went to a Beverly Hills restaurant/bar, and we each got "picked up" by other partygoers. She met a good-looking guy with whom she was making out on the dancefloor, while a blonde bombshell who literally was Marilyn Monroe's doppelganger lured me onto the dancefloor as well. (At one point, "Marilyn" pulled out her rather large tits and waved them at me!)

KK dated the guy briefly, until he started lecturing her about his intense beliefs in Christianity. I had two dates with "Marilyn Monroe," but when I saw her home after the end of date 2, I freaked out. I'd never seen a bigger pigsty in my life, so I never pursued her again.

Shortly thereafter, KK hooked up with one of the music industry's most prominent and wealthy record producers and ended up living with him in a huge mansion for years. When I'd see her during that era, all she would do was complain about how much this guy was ruling and controlling her. After months and months of enduring those talks, I simply told her I never wanted to hear her talk about that asshole ever again.

We then had a text fight and "broke up."

I did see her one last time, on New Year's Eve (2021/2022,) when she invited me to her new apartment – she'd since broken up with music guy. We drank, ate, watched movies, and she told me, for hours in detail, about all the sex she was having with a number of "incredibly handsome guys."

I was completely offended by her confessions to me about her remarkable sex life (while I was in a complete "sex-drought,") and doubly so after she fell asleep against me on her couch. I quietly slipped out from against her body and tip-toed out her apartment door. While I only wish KK the best of everything in life in the future, I don't need to have her rub her overly-descriptive sexcapades in my face.

In spring 2017, my daughter moved out of my apartment and into a new place with a new boyfriend, Ryan, in Burbank. Almost concurrently, my dad passed away at age 87 from stage four prostate cancer and Alzheimer's. It was a one-two punch for me, losing my beloved father and also having my daughter now living an hour away. So how did I respond to those challenges? I decided to re-employ my call girl hobby.

I started having call girls of all shapes, sizes and colors coming to my apartment to entertain me. I didn't care about the money spent nor did I have the least bit of shame or embarrassment in "re-visiting" my sexual addiction in this manner.

What did bother me then, though, was the fact that my penis no longer seemed to be willing or able to cooperate with me and my "lady friends." I was tested by a doctor who revealed that my testosterone levels were on the low side. And while the same doctor prescribed testosterone injections for me (which I could apply at home,) I decided not to become dependent on such a powerful aide simply to get good boners.

In fall 2018, my daughter had a bad breakup with her boyfriend, and came sobbing back to my door. Of course, I helped her move out from their shared place and she returned back to my pad. While this curtailed my call girl hobby, I didn't care. My daughter is the most important woman in my life, and her happiness will always come first for me.

The following year, I chased after three "Carrots" in a row, all of whom were actresses. I was hired to do the PR for a funny, all-female play in West LA about five housewives who were going through menopause and having to deal with their daily life problems. The writer and creator and star of that show was an attractive singer/actress named Tina. In a short period of time, we developed crushes on each other, and dated a few times, going out for dinners or movies, or both. After one of those dates, we got into my car and fooled around in the backseat. I then told her how badly I wanted to have sex with her.

"Oh, for that, I'd have to charge you money," she responded. "You don't think I make enough money to survive just from my plays, do you?"

Quite literally shocked, I drove home, alone, my balloon deflated that such an attractive and talented woman, who'd seemed to really like me, had to be paid for her sexual services.

I re-connected with Caryn Richman, my long-lost friend and star of *The New Gidget* TV show. I took her out to several dinners with drinks, and to the play starring Tina. I finally told her that I'd had a crush on her since 1986 and that, maybe, it was time for the two of us to date each other?

"Sorry, Dan, I can't," she said. "I'm living with a guy named Tom. He's really good to me. I just don't think you and I are ever going to both be single at the same time."

I introduced Caryn that year to my daughter and closest friends for one of my birthday dinners. While she will forever remain a true "Carrot," I will also, forever, have a crush on her from afar.

I met a terrific woman named Kayla, a fiery redhead with a feisty personality, during an event I was producing at The Grammy Museum near downtown LA. We quickly became very close, albeit short-lived, friends. During our first date together, she and I were at an art walk event downtown where thousands of people had congregated. As we were leaving a private party, two perfect, stunning blondes, both of whom resembled the lead singer from ABBA, approached me. They said, "Ve are from Sveden. Vhere should ve go now?" Since I'd never had two "10's" stop me on the street before in the history of my life, I froze in my tracks, unprepared for the experience.

Kayla, standing just a few feet away from me, was furious – steam shooting out of her ears. She stormed off. I curtailed my conversation with the Swedes, ran after her, and asked what was wrong. "If you ever had a chance of sleeping with me before, forget it, buddy. It's gone forever. You're like a 12-year-old boy with his tongue hanging out when you see a pretty girl. You're so immature. I was hoping you were a man."

After apologizing profusely, Kayla gave me a second chance, and we wound up having dinners and seeing movies together for the next several months. (She even attended a mini-family reunion of mine and spent one of my birthdays sightseeing with me in Santa Barbara.) While we were certainly bonding as friends, we rarely kissed, and we weren't having sex.

One night along the way, Kayla told me that she was very attracted to me, but she would become my lover ONLY if I promised to give her a baby. (Shades of The Ten, years earlier!) She realized I was much older than her (20 years), but she thought, perhaps, I might consider the possibility, regardless.

I really enjoyed my time with Kayla and could easily have developed feelings for her. I did give the baby idea some thought, then asked my daughter her opinion. "Dad," she said, "do you REALLY WANT another KID?" Without hesitation, I answered, "No, of course not." "Then, that's your answer," Anjuli replied. "It's a no brainer."

After a long talk with myself, I realized that since I'd already had a vasectomy and two adult children, I simply did not have the wherewithal to grant Kayla her wish. In spite of the fact that I was truly smitten with this woman at the time, and even in spite of the possibility that, perhaps, she was "The One," there just ain't no way this guy's gonna make any woman "Baby Number Three" anytime soon.

I visited my mom in New Jersey for her 87th birthday, and while there had a mini-reunion of sorts with Lori, my friend from high school and Rutgers. She's the girl who'd asked me "Who's Alice Cooper?" and the "Carrot" who would not remove her danskin the night we fooled around after our joint party at my Long Branch apartment.

We had a pizza meal together along with her husband, Tom, a great guy. And at one point, when Tom went to use the restroom, I said, "Lori, remember the time we fooled around after the party we threw back in 1979? That was so hot!" Much to my surprise, she had ZERO memory of that evening – one of the more romantic nights of my younger years! "Are you kidding me...we did? Wow, I have absolutely no recollection of that! That's hilarious!"

I must admit that this deflated my ego a bit, but then again, after all, she always was, and remains still to this day, a friendly "Carrot" of the highest order.

I was having dinner with my dear, close friend Shauna at a restaurant in Beverly Hills, when our very attractive, brunette waitress came to our table. I quickly flirted with Penny, got her number, and began pursuing her. While she was a waitress in "real life," she was also an aspiring actress and wanna-be TV producer. She was hoping to sell a TV series about restaurants and bars in Los Angeles in which she would also star.

I quickly came to learn that Penny had a serious boyfriend and that there was no chance she'd end up with me. However, I was so enticed by her that I did try to help her sell that TV show idea to a network (no luck.) I also wined and dined her at the top restaurants in town. During those meals, we each revealed to the other some very interesting (and hot) sex life details, which made me want her even more. (At the end of one of those dates, I kissed her in her car. That didn't go over too well.)

A week later, Penny invited me to her birthday party in West Hollywood. I got very drunk there, and flirted (obnoxiously, I might add) with several of her girlfriends. At the end of the night, when I went to leave and hug her goodbye, she said, "Hey, you were a real shithead tonight to my friends. And, by the way, I haven't forgiven you for trying to kiss me the other day. Please don't call me again."

Another "Carrot" – and quite possibly THE VERY LAST ONE – for the foreseeable future.

Just before the start of the Covid-era (2020,) I'd begun taking in-person (and then, later, online) classes at the Kabbalah Center, located just blocks from my home. Kabbalah, meaning "to receive," is an ancient wisdom that reveals how the universe and life work. It is the study of how to receive fulfillment in our lives through the technology of how the universe works.

The center offers a class entitled "Kabbalah and Sex." From the course book, I've learned that the real adventure in regard to sex is not in the number of partners someone sleeps with, nor in the elaborately choreographed chase of an alluring potential bedmate. Disconnected, tuned-out sex between self-absorbed partners is incomplete sex, shrinking intimacy to its most limited possibilities.

Sex that's divorced from one's inner self and from the soul of one's partner prevents you from experiencing the kind of connection that can evoke a sense of heaven on Earth. Sadness, depression, and self-loathing occur when there is a lack of Light in one's life, which spills over, deeply affecting one's sex life.

Thus, I've begun my newest journey – I've begun seeking the Light. I firmly believe that, at the tender age of 66, I no longer need to allow my sex drive and my dopey, limp penis to rule my universe.

There are other things to do in life besides chase after women, try to lure them into sex and begging them to help make you cum.

CHAPTER THIRTY-SIX

The "Energizer Donkey" Retires

There is a Yiddish word, "bashert," which means "inevitable" or "pre-ordained," and is used most often in terms of a single person who prays to meet their "life partner," their "other half," in whose presence they are assured to find love and fulfillment. According to my research, several Rabbis believe that people may, in fact, have more than just one "bashert." However, these life partners can become lost due to bad actions or destructive words or deeds. Worst of all, they can also be lost through inaction—when they fail to be recognized by their "pre-ordained" soulmate while crossing the other's path.

Have I already met my "bashert?" I don't know…maybe. Perhaps it was Kim 1, or Kim my wife? Or Candy? Ellen? Sharon? Marti? Bella? Bethany? Kayla? The Ten? Was one of these women my true "bashert?" Was I too blind to recognize her at the time?

I once heard a famous expression: "For every pot, there is a lid." That's a sweet sentiment, and one that I wish were true. It's taken me a long time, but I have finally come to peaceful terms with this fact – there simply does not exist a female "lid" for me.

My childhood buddy, Steve, recently came to LA for a visit. While his bedpost notch count could likely rival that of Wilt Chamberlin's, remarkably, he's never been engaged, married or even lived with a woman. "Being single is completely underrated," he told me. "Maybe it's selfish, but if you're single, you can do whatever you want, whenever you want, and don't have to ask permission or coordinate schedules. You want to eat Italian? Eat Italian. You want Chinese? Eat Chinese. You can see any movie, watch any TV show, and come and go at all times, solely as you please. My married friends all tell me I was the smart one. I stayed single. They're all completely miserable."

Having now been single for 30-plus years, I realized he was right. While it would be nice to have something to hug in bed at night besides a pillow, being alone isn't such a bad state of affairs. There is only one thing in life that a man just cannot do by himself – "make love." However, even this handicap can be overcome through creativity, ingenuity, and, sometimes, just a whole lotta cash.

In retrospect, I've had more than my share of sex, both real and imagined, and while the idea of sleeping with a new, attractive woman will always be a siren's call, I no longer have the patience, energy, or desire to seek out new women to woo. Since my testosterone levels are on the low side, I have accepted this fact with great relief. I have become much less interested in the pursuit of sex than ever before. Fortunately, for me with age, I've become almost entirely "horny free."

I attended innumerable singles parties and events in the decades following my divorce. Even if I were to go out tonight, show up at another such gathering and bring home three new phone numbers, I already know that nothing significant would come of that wasted effort.

If you own a dog, call him over to you, then kick him as hard as you can, he'll likely not want to come racing back to you the next time you call. Every new woman I've met, every new phone number I've secured, has been the equivalent, for me, of getting a fresh, new kick in the ribs, every single time.

While working closely with my various therapists, I've developed a number of "Outer Circle" behaviors – new interests that don't involve my penis, testicles, or an endless quest for the ultimate orgasm:

** Walking: Every other day, I walk exactly 5.1 miles through Beverly Hills and West Hollywood. I listen to my iPod mini, which my son uploaded with over 300 of my all-time favorite songs. I will never get sick of hearing "Light My Fire," "Good Vibrations," or "Baba O'Reilly."
** Pets: I got myself two baby West African tortoises, who eat massive quantities of food, and who have grown exponentially over the years. They remind me of my late, beloved father, as he and I used to collect turtles together when I was a child.
** Men's Club Nights: My best buddies Ron and Toby and Ray (and Shauna – not a man but who totally understands them!) and I do our best to attend at least one "Men's Club" dinner a month, usually at one of my favorite restaurants. It's our way of keeping each other up to date on work, significant others, kids, current events, etc.
** JFK: I have been avidly studying the assassination of President John F. Kennedy for over 40 years. I've become ravenously interested in every aspect of his death, the greatest "murder mystery" ever in history. I've since read well over 100 books on the subject, and can describe, in detail, every conspiracy theory and how each can be debunked. Endlessly fascinating, this subject, along with my on-going UFO studies, keeps my curiosity occupied when there's nothing else to do and when no one else is around.

I've also become a major aficionado of true crime stories, watching every TV show and documentary and reading every book on the subject I can get my hands one. Currently, I'm fascinated by the murder of Elizabeth Short, the "Black Dahlia," in LA back in 1947. I've been reading a series of books by author Steven Hodel, who claims his late father was a serial killer.

In summary, has my lifelong "Carrots Curse" situation been real? Imagined? An unwanted relic from a past life? According to the various paranormal experts with whom I consulted, something is clearly amiss with my karmic past. Since I probably won't know this for sure until I die (and the truth is revealed to me at the Pearly Gates,) I just have to believe that sometime in a past life, whoever "I" was, was involved in violent or peculiar acts, with repercussions that "bled" over into my 1956-present lifetime.

Sure, I'll admit it. I blew it COUNTLESS TIMES with many of the women recounted in this book. Quite often I was too shy, too stupid, too naïve, too cocky, and more often than not, too drunk, to do the right thing. I was "Mr. Self-Sabotage" countless times during drunken stupors.

Perhaps, in the end, the "Carrots Curse" was simply a lifelong phenomenon manufactured by my own hand, aided and abetted by lifelong, chemical depression, colored by various childhood traumas, and embellished by my young mother's troubled years defending herself against an abusive father.

But then again – the possibility that I was an evil psychopath in a past life certainly didn't do me any favors in this one, either!

For all intents and purposes, however, now in 2022, my pursuit to find my 'Bashert,' my one true love, and live "happily ever after," has come to a close.

This "Energizer Donkey" – this ridiculous, orgasm-obsessed lunatic, who's been chasing after the ultimate "Carrot on a Stick" since 1956 – now declares himself officially, and finally, retired!

Afterword

I first wrote "Carrots" as a screenplay on my mother's dining room table during the summer of 1980, following my brief position in the PR department of Columbia Pictures in New York City. At one point the following year, Jerry Seinfeld's agent represented the project, but no sales resulted from his interest.

I decided to re-shape "Carrots" into a book in the fall of 2009, after I'd come close to securing a publishing deal for supermodel Amber Smith. I realized, then, that my stories about love, sex, and romance were far more interesting than hers.

Two aspects of writing this book were by far the most difficult to overcome:

** Deciding which of the HUNDREDS of "Carrots" stories, from the course of 66 years, to EXCLUDE from this material; and
** Dealing with the gut-wrenching pain caused by reliving so many "What If" experiences, if just some of these seminal moments in my life had been handled differently. "What If" I'd been able to embrace Cheryl in her car during high school; or actually speak to Long Red, or ask Morgan out for a date; or make love to Carol in Boston during "Moondance," or ask any of the super sweet women I dated following my divorce to marry me. Would my lifelong interactions with women have brought me more happiness and joy than I ever allowed myself to experience???

I'm very sorry to add, in closing, that I had a major falling out with my son, Jordan, in 2019. As of the writing of this book, we have not had a conversation in years. I wish him well, I will always love him, and I truly hope he finds what he's out there in Alaska searching so hard to find.

At the end of this nonsense, and when all is said and done, I did manage to create an incredibly brilliant, accomplished, beautiful and artistically gifted daughter to show for my time here. That's more than many others I know have achieved, and I'm truly and unbelievably grateful that she exists.

If Anjuli, alone, was the sole reason I was meant to spend over six decades on Planet Earth tortured and tormented by hundreds and hundreds of elusive "Carrots," then perhaps my life hasn't been such a colossal waste of spilled semen after all.

PHOTO CREDITS

Most of the photos contained within this book are courtesy of the Author's Personal Collection: 1956–2022.

Additional Photo Credits:

- ** Photo of "Long Red" – Courtesy of Meryl Hausner Stollar, 1974
- ** Photo of Two Girls in New York City wearing "Ass Shorts" – Courtesy Columbia Pictures, 1980
- ** Photo of Author with Playboy Playmates Lynda Weismeier and Kym Malin – Courtesy Sam Maxwell, 1984/85
- ** Photo of Author with Caryn Richman/The New Gidget – Courtesy of Columbia Pictures Television, 1986
- ** Photo of Author with Jennifer the Trainer – Courtesy of Jennifer Cohen, 2001
- ** Photo of Author with Amber Smith – Courtesy of Amber Smith, 2009

www.ingramcontent.com/pod-product-compliance
Lightning Source LLC
Chambersburg PA
CBHW050329230426
43663CB00010B/1794